The School Library Media Manager

Recent Titles in Library and Information Science Text Series

THE SCHOOL LIBRARY MEDIA MANAGER

Fourth Edition

Blanche Woolls

Library and Information Science Text Series

LIBRARIES
UNLIMITED

A Member of the Greenwood Publishing Group

Westport, Connecticut • London

Library of Congress Cataloging-in-Publication Data

Woolls, Blanche.
   The school library media manager / Blanche Woolls. — 4th ed.
      p. cm. — (Library and information science text series)
   Includes bibliographical references and index.
   ISBN 978-1-59158-648-7 (alk. paper)
   ISBN 978-1-59158-643-2 (pbk. : alk. paper)
   1. School libraries—United States—Administration.   2. Media programs
(Education)—United States—Administration.   I. Title.
   Z675.S3W8735   2008
   025.1'978—dc22   2008018081

British Library Cataloguing in Publication Data is available.

Library of Congress Catalog Card Number: 2008018081
ISBN: 978-1-59158-648-7
      978-1-59158-643-2 (pbk)

First published in 2008

Libraries Unlimited, 88 Post Road West, Westport, CT 06881
A Member of the Greenwood Publishing Group, Inc.
www.lu.com

Printed in the United States of America

The paper used in this book complies with the
Permanent Paper Standard issued by the National
Information Standards Organization (Z39.48–1984).

10 9 8 7 6 5 4 3 2 1

Contents

Preface

This volume moves the school library media manager from the first school libraries, small collections of books on the teacher's desk, into access to global information. The computer is placed not only on the corner of the teacher's desk, but on every student's desk. The multistoried facility with large physical collections of print and nonprint items has been remodeled with computer laboratories and wireless networks installed. Information available in-house is supplemented by telecommunications to databases, other school classrooms and libraries, other academic institutions; and beyond student and teacher homes into homes and offices of experts. Knowledgeable persons, previously available only through their writing or other publications, a telephone interview, or an on-site visit, are now accessible through e-mail, Web sites, and real-time transmission into the library and classroom. It is truly an exciting time for information professionals, including school library media specialists.

The present volume includes references to the new American Association of School Librarians guidelines. These new guidelines will reflect much of *Information Power: Building Partnerships for Learning*; in fact, a comparison between the two is found in the text. However, the focus of these new documents on information literacy meant that references to previous guidelines remain necessary in discussing other aspects of the library media program—especially facilities, the reading program, and media center staff.

The format is similar to the previous editions. Chapters 1 and 2 offer a brief history of school library media programs; and they describe the role of the media specialist in new technology. The relationship with public libraries helps media specialists understand the reality of combined libraries and the recurring discussion of one or the other replacing both. The expansion of communication links between individuals and libraries leads to a discussion of teleconferencing and distance education.

The third chapter describes preparation programs and job-seeking behavior for the potential library media specialist. Chapter 4 discusses the first week on the new job. Included are information needed and where it may be located, as well as a brief introduction to the analysis of the facility, the collection, and personnel matters affecting administrators, teachers, and students.

Chapter 5 is a more detailed presentation of the tasks required in managing the school library media program facility. Managing the planning and scheduling of the library media center and reviewing the ambiance of the facility itself are considered in chapter 6. Chapter 7 explains the interaction of personnel, including media center staff, students, and volunteers. Steps in the management of the media center with administrators and teachers are described in the context of trends in educational administration.

Access to information is the subject of chapter 8. The right to privacy of all media center users is presented, and the need for expertise in copyright law is explained. Technology decisions and integrating library systems are discussed. Defending the contents of the collection—print, nonprint, and electronic—is stressed, as well as the importance of de-selecting materials from the media center.

Chapter 9, on managing the budget, includes sample forms, records, and other examples to aid the library media specialist. The fiscal year is described, and details are given for writing specifications and preparing proposals for funding and program expansion.

Chapter 10 discusses a decision process for determining which services should be offered. This sequence is set in the context of teaching methods, classroom assignments, the media specialist in the classroom, and the media center as classroom. Chapter 11 has been expanded from a section in the earlier part of the book. Facilitating reading was the raison d'être for early school libraries, and it remains one of the most important assignments of the media specialist. The research behind teaching methods and ways for the library media specialist to carry out this mission are changing constantly.

The evaluation of all aspects of the media center is the subject of chapter 13. Divided between qualitative and quantitative measures, it also includes a discussion of staff performance appraisal. Added here is the assessment of student learning. Chapter 14 traces cooperation, networking, electronic publishing, and social networking.

Chapter 15 offers suggestions for the school library media specialist as a leader in the school district and in local, state, national, and international professional associations. This final chapter makes some predictions for the future of the school library media center and provides a list of activities the media specialist can undertake for a successful school library media center program.

Each chapter presents an exercise for use in the classroom and in a workshop setting. Those designed especially for the library and information science classroom presume that students have ready access to at least one school library media specialist serving in an active media center with an integrated program. Beginning school library media specialists as well as veterans should be shown examples of teaching teams who are collaborating to develop and teach well-planned units of instruction that will prepare students for lifelong learning. Such examples must also include the information needed to assess student learning.

Acknowledgments

This volume, and its predecessors, is dedicated to the many school librarians and school library media specialists I have taught in classrooms in Indiana, Maryland, New Mexico, Pennsylvania, Texas, California, and in the summers in Vilnius, Lithuania. You, and the school librarians I have met in other states and other countries, have provided both the suggestions for content and the impetus for writing. I would also like to acknowledge my niece, Marylynn Boatright, and my nephew, Robert Sutton, who to varying degrees followed in their aunt's footsteps.

Special thanks to a series of graduate assistants—Bonnie Black, Sandi Bianculli Miller, and Wendy Bethune—who worked with me on the first volume; Jo Falcon, who shared the second edition; and Dale David, for the third. For this fourth edition, Janice Gilmore-See provided not only research help, but she filled in some needed sentences when they were missing. These superb researchers found information, input data, checked headings, confirmed URL addresses, and brought sanity to chaos.

Finally, Sharon Coatney, editor extraordinaire for the last two volumes, is due my gratitude. She reads manuscripts thoroughly, makes suggestions for changes gently, and is always right.

The School Library Media Center in Today's Global Environment

As an integral part of the education world, the school library media center responds to requirements of the educational environment. In the global community, collections of materials housed in a central location are seen as an educational positive, but few nations have been able to afford the cost of providing materials beyond textbooks. The relationship of school library media specialists to their counterparts in other nations is discussed in chapter 15. The role is described here in relation to U.S. education.

EDUCATION IN THE UNITED STATES

American education has been, is, and always will be in a state of change. New theories are developed, refined, implemented—usually before they are tested adequately—then discarded in a cycle that finds educators reinventing wheels. Administrators accept innovation; teachers follow administrative leadership; and students become recipients of each educational teaching theory, mode, and method currently in vogue.

In the first schools in the United States, education was individualized, with the headmaster asking students to copy materials. They did not necessarily learn how to read or write independently from what they were copying. Schooling was labor-intensive and open only to those who could pay; and our fledgling nation was basically illiterate among the poor.

To overcome illiteracy in some of the larger cities, societies were formed to provide free education. These nineteenth-century societies adopted a method called the Lancasterian system, in which many students were taught at the same time. The method was developed in India by Andrew Bell, who used it to teach Indian children whose fathers were in the British military.[1] To maximize instruction, students were organized into groups based on ability.

Joseph Lancaster taught older children, who, in turn, drilled the younger ones. Students sat in desks lined up in large rooms where they observed their monitor, who would state a fact and write an example on the blackboard. Students copied the fact, spoke it, and drilled it until they "knew" it.

This system of instruction through monitors meant the headmaster was freed from working with one student at a time and became responsible only for what was to be taught—that is, stated, written on the blackboard, copied, and drilled—and for training the first level of monitors. This type of instruction did require a trained teacher to plan the lessons, but ability grouping and rote learning became the norm. Also, free education for the masses began.

As the nation grew, theories of education were proclaimed, adopted, modified, or dismissed. These theories moved into the twentieth century with the creation of kindergarten, adjustments to the legal age of leaving school, and changes in the length of the school day and term. In the early part of the century, the theories of Edward L. Thorndike and John Dewey led the way.

Thorndike believed that human nature, whether good or bad, depended on learning. He advocated a stimulus-response environment in which patterns of behavior could be established when a satisfying stimulus produced a satisfying response. Conversely, Dewey believed that education was life and that learners react to their environment, solving problems posed from their environment.

In Dewey's Laboratory School at the University of Chicago, drill and practice disappeared along with straight rows of desks in classrooms. Although Dewey believed he was not as successful as he wanted to be, he did establish that the first goal was for children to "learn" rather than memorize.

The modern-day approach of project learning was based on a revision of Dewey's theories by William Heard Kirkpatrick. In Kirkpatrick's classroom, the teacher was responsible for beginning an activity, seeing that it was carried forward, and evaluating the results. The students were expected to define how to execute the assignment by solving the problem.

Theorist Maria Montessori's work led to the establishment of Montessori schools, which offer a private alternative to public day care and kindergarten. Montessori encouraged educators to focus on the sensory perceptions of individual learners and allow each child the freedom to investigate. The teacher was responsible for providing relevant opportunities, encouraging independence, and allowing children to expand their inherent interest in learning. In some cases, older children were allowed to help younger children, but independence as quickly as possible was stressed.

Individualized instruction returned in 1919 with the Winnetka Plan in Illinois and the Dalton Plan in Massachusetts. Students were tested, allowed to proceed at different rates depending on ability, self-tested, and retested to check the progress made. Although group work was acceptable, the emphasis was on individual learning.

One of the greatest impacts on education in the twentieth century was the ebb and flow in school enrollments. In the 1950s, schools were built to accommodate the baby boomers, children of GIs born after World War II. President Lyndon B. Johnson's Great Society programs instituted Head Start, free school lunches, and funding for new teaching methods.

By the 1970s, it was apparent that enrollments were steadily decreasing. Schools in the late 1970s and early 1980s were closed and demolished or sold to the community. Neighborhoods changed as all the school-age children finished basic education. Funds for education were drastically cut as legislators responded to citizens' opposition to heavy taxes. The 1990s began with a society concerned about both the cost and the quality of education.

Events in the 1990s—including the fall of the Berlin Wall, the breakup of the Soviet Union, the creation of the European common market, and the rapid expansion of technology and the Internet—placed U.S. education in the international environment. The U.S. policy of free universal schooling, beginning in the nineteenth century, taught citizens to read, write, and do math; it provided increased opportunities for personal, social, and economic well-being. Other nations followed the U.S. lead and some not only caught up but also surpassed the achievements of U.S. students.

The Education Summit convened by then-President George Bush with the nation's governors in 1989 adopted a set of national education goals. This framework, set forth in *America 2000*,[2] was designed to transform the United States into "A Nation of Students," and to make learning a lifelong endeavor. This document proclaimed the need for "A New Generation of American Schools":

> We will unleash America's creative genius to invent and establish a New Generation of American Schools, one by one, community by community. These will be the best schools in the world, schools that enable their students to reach the national education goals, to achieve a quantum leap in learning and to help make America all that it should be.[3]

The writers of *America 2000* cited three educational plans that they considered exemplary. The first example, the Coalition of Essential Schools (CES), a project organized in 1984 and cosponsored by the National Association of Secondary School Principals and the National Association of Independent Schools, was chaired by Theodore D. Sizer, a faculty member at Brown University. The common principles of the Coalition were

- an intellectual focus
- simple goals
- universal goals
- personalization
- student as worker
- student exhibitions
- attitude
- staff
- budget[4]

Students were to learn to use their minds; therefore, schools were not comprehensive at the expense of individual students. Students should master "essential skills" in school, with goals applying to all students. Teaching and

learning were personalized, with students participating in the learning process rather than absorbing what the teacher delivers as instruction. Final
evaluation of students' performance before leaving high school becomes an
exhibition of what has been learned.

Teachers in these schools were expected to trust students and, in turn, to
anticipate collaboration with parents in establishing values. Teachers were
expected to be generalists first and subject-area experts second. Finally, budgeting would allow for planning time, restrictions on numbers of students
each teacher is expected to teach, and competitive salaries, among other goals.
Meeting these goals should cost no more than 10 percent of what a traditional
school program costs. After more than 20 years in existence, the CES Network
Web site (www.essentialschools.org) states that it has hundreds of schools as
members, offers more than two dozen Affiliate Centers, and continues to promote personalized teaching and learning.

The *National Education Goals Report: Building a Nation of Learners 1997*[5]
found that national performance had improved significantly in six areas and
declined in seven. Three areas addressed Goal 1 and showed a decrease in
the proportion of infants born with one or more health risks, an increase in
immunization of two-year-olds against preventable childhood diseases, and
more families reading and telling stories to children. Further, mathematics
achievement had improved among students in grades 4, 8, and 12, with more
students receiving degrees in mathematics and science. Incidents of threats
and injuries to students had further decreased.

Declines in national performance were

- Reading achievement at grade 12 declined (Goal 3).
- Percentage of secondary school teachers who hold a degree in their
  main teaching assignment decreased (Goal 4).
- Fewer adults with a high school diploma or less were participating
  in adult education compared to those who have postsecondary
  education (Goal 6).
- Student drug use increased (Goal 7).
- Threats and injuries to public school teachers increased (Goal 7).
- More teachers reported that disruptions in their classrooms interfere
  with their teaching (Goal 7).

THE EDUCATION ENVIRONMENT TODAY

The education environment today is one of economic concern. One facet of
the educational goals stated above is even more acute: the need for more and
better trained teachers. In 1996, the National Commission on Teaching and
America's Future stated

> Although no state will allow a person to fix plumbing, guard swimming
> pools, style hair, write wills, design a building, or practice medicine
> without completing training and passing an examination, more than
> 40 states allow school districts to hire teachers on emergency licenses

who have not met these basic requirements. States pay more attention to the qualifications of veterinarians treating the nation's cats and dogs than to those of teachers educating the nation's children and youth.[6]

Many school library media specialists and teachers began with emergency licenses because of the great need for persons to fill new positions due to teachers leaving the profession, retirements, an unusual influx of students due to new home construction, and, in some areas, for class-size reductions. In many states, teachers were assigned to classrooms after introductory summer programs and were assigned to a mentor teacher who could help them while they continued to take classes. Completing the requirements for certification should better prepare individuals to assume a place in the ever more complex world of the information professional. The effect of these short-term programs on teaching staff has not been determined.

The shortage of teachers continues and is further impacted by the numbers of persons who teach for a short time and then leave the teaching profession. School administrators find it difficult to keep those teachers they are able to recruit because of conditions in the schools, ranging from student problems to lack of teaching materials to poor classroom furniture. Others leaving the profession cite excessive paperwork and bureaucracy, teaching to a blueprint or "scripted teaching," pressure to perform brought about by the No Child Left Behind initiative, teaching with an emphasis on standardized test performance, lack of control over the curriculum, and no time to develop the whole child through art, music, and enrichment because teachers of those subjects have been cut from the budget.

Education in the United States at the beginning of the twenty-first century is plagued by loss of funds, making it difficult for school districts to plan. *Environmental scanning* is the term used to describe the gathering of statistics about key factors influencing the school district and any strategic plan to be created. Obviously, the external setting—political climate; economic condition of the nation, state, and city; primary and secondary cultures in the community; numbers of children to be educated; their family structure, income, and educational background of parents; and the geographical location—must be taken into consideration.

Among the external factors, the rising costs of consumer goods erode buying power. The transfer of services to other countries through expanded communication links means questions about charges to credit cards may be answered from across an ocean. Costs of international conflict further erode the ability of the government to fund programs.

Internal factors include the economic condition of the schools; the staff and their educational backgrounds; facilities, materials, and equipment; and the administration. The students themselves, including their performance on tests, the numbers leaving before graduation, and numbers going to college, affect strategic planning. A major consideration is the general mobility of the students. Schools must accommodate constant transfers of students for many reasons, ranging from the need to move before the rent is due to parents' job changes.

As we move into the twenty-first century, in a noticeable change from the past, most students come from homes where both parents work or from single parent households. In 2006, 30,717,000 children came from homes where both parents worked, and 12,905,000 children came from single parent homes.[7] Few houses in any town or city have adults at home when the child is waiting to go to school or at home when the school day ends. In light of changing family dynamics, schools have restructured by providing extended services such as before- and after-school care, breakfasts and snacks, and flexible conferencing. School schedules now range from the traditional September to June to year-round and other modified schedules that suit the needs of families. Some school districts have adopted a movement called Small Learning Communities: schools within schools where teachers and students are grouped into more manageable-sized teams to facilitate connection, communication, and belonging.

Schools have also taken an interest in preschool connections and offer assistance in getting students ready for school. This interest can be traced to significant changes in kindergarten, which has moved from a primary focus on social skills and half-day schooling to teaching students to read and write. This means that students must enter kindergarten with significant skills that were not necessary in the past. Many school districts provide preschool programs with their elementary programs.

Preschool programs introduce foundation skills such as school readiness. Students become emotionally ready for school, able to leave their family and accept other authority figures. Children must be socially ready, able to tell adults their needs, to get along with their peers, work in groups, and control their impulses. Teachers hope they will be behaviorally ready and able to sit in a circle, at a desk, on the floor with a group, and walk in a line. They should be able to answer simple questions, put together puzzles, and use pencils, crayons, scissors, and glue.

Library media specialists with preschool classes are a very important part of the teaching staff. They reinforce letter recognition, numbers, shapes, and colors, and also introduce nursery rhymes, songs and dances, and creative play. They work with public librarians who also offer programs to help preschool students become cognitively ready to recognize the alphabet, numbers, shapes, colors, and body parts.

Schools have undergone major restructuring, especially in leadership. In school-based management or site-based management, school programs were decentralized and the decision-making process is placed with teachers, staff, and parents in individual buildings. No longer are central office administrators and staff making decisions across the district. In chapter 4, an organizational chart depicts one school district before and after restructuring and the reduction of central office staff. Those persons who remain become generalists rather than subject-area specialists.

Perhaps one of the reasons for this restructuring is the change in tenure and tasks of superintendents. In 1993, the longest tenure of a school superintendent in a major city in the United States was six years. The American Association of School Administrators (AASA) publishes studies every six years. Its 2000 study dispelled the rumor that superintendents have a short tenure, maybe two and a half years. Rather, they usually have 14- to 17-year careers, but they work in two or three school districts, averaging five to six years in each. The AASA perceives that school districts are sorely underfinanced. High-stakes testing and standards make their jobs more difficult.

The tasks facing many superintendents and assistant superintendents have become more business oriented, causing them to concentrate their efforts on relationships with teacher unions and the community at large. They now justify funding and seek outside sources of revenue, maintain buildings, negotiate with bargaining units, and oversee legal matters relating to students and teachers, among other tasks. They have little time to focus on curriculum and even less time to direct curricular reviews. In fact, one current idea is to replace the superintendent with a business person rather than an educator.

Another trend that is affecting schools and school staff is redesigning the evaluation of student performance, placing it back in the hands of developers of standardized tests. "Developers of scholastic tests have inadvertently become the overseers of a very powerful instrument of education policy making: achievement tests."[8] This means that "local control over schools is also being lost to private organizations, namely test developers. Despite the significant and growing role that their products play in educational decisions, these testing companies face little government regulation or supervision . . . governed by virtually no regulatory structures at either the federal or state levels."[9]

Standardized achievement test developers create their tests on a generally similar curriculum scope and sequence found only in some U.S. elementary and secondary educational programs[10] because the nation does not have a national curriculum. These tests have been criticized for their lack of relevance to students as individuals and to teachers and their quality of teaching. In the past, the assumption of mass testing was that the education and thought processes of students were similar. Haney and Madaus suggest that "the term *educational testing* is something of a malapropism, since most standardized testing has far less to do with the teaching of individual teachers and the learning of individual students than it does with the bureaucratic organization of schools."[11] However, with the current focus on No Child Left Behind, we are in an era of testing student performance. Teachers teach to the test, and anything not related to potential test questions has little interest to teachers, especially because salary increases in some districts are based on students' test performance.

As schools restructured in the past, the bureaucratic organization of schools changed. Curriculum that was designed to meet the needs of the students in those schools did not rely on national testing. The efforts to prepare students for the workplace and to make curriculum meaningful in their daily lives with its perspective on whether students have achieved the progress anticipated are being replaced by test scores, sometimes with teacher retention or merit salary increases based on these test scores.

This dismissal of any learning occurring outside the classroom has made it more difficult for school library media specialists to collaborate with teachers in unit planning and the use of materials found in the media center. The new American Association of School Librarians (AASL) *Standards for the 21st-Century Learner* are based on the premise that learners use skills, resources, and tools and that school libraries are essential to the development of these learning skills. The outline was shared with school library media specialists in attendance at the AASL conference in October 2007.

The new *AASL Standards for the 21st-Century Learner* have a relationship to the former standards, and Deborah Levitov has shown this relationship in *School Library Media Activities Monthly* (*SLMAM*):

SLMAM Skills Correlations—New (2007) To Old (1998) AASL Information Literacy Standards

AASL Standards for the 21st-Century Learner (2007), http://www.ala.org/aasl/standards, correlated to AASL/AECT, *Information Literacy Standards* (1998) and AASL/AECT, *Information Power: Building Partnerships for Learning* (Chicago: American Library Association, 1998).

The following correlations are made to help library media specialists match their previous knowledge of nine AASL Standards to the four new standards through a correlation process between "Indicators" from the 1998 Standards and "Skills" from the 2007 Standards. Although this only addresses skills, attention should also be given to the "Dispositions," "Responsibilities," and "Self-Assessments" outlined in the new standards.

Learners Use Skills, Resources, and Tools To

1. Inquire, think critically, and gain knowledge.
   - 1.1.1 Follow an inquiry-based process in seeking knowledge in curricular subjects, and make the real-world connection for using this process in own life. (1998: 1.5)
   - 1.1.2 Use prior and background knowledge as context for new learning. (1998: 3.2)
   - 1.1.3 Develop and refine a range of questions to frame the search for new understanding. (1998: 1.3)
   - 1.1.4 Find, evaluate, and select appropriate sources to answer questions. (1998: 1.1, 1.4, 1.5, 2.4)
   - 1.1.5 Evaluate information found in selected sources on the basis of accuracy, validity, appropriateness for needs, importance, and social and cultural context. (1998: 1.2, 2.4)
   - 1.1.6 Read, view, and listen for information presented in any format (e.g., textual, visual, media, digital) in order to make inferences and gather meaning. (1998: 1.4)
   - 1.1.7 Make sense of information gathered from diverse sources by identifying misconceptions, main and supporting ideas, conflicting information, and point of view or bias. (1998: 1.2, 2.2, 2.3, 2.4, 7.1)
   - 1.1.8 Demonstrate mastery of technology tools for accessing information and pursuing inquiry. (1998: 1.5)
   - 1.1.9 Collaborate with others to broaden and deepen understanding. (1998: 9.3)

2. Draw conclusions, make informed decisions, apply knowledge to new situations, and create new knowledge.
   - 2.1.1 Continue an inquiry-based research process by applying critical-thinking skills to information and knowledge in order to construct new understandings, draw conclusions, and create new knowledge. (1998: none)

2.1.2 Organize knowledge so that it is useful. (1998: none)

2.1.3 Use strategies to draw conclusions from information and apply knowledge to curricular areas, real-word situations, and further investigations. (1998: 5.2)

2.1.4 Use technology and other information tools to analyze and organize information. (1998: 9.1)

2.1.5 Collaborate with others to exchange ideas, develop new understanding, make decisions, and solve problems. (1998: 9.1, 9.3)

2.1.6 Use the writing process, media and visual literacy, and technology skills to create products that express new understandings. (1998: 5.3, 6)

3. Share knowledge and participate ethically and productively as members of our democratic society.

3.1.1 Conclude an inquiry-based research process by sharing new understandings and reflecting on the learning. (1998: none)

3.1.2 Participate and collaborate as members of a social and intellectual network of learners. (1998: 9.4)

3.1.3 Use writing and speaking skills to communicate new understanding effectively. (1998: 3.4, 5.3, 6, 9.1)

3.1.4 Use technology and other information tools to organize and display knowledge and understanding in ways that others can view, use, and assess. (1998: 9.1)

3.1.5 Connect learning to community issues. (1998: none)

3.1.6 Use information and technology ethically and responsibly. (1998: 7.2, 8.1, 8.2, 8.3)

4. Pursue personal and aesthetic growth.

4.1.1 Read, view, and listen for pleasure and personal growth. (1998: 3.4, 4.1, 5.1)

4.1.2 Read widely and fluently to make connections with self, the world, and previous reading. (1998: 4.1, 5.1)

4.1.3 Respond to literature and creative expressions of ides in various formats and genres. (1998: 7.1)

4.1.4 Seek information for personal learning in a variety of formats and genres. (1998: 4.1, 7.1)

4.1.5 Connect ideas to own interests and previous knowledge and experience. (1998: 4.2)

4.1.6 Organize personal knowledge in a way that can be called upon easily. (1998: 3.4, 6)

4.1.7 Use social networks and information tools to gather and share information. (1998: 9.4)

4.1.8 Use creative and artistic formats to express personal learning. (1998: 4.2)

From: *School Library Media Activities Monthly* 24(6) (February 2008). Permission to publish granted by the American Library Association to *School Library Media Activities Monthly* 24, no. 6, February 2008 and to *School Library Media Manager, 4th Edition.*

The lack of a national curriculum, mentioned earlier, led to the development of content standards by various national associations such as the National Council of Teachers of English and the National Council for the Social Studies, among others. Standards have been proposed at the national level for fine arts, language arts, mathematics, physical education and health, science, social sciences, and technology, but they can only be useful if individual state departments of education adopt them as requirements for their schools. Some of this turmoil has led to a variety of alternatives to traditional education such as charter schools.

ALTERNATIVES TO TRADITIONAL EDUCATION

During the 1990s, an effort began to provide public funding for private education, long a greatly debated issue in the United States. One compromise was legislation for charter schools, a system in which private individuals are given the same funds per pupil for an approved school as would be given to the public school were the children attending there. This new system is still in place, although the evaluation of this alternative is incomplete.

Charter schools, while publicly funded, are governed by a group or organization under a contract with the state. The charter exempts the school from some local or state rules and regulations. In return, charter schools must meet accountability standards, and their contracts are reviewed at intervals (usually every three to five years. If guidelines on curriculum and management or the established standards are not met, a charter school's contract may be revoked.

In the 2004–2005 school year, 3,294 charter schools made up 4 percent of all public schools, compared with 90,001 conventional public schools in the United States. Forty states and the District of Columbia allow charter schools. Students served differ from more conventional schools; charter schools enroll larger percentages of minority students and lower percentages of white and Asian/Pacific students.[12]

Although the first charter schools were privately funded, public school districts determined to initiate charter schools to keep education funds from the state within the district. Administrators and teachers were given freedom to develop what would be an attractive curriculum for parents and their children to keep them in the local schools.

Another alternative to traditional education has been home schooling. Many parents have adopted home schooling as an alternative because they feel they can offer more individualized instruction at home. They do not believe a lock-step curriculum matches the learning styles of their children. Others home school because of a desire to provide more religious training for their children. Many students who are home schooled take part in some school activities such as band or chorus and use materials from the school media center. Meeting the needs of the home schooled children is a new challenge for the library media specialist.

Proposals to offer parents vouchers to send their children to a specific school, either public or private, come and go. Parents can take a voucher for the funds allocated to their child for any school, public, private, or even church related.

THE MEDIA CENTER IN THE EDUCATIONAL ENVIRONMENT

The school library, an innovation of the twentieth century, has escaped complete recycling during its 100-year history, but many changes have occurred along the way. When the library was transformed at mid-century into the school library media center, the media specialist's role changed, more as a result of rapid changes in technology than a total change in concept, perhaps because education itself has not maintained consistent alterations imposed with new and renewed methods of teaching. The role was defined in 1988 with the AASL's publication, *Information Power: Guidelines for School Library Media Programs.* This mission statement written in 1988 was reconfirmed for the media center in 1998 with *Information Power: Building Partnerships for Learning.* "The mission of the library media program is to ensure that students and staff are effective users of ideas and information."[13]

The mission is expanded with the ways this will be accomplished:

- by providing intellectual and physical access to materials in all formats
- by providing instruction to foster competence and stimulate interest in reading, viewing, and using information and ideas
- by working with other educators to design learning strategies to meet the needs of individual students.[14]

The 1988 *Information Power* lists seven goals that include providing access to information through learning activities as well as physical access. Learning experiences should help students become "discriminating consumers and skilled creators of information." Further, the library media specialist should lead, collaborate with, and assist teachers in applying principles of instructional design. Resources and activities are planned that contribute to lifelong learning. The library media program should function as the information center of the school with resources and activities and provide "a diversity of experiences, opinion, and social and cultural perspectives."[15]

Supported by the mission and objectives in both sets of these guidelines, school library media specialists began taking a stronger leadership role in the education of students in their schools. This role was not new, but it was one that was changing. For school library media specialists to provide leadership for their individual programs, they must manage programs well. To meet the needs of students, teachers, and curriculum as defined by the school community and to be an effective manager, the library media specialist should build both from the perspective of the past and from a vision of the future.

The leadership role can be very effectively instituted through collaboration with classroom teachers. Taking the initiative to place the resources of the media center into the curriculum means that students will have two teachers working with them on a unit of instruction. To build this joint relationship, the library media specialist must make it clear to the teacher that the partnership will not substantially increase the workload of the teacher and will substantially increase the learning of the students. With the focus of the new *Standards for the 21st-Century Learner,* it should be easier to demonstrate how a strong

media program will help the learner, a premise that is essential when allocation of funds becomes building-based. At this time, the media specialist must
become an integral part of the leadership team.

To initiate a charter school or to restructure an existing public school,
the emphasis on building-based planning provides the building staff with an
opportunity for leadership. Because in many districts, central staff positions
are being eliminated or turned into generalist positions, district-level support
of the library media program may be eliminated, or the former supervisor of
media centers may be given other responsibilities. When this is combined
with radical changes in district resource allocation, the role of the media
specialist comes under scrutiny. Library media specialists must take on a
leadership role, especially when restructuring the media program may result
in its being reduced or eliminated. A constant reminder of the role of the
media specialist in the use of technology and the finding of resources outside
the school helps others remember the importance of the media center in
students' learning.

The emphasis on reading books provided in the school library at the
beginning of the twentieth century has been maintained, but it now embraces
a variety of formats including e-books, audio books, animated books, and
interactive books. Additionally, student researchers now rely less on printed
reference materials and more on electronic sources such as databases, online
encyclopedias, atlases, dictionaries, and information found on the Internet.
The challenge remains to meet the national goal for literacy by graduating
students who are literate and will become adults who are not only literate, but
also who "possess the knowledge and skills necessary to compete in a global
economy and exercise the rights and responsibilities of citizenship."[16]

HISTORY OF SCHOOL LIBRARIES AND LIBRARY MEDIA CENTERS

The history of the development of libraries and library media centers in
schools is relatively short compared with the history of other types of libraries. They are indeed an educational innovation of the twentieth century. The
first professionally trained school librarian, Mary Kingsbury, was appointed
in 1900.

Prior to 1900, schools had built collections of books into libraries to the
point that, in 1876, *Public Libraries in the United States* reported 826 schools
of secondary rank with libraries containing nearly 1 million volumes, or a little
over 1,000 volumes per library.[17] Between 1876 and 1900, statistics reported
the number of volumes but not the numbers of high school libraries, so further
comparisons are not possible.

Growth in the number of libraries was slow, and growth of the collections
was even slower. In 1913, Edward D. Greenman wrote, "Of the 10,000 public
high schools in the country at the present time, not more than 250 possess
collections containing 3,000 volumes or over."[18] He continued, "The libraries
are well managed, and are frequently under the supervision of a trained
librarian. The students are given practical training in the use of the library, in
cataloging, classification and in the value of reference books."[19]

The condition of school libraries was further described in 1915 by Mary E. Hall, the second person to be appointed a school librarian in the United States, when she was named to the Girl's High School in Brooklyn in 1903. She wrote that

> to realize what we mean by a "modern" high school library one must actually see it in action. . . . To have as your visitors each day, from 500 to 700 boys and girls of all nationalities and all stations in life, to see them come eagerly crowding in, 100 or more every 40 minutes, and to realize that for four of the most important years of their lives it is the opportunity of the library to have a real and lasting influence upon each individual boy and girl, gives the librarian a feeling that her calling is one of high privilege and great responsibility.[20]

The activities were rapidly outgrowing a single reading room, and new facilities were being built that included a librarian's office or workroom. At Mary Hall's school, a library classroom was proposed.

> The library classroom adjoins the library reading room and should be fitted up to have as little of the regular classroom atmosphere as possible. It should be made quite as attractive as the reading room and have its interesting pictures on the walls, its growing plants and its library furniture. Chairs with tablet arms on which pupils can take notes, one or more tables around which a small class can gather with their teacher and look over beautiful illustrated editions or pass mounted pictures and postcards from one to another, should surely form a feature of this classroom. . . . There should be cases for large mounted lithographs . . . for maps and charts, lantern slides, mounted pictures, and clippings. A radiopticon or lantern with the projectoscope in which a teacher can use not only lantern slides but postcards, pictures in books and magazines, etc. . . . For the English work and, indeed for German and French, a Victrola with records which make it possible for students to hear the English and other songs by famous singers, will help them to realize what a lyric poem is. . . . This room will be used by the librarian for all her classes in the use of reference books and library tools, it will constantly service teachers of history, Latin, German, French, and be a boon to the departments of physical and commercial geography. After school it will be a center for club work. Reading clubs can be made more interesting. . . . Classes will be scheduled for a regular class recitation there when a teacher wishes the aid of the room in awakening interest.[21]

Hall goes on to say that this library had come a long way from "the dreary room with its glass cases and locked doors, its forbidding rows of unbroken sets of standard authors, its rules and regulations calculated to discourage any voluntary reading."[22]

Despite the enthusiasm of Mary Hall and others, school libraries developed slowly. The impetus to expand secondary school libraries accelerated in the mid-1920s, when regional accrediting agencies specified a high school library with a trained librarian as a requirement for all schools seeking to be accredited by their associations.

Although elementary school library standards were published in 1925, not many elementary schools had libraries or librarians. If monies were allocated for the purchase of library books, these books were kept in individual classroom collections. The size and quality of such collections depended on four criteria. The first two were the budget allocated and the skill of the teacher in selecting suitable books. The third was the stability of the teacher's grade assignment. Many books ordered by a teacher for students in an above-average fourth grade arrived at the end of the school year. In the fall, the teacher's assignment might change to a below-average third grade for whom these selections were inappropriate. The last criterion was the longevity of the teacher in a particular classroom. When teachers left a school, their classroom collections, if not redistributed by the teachers before their departure, were raided by other teachers before replacements arrived. The demise of the classroom collection was a slow and painful process for many teachers who did not wish to lose control over their old favorites.

The Soviet Union's launch of the Sputnik satellite in the 1950s produced an upheaval in U.S. education and caused Congress to provide funds for workshops, special programs, and institutes for training and retraining teachers. Funds also became available for materials and equipment to supplement classroom textbooks, especially in math, science, and foreign languages.

Several events in the early 1960s had great impact on the expansion of school libraries and the initiation of the concept of elementary school libraries in the United States. The first was the completion in 1960 of *Standards for School Library Programs,* which updated *School Libraries for Today and Tomorrow,*[23] published in 1945.

Immediately following the 1960 publication of *Standards,* the American Association of School Librarians received a grant from the Knapp Foundation to assist in the development of school libraries. The motion picture *And Something More* was produced to show an excellent example to parents and community members and to encourage support for an elementary school library program. In December 1962, the Knapp Foundation awarded the AASL a grant of $1.13 million for a five-year demonstration program to be conducted in three phases.

Another event that affected the development of school libraries was the publication in 1964 of a report by Mary Helen Mahar and Doris C. Holladay for the U.S. Office of Education showing that fewer than 50 percent of U.S. elementary schools had libraries.[24] The report attracted the interest of private industry, and additional materials were prepared to bring the plight of school libraries to the attention of the public.

These efforts in the early 1960s also caught the attention of Congress. Cora Paul Bomar, head supervisor in the Library and Instructional Materials Section of the North Carolina Department of Public Instruction (1951–1969), in her discussions with members of Congress, put on the "saddest face one could ever imagine" because she had "a vision of 10 million children going to 40,000 schools with no library."[25]

The lobbying efforts of the American Library Association's Washington office and the concentrated efforts of key school librarians across the country resulted in passage of the Elementary and Secondary Education Act (ESEA) in 1965. Funds were placed in Title II specifically to purchase library materials. These funds were then combined with local initiatives and volunteer efforts to build school libraries in elementary buildings and to expand libraries in secondary schools.

Modifications in this law found federal funding guidelines rewritten and categorical restrictions lessened. Library media specialists now competed with other programs, not only for declining federal dollars but also for declining state and local funding. The monies spent for microcomputers further decreased funding for other types of materials and equipment in school libraries, and, in the early 1980s, the school library media picture seemed bleak.

In the late 1980s and early 1990s, site-based management changes meant that many staffs did not include a library media specialist as part of the essential programs for students. In other states, certification requirements came under review, and it was no longer considered necessary for the media center staff person to hold teacher certification.

Mid-decade, the DeWitt-Wallace/Reader's Digest Foundation funded a $40 million initiative to create model elementary and middle school libraries.[26] This Library Power project, administered by the American Association of School Librarians, involved 19 districts that received up to $1.2 million over three years to increase their collections, train staff, and improve facilities. Schools were required to commit to full-time library media specialists, a flexible schedule in the library, and to encourage collaboration between teachers and library media specialists. The Foundation ended this phase of funding in 1998, but the impact of these models has helped library media specialists make a case for strong school libraries. Benefit has also come from the studies conducted by Keith Lance and others that demonstrate the value of a school library media specialist in the achievement of students. The Lance studies will be discussed in chapters 12 and 13.

Forty years after ESEA Title II and the loss of enrollment toward the end of the twentieth century, school populations are now growing steadily (see Figure 1.1). This increase in enrollment has created overcrowded schools, and the need to hire teachers has put already limited budgets even more at risk. This situation and the impact of No Child Left Behind and its emphasis on testing students make the role of the media specialist vulnerable. Learning how to assess programs and report assessments to the appropriate audiences will be covered in chapter 13, Managing Program Evaluation and Assessment.

RELATIONSHIP WITH PUBLIC LIBRARIES

Schools and public libraries have a long history of contact, communication, and cooperation. The length of time such cooperation continues and the degree or the depth of the relationship varies from year to year and from location to location. A public library at one time could have close communication with a public school system and, at another time, no contact at all. In an 1876 speech, C. F. Adams, a trustee of the Quincy Public Library, noted that, "Yet though the school and library stand on our main street, side by side, there is, so to speak, no bridge leading from one to the other."[27]

Adams ended his presentation with

I want very much indeed to see our really admirable Town Library become a more living element that it now is in our school system. . . . To enable you to do this, the trustees of the library have adopted a new rule, under

Total	1980	1990	1995	2000	2002
Elementary Secondary	58,305,000	60,269,000	64,764,000	68,671,000	71,215,000
Public Elementary/ Secondary	40,877,000	41,217,000	44,840,000	47,204,000	48,202.000
Public K–8	27,647,000	29,878,000	32,341,000	33,688,000	34,135,000
Public 9–12	13,231,000	11,338,000	12,500,000	13,515,000	14,067,000

Figure 1.1 Numbers of Children in Elementary and Secondary Schools in the United States, 1980–2002

Source: U.S. Department of Education, National Center for Education Statistics, Statistics of Public Elementary and Secondary School Systems, 1980; The NCES Common Core of Data (CCD), "State Nonfiscal Survey of Public Elementary and Secondary Education," 1985–86 through 2002–03; Private School Universe Survey (PSS), 1995–96 through 2001–02; Projections of Education Statistics to 2014; Higher Education General Information Survey (HEGIS), "Fall Enrollment in Institutions of Higher Education" surveys, 1980 and 1985; and 1990 through 2002 Integrated Postsecondary Education Data System (IPEDS), "Fall Enrollment Survey," (IPEDS-EF90–99), and Spring 2001 through Spring 2003.

which each of your schools may be made practically a branch library. The master can himself select and take from the library a number of volumes, and keep them on his desk for circulation among the scholars under his charge. . . . From that time, both schools and library would begin to do their full work together, and the last would become what it ought to be, the natural complement of the first—the People's College.[28]

Differences exist between school library media centers and public libraries in almost every area of facilities, management, clientele, and services. Schools should have their media center located in the center of the building, accessible to all, while public libraries should be in the center of the greatest population movement, whether downtown or a branch. Public librarians report to a board of trustees, while school librarians report to their principal. The youth librarian at a public library reports to the director (another librarian), while the school library media specialist reports to the principal (an educator).

School library media centers serve the students who are assigned to their attendance center; the students are a captive audience because they are sometimes sent or taken there during the teacher's contractual preparation period. Public librarians must seek out their clientele. Another challenge exists when a public library serves a different geographic district than the school and may not be able to serve all the students attending a single school.

Media centers in schools exist to integrate learning resources and references into the curriculum, while the public library is more of a research library to serve the needs of all the clientele in its community. The need to share the topics assigned at the school each year becomes one of the most critical needs for cooperation between schools and public libraries so that materials can be available to everyone who needs them.

School and public library boards often suggest combining these two entities. Aaron has examined the pros and cons for combining school and public libraries. Her three-phase study[29] concluded that the successful programs had the following characteristics:

A separate area was set aside in the library exclusively for adult use.

There was much community involvement in and commitment to the decision to have a combined library, including citizens as well as the two legal boards in the planning process.

A single board was established to assume governance.

A formal written agreement was adopted.

A head librarian with the required expertise and commitment to the concept was selected.

A location suitable to both school and public library was chosen.

Professional library personnel and others planned with the architect for both development and construction.

Efforts were made to get people to consider this as an integrated whole rather than separate school and public library programs.

Both boards contributed funds.

Materials for children and adults were shelved in separate areas.

No restrictions were made on materials that children, young adults, or adults could check out or examine in the library.

Emphasis was given to achieving a well-balanced collection to support use by both clienteles.

Many more recommendations are given, with one interesting note worth repeating: There were no restrictions placed on materials selection.

Many more recommendations are given, with one interesting note. "There was no documented evidence that this organizational pattern was more economical than separate programs."[30]

Jaffe, in a later study, found that "Combined school/public libraries invariably cited their need for additional space."[31] Also reported as challenges were adequate staffing, the need for a formal agreement, and worry among some librarians about access by children to the adult collection. Although this is a violation of the Library Bill of Rights as it affects access, it often is a real concern.

In 1995, Bauer conducted a case study to identify factors affecting operations of a combined school/public library program. Her conclusions were that

- Proactive planning provides the most practical perspective for planning a combined library program.

- Planning processes that allow for participation by all important stakeholder groups are the best hope for meeting the information needs of both public and school library users.

- Intergroup conflict between the separate public and school library programs is affected by factors that the organization can influence.

- Programming excellence, the product of a talented and committed library manager, is the key to successful articulation between school and public library programs.

- Governance of a cooperative program must involve stakeholders' representatives in true decision-making processes.[32]

This study implied that the effectiveness of an organization, when dependent on a single individual, can prove disastrous if no plan exists for dealing with personnel changes. In fact, the library from the Jaffe study cited above did lose its librarian, and the combined branch closed. The personnel factor should be considered if the proposal is to merge two successful individual organizations.

One recent effort by public librarians that is helping the education community is the establishment of homework centers to accommodate students who do not go home immediately after school. Library media specialists working with public librarians can encourage high school students who are doing community service to tutor younger students. Providing copies of assignments to the public librarian makes this time of more value to students.

School and public libraries need to cooperate at all times, but in the present funding climate, this remains essential. The current trend seems to be to fund projects that combine the efforts of several agencies, thereby increasing the numbers and variety of persons who will benefit. Guidelines for federal and private dollars are predicated upon shared efforts that will get the most bang for the bucks. Agencies should join hands, choose project ideas that will benefit all, and apply for funding as a consortium.

School and public libraries are natural friends because they serve the same children. Among other opportunities, joint proposal writing provides a convenient mechanism for joining forces to interest a funding agency, to help raise any required matching funds.

> No single library collection can or should attempt to meet all the needs of students in schools. Library services to students is the joint responsibility of school and public libraries with school library media center activities concentrating upon curriculum-oriented programs and the public library offering its wide range of reading and other varied program possibilities. Much has been done to solve the needs for materials and services for students. Much more can be accomplished if both agencies communicate and cooperate.[33]

This chapter has covered the influence of the education environment on library media programs, including alternatives to traditional education. The relatively short history of school libraries offers a challenge to persons just entering the profession to make a bigger difference in the education of students. Finally, media specialists are urged to work with public librarians to offer resources to their clienteles.

Exercises

1. Study your local newspaper closely for one week, reading from cover to cover. Clip each article that would have an impact upon schools and school library media centers. It may be as simple as a change in area code for telephones that would necessitate reprinting stationery for the school or as major as a report of a school board meeting that announces the closing of a school building or a change in grade level for that attendance center; an even more compelling announcement might

be a manufacturing company that was downsizing, which would predict both loss of income for schools from business profits and from salaries of employees. Also, if change is drastic, real estate values will decrease, further decreasing tax revenues for schools.

2. Analyze the current level of cooperation between your local public library and the local schools. What communication exists between these two agencies? If either the school board or the public library board were to propose a combined library, what would you see as the major challenges?

3. Prepare an entertaining presentation for a service club such as Rotary or Kiwanis that includes the history of school libraries and the history of your school library.

4. Plan an in-service program for your teachers to show how you can cooperate with them to increase students' reading skills in elementary, middle, or high school. Prepare an annotated bibliography of the reading research results you will share with them at this program.

NOTES

1. Blanche Woolls, *Ideas for School Library Media Programs* (Castle Rock, CO: Hi Willow Research and Publishing, 1996).

2. U.S. Department of Education, *America 2000: An Education Strategy Sourcebook* (Washington, DC: U.S. Department of Education, 1991).

3. Ibid., 25.

4. Theodore R. Sizer, "Rebuilding: First Steps by the Coalition of Essential Schools," *Phi Delta Kappan* 68 (September 1986): 41.

5. National Education Goals Panel, *National Education Goals Report: Building a Nation of Learners 1997* (Washington, DC: U.S. Government Printing Office, 1997), 25–26.

6. National Commission on Teaching and America's Future, *What Matters Most: Teaching for America's Future* (New York: Teachers College, Columbia University, September 1996), 14–15.

7. U.S. Census Bureau, Housing and Household Economic Statistics Division, Fertility & Family Statistics Branch, *America's Families and Living Arrangements: 2006,* http://www.census.gov/population/www/socdemo/hh-fam/cps2006.html.

8. D. Monty Neill and Joe J. Medina, "Standardized Testing: Harmful to Educational Health," *Phi Delta Kappan* 71 (May 1989): 688.

9. Richard J. Shavelson, Neil B. Carey, and Noreen M. Webb, "Indicators of Science Achievement: Options for a Powerful Policy Instrument," *Phi Delta Kappan* 72 (May 1990): 692.

10. Victor Willson, ed., *Academic Achievement and Aptitude Testing: Practical Applications and Test Reviews* (Austin, TX: Pro-Ed, 1989), 1.

11. Walter Haney and George Madaus, "Searching for Alternatives to Standardized Tests: Whys, Whats, and Whithers," *Phi Delta Kappan* 71 (May 1989): 684.

12. U.S. Department of Education, National Center for Education Statistics, *The Condition of Education 2007* (NCES 2007–064), Indicator 32 (Washington, DC: National Center for Education Statistics, U.S. Department of Education, 2007).

13. American Association of School Librarians and Association for Educational Communications and Technology, *Information Power: Guidelines for School Library Media Programs* (Chicago: American Library Association, 1988) and American Association of School Librarians and Association for Educational Communications and Technology, *Information Power: Building Partnerships for Learning* (Chicago: American Library Association, 1998).

14. AASL and AECT, *Information Power: Building Partnerships for Learning*, 6.

15. Ibid., 6–7.

16. Jerry Odland, "Education Reform and Goals 2000" *ACEI Exchange* 70 (Fall 1993): p. 32.

17. U.S. Office of Education, *Public Libraries in the United States: Their History, Condition, and Management,* Special Report, Department of the Interior, Bureau of Education, Part I (Washington, DC: U.S. Government Printing Office, 1876), 58. Reprinted in Melvin M. Bowie, *Historic Documents of School Libraries* (Englewood, CO: Hi Willow Research and Publishing, 1986).

18. Edward D. Greenman, "The Development of Secondary School Libraries," *Library Journal* 38 (April 1913): 184.

19. Ibid., 184, 186.

20. Mary E. Hall, "The Development of the Modern High School Library," *Library Journal* 40 (September 1915): 627.

21. Ibid., 629.

22. Ibid.

23. American Association of School Librarians, *Standards for School Library Programs* (Chicago: American Library Association, 1960); Committee on Post-War Planning of the American Library Association, *School Libraries for Today and Tomorrow: Functions and Standards* (Chicago: American Library Association, 1945).

24. Mary Helen Mahar and Doris C. Holladay, *Statistics of Public School Libraries, 1960–61, Part 1, Basic Tables* (Washington, DC: U.S. Office of Education, 1964).

25. Cora Paul Bomar, quoted in Bertha M. Cheatham, "AASL: Momentous in Minneapolis," *School Library Journal* 33 (November 1986): 38.

26. "Can Library Power Survive without its Chief Funder?" *School Library Journal* 43 (April 1977): 10.

27. C. F. Adams, "The Public Library and the Public Schools," *American Library Journal* 1 (August 31, 1877): 438.

28. Ibid., 441.

29. Shirley L. Aaron and Sue O. Smith, *A Study of the Combined School Public Library,* prepared for the State Library of Florida (Tallahassee, School of Library Science, Florida State University, 1978).

30. Shirley L. Aaron and S. O. Smith, *A Study of the Combined School Public Library Phase I* (Tallahassee: Florida State University, 1977); Phase II and Phase III, 1978.

31. Lawrence L. Jaffe, "Collection Development and Resource Sharing in the Combined School/Public Library," in Brenda H. White, ed. *Collection Management for School Library Media Centers* (New York: Haworth Press, 1986), 208.

32. Patricia T. Bauer, *Factors Affecting the Operation of a Combined School/Public Library: A Qualitative Study* (Ph.D. diss., Florida State University, 1955), 102–104.

33. Esther B. Woolls, *Cooperative Library Services to Children in Public Libraries and Public School Systems in Selected Communities in Indiana* (Ph.D. diss., Indiana University, 1973).

2

School Library Media Centers Today

For the past 30 years, progress in school library media centers has been affected by the development of new technologies. During the 1980s, the development of the microcomputer made the use of computing power, which had previously been limited to large academic and large public libraries, available to the smallest school library media center. School library media specialists who were responsible for audiovisual resources as instructional technology in their schools were given the expanded assignment for microcomputers and related applications. Automated circulation systems appeared, and in a short time the card catalog disappeared, replaced by online public access catalogs (OPACs) that were connected to the circulation systems. Access to electronic resources outside the walls of the library media center also became available. Citizens in most parts of the United States now enjoy electronic access to statewide databases and identify and borrow resources from public, academic, and other school district libraries across the country.

School library media specialists have also assumed a leadership role in restructuring schools and creating strategic long-range technology plans for school districts. Such educational modifications are placing an even greater emphasis on integration of the media center into the curriculum. This has become especially difficult with the pressures on student achievement and testing that have come with the standards movement and the No Child Left Behind initiative. In editing their landmark book, *Curriculum Connections through the Library*,[1] Barbara Stripling and Sandra Hughes-Hassell gathered articles from leaders in the field who discuss building independent learners, mapping the curriculum, teaching and assessing, and creating collaborative learning communities. They suggest that, "in order to build independent learning skills, educators must offer a series of experiences in which students develop and use these skills to learn important content."[2]

The school library media specialist has a primary role in helping teachers teach independent learning skills and helping students become independent learners. School libraries offer the laboratory for experimenting. Media specialists must know the curriculum well and lead in the integration of all the literacy skills, information, technology/digital, and health, among others, in all areas of the school. Media specialists lead in fostering collaborative instructional opportunities.

COLLABORATION AND INTEGRATION WITH THE CURRICULUM

The fact that strong media programs with professional library media specialists have an impact on student achievement has been shown repeatedly and will be discussed throughout this book. Much of the impact occurs when teachers and media specialists collaborate. Collaboration, according to Hughes-Hassel and Wheelock,[3] has three stages: cooperation, coordination, and collaboration. The level of planning with teachers increases at each step. Cooperation can be as simple as setting aside materials when teachers bring classes to the media center. Coordination is shared work on a unit, while collaboration is shared in the whole process of instruction, not just teaching. However, in reviewing the research, Eric M. Meyers proposes that school library media specialists might be better at managing instruction rather than teaching. He proposes:

> Freeing the teacher-librarian from the onus of direct skills instruction. . . . the teacher-librarian must also work at the network level, managing curriculum instead of discrete lessons, integrating skills as well as resources into the activities of the classroom on a different scale. The teacher-librarian then becomes a curriculum coach and a manager of information literacy instruction, as well as a partner in assessing the outcomes of instruction.[4]

However, the role of school library media specialists is a judgment call, and the media specialist who is a true leader can manage instruction, becoming a curriculum coach for teachers as well as students, while another might choose to collaborate with teaching. The third choice is to do both—leading when appropriate and teaching collaboratively at other times.

Collaboration is the key, but collaboration takes time. Teachers and media specialists must find the time to collaborate, and this has many obstacles to implementation. The latest has been the emphasis on testing. Teachers who must ensure that their students do well on standardized tests are reluctant to spend time away from what they perceive are the best methods to raise test scores. Teaching information, technology, and health literacy, while essential, may take a second place in a teacher's primary goals. While waiting for the eventual demise of the emphasis on testing, media specialists will remain responsible for teaching information as the general term as well as other forms of literacy.

INFORMATION AND TECHNOLOGY/DIGITAL LITERACY

School library media specialists are now responsible for information and technology/digital literacy. The first role helps students become information literate.

Information Literacy

The term *information literacy* was first used by Paul Zurkowski, president of the Information Industry Association, more than 30 years ago. He described persons who were information literate as "people trained in the application of information resources to their work. . . ." They have learned techniques and skills for utilizing the wide range of information tools as well as primary sources in molding information-solutions to their problems.[5]

In Loertscher and Woolls, the concept of information literacy with other educators has a different terminology:

Educators interested in school reform, constructivism, problem solving, gifted education, learning styles, content areas such as math, social studies, and educational psychology are all discussing their own brand of information literacy principles under different terminology.

New ideas in education, however, have come under increasing attack by governments and groups proclaiming that achievement as measured by standardized tests is not high enough and that all the talk about reform has not changed practice in a positive direction. The resulting conflict has produced a great deal of rhetoric, new state laws demanding accountability, and new standards of testing. The debate does not seem to be at an end as a new millennium begins.

Nonetheless, school library media specialists are suddenly realizing that because of expanding information resources and the technology to access it, the world has changed. Gone are the days of access to a few books and magazines located through the card catalog or the printed periodical index. In the last ten years, the speed at which schools are becoming wired, computer networks created, and classrooms and librar- ies retrofitted creates many "where to next?" questions.[6]

Information literacy, the foundation for *Information Power: Building Part- nerships for Learning*, is defined as follows: "Information literacy—the ability to find and use information—is the keystone of lifelong learning."[7] Although these guidelines are being replaced, they are similar and they remain a basic part of work with students. *Information Power* offers a set of nine information literacy standards designed to "guide and support library media specialists' efforts in three major areas: Learning and teaching, Information access and Program administration,"[8] divided under three headings: information literacy, independent learning, and social responsibility.

Implementation of information literacy instruction, as a role of the library media specialist, lies along a continuum from nonexistent to exemplary. In libraries with basic levels of service, skill-based lessons may occur. Usually this library curriculum, which is created by district library staff, is taught in isolation of the core curriculum This can happen when schools use the library media specialist to provide for teacher release time, and it is a primary reason to urge flexible scheduling. The role of the library media specialist in the implementation of information literacy instruction confirms that any "library lessons" are integrated into the curriculum. As the teaching role of the library media specialist increases and collaborative teaching partnerships are created, the method of presentation and content of library lessons are drastically modified. Media staff presents literacy skills when the instructional need occurs, generally a time when a related assignment within a unit of regular classroom instruction is needed to cover the core curriculum in science, history and social science, math, and language arts. For example, students are taught how to develop search strategies, locate citations, and request materials not available in their media center from other libraries only when they have a need for information or when their teachers have given a research assignment. For this to become a reality, school districts need to develop their own literacy standards. Joie Taylor[9] suggests answering the following questions before beginning to develop local standards:

- Are the standards to be district or building standards?
- Have standards already been developed that can be adopted?
- In what format will the standards be written?
- What terminology will be used?
- At what grade level and subject areas will benchmarks be established?
- How will standards be assessed, and who will do it?
- Who has the final authority on the local standards?
- Who needs a copy of the standards?

When instruction is totally integrated into the curriculum, the library media specialist helps assess the quality of student research papers or other projects based on joint planning and teaching of the research process, with expectations and assessment for student outcomes mutually determined.

Sharon Coatney[10] suggests that assessment or progress can be made as students work, or it may be done from the finished product to assess their knowledge and skills. This assessment should provide information for adjustment to assignments as well as to determine which students need additional help. Assessment may also include the results of a standardized test. Regardless of the assessment procedures, the school library media specialist is involved in the process and learns the results.

Although the sequence of instruction may be planned and taught in a single school, library media specialists within a district are aware of the probable skills taught in previous years. That is, an introduction about how to use the index in a book may be a skill taught initially in third grade in each elementary school library media center in the school district, but it may need to be reintroduced in middle school and reinforced again in high school. All of this type of instruction falls under the rubric of information literacy.

Library media specialists have begun to address the way they present library skills to implement an information literacy curriculum that will lead to learning research skills. Loertscher drew the research process as circular, beginning with questions and wonders, followed by finds and sorts, consumes and absorbs, thinks and creates, summarizes and concludes, communicates, reflects on process and product, and then again questions and wonders.[11] Teaching information literacy is discussed again in chapter 10.

Technology/Digital Literacy

Swift technological development and the natural implementation of these information resources in the library have set the stage for library media specialists to assume another leadership role in the school. Students cannot access, evaluate, and use a full range of information sources without adequate technology knowledge and skills. At the same time, the increased use of technology for research and scholarship has raised important concerns about plagiarism and copyright infringement. Students need to analyze the information they find with electronic sources and tools, and library media specialists have traditionally been the ones to teach critical evaluation of sources, whether text or electronic.

Many of the underlying principles of information literacy also apply to the educational use of technology, specifically the idea that students will be using technology and information to learn their core curriculum, not learn technology and information literacy as subjects in and of themselves. For example, one technology standard reads that students will use technology to access, evaluate, and use information to solve problems and think critically. This natural blending of technology and information literacy means the library media specialist plays an integral role when collaborating with teachers. Extended inquiry-based learning activities engage students to not only gain information and technology literacy knowledge and skills, but also to strengthen student achievement in social studies, science, language arts, and mathematics.

Computers have been moved into laboratories attached to and throughout the library media center making it possible for library media specialists to instruct both teachers and students in a wide variety of technology uses:

- Word processing to create reports and correspondence
- Spreadsheet applications to create tables, graphs, and organize information
- Presentation programs to share research and projects
- School, library, and teacher Web site construction and maintenance
- Courseware to manage distance learning
- Portfolios saved on flash drives
- Searching strategies to use with databases, the Internet, and World Wide Web
- Maintaining blogs
- Creating wikis as collaborative learning spaces

This list is directly related to school library media specialists; however, the National Forum on Information Literacy defines several types of literacy, including business, computer, health, information, media, technology, and visual. While information and technology literacy are important to the library media specialist's role, the others are not as critical. As an example of one of these additions to the literacy list, a quote beginning a book by W. Bernard Lukenbill and Barbara Froling Immroth sets the stage:

> Health is an important issue for everyone in today's complex world. Having appropriate information about health is especially important for youth and their parents and caregivers in all parts of the world. No country or society can exist successfully without good health care and health information for all its citizenship, including children and adolescents.[12]

They advocate helping students to become health literate and point out that health issues are critical. These include emotional and behavioral issues, obesity as an epidemic in children, and child and teen suicide. Students at ever younger ages need information about reproduction and sexually transmitted diseases (particularly HIV-AIDS), topics often resisted by parents. However, in terms of a literacy implementation, this is more an area for collaboration rather than the responsibility of the school library media specialist.

WRITING A TECHNOLOGY PLAN

Media specialists oversee information technology systems. This could be as basic as setting up and maintaining the computers in the library media center or as complex as managing the servers that handle the school's electronic mail (e-mail) traffic and host Web sites for administrators, teachers, and students. Wireless carts with laptop computers move from media center to classrooms. This broad expansion of the use of technology by teachers and students makes it more important that the media specialist conducts staff development for teachers and instructs students to make sure everyone knows how to use new equipment, search new databases, and is aware of the possibility offered by each new technology. This is the instructional use, not the technical applications, yet the school library media specialist needs to be involved in developing the district's technology plan.

School districts develop technology plans, and these are often developed to meet state requirements. The committee writing the technology plan includes administrators, teachers, students, parents, and members of the community, particularly if the plan is for the district and not just for the individual school. Because the library media specialist is a critical member of this team, it presents a good opportunity to exert leadership and volunteer to chair the committee.

Ideally, the library and technology plan are written in one combined document. Regardless of whether this happens, the library media specialist must communicate to the committee how technology is integrated into library services. This might be a description of collaborative learning activities, professional development to teachers, or information literacy instruction. In this way, the library media specialist not only advocates for the library media center, but ensures that appropriate technology is available inside and that the technology available outside the media center is compatible and of good quality.

An effective instructional technology plan can take a year or longer to write and bring through the approval process. As Larry Anderson points out:

Technology planning is an activity that provides direction and helps users understand clearly where they are now and *imagine* where they want to be. The most common technique used to formalize technology planning is the creation of a document. A technology planning document is to technology planning as a road map or a navigational chart is to a journey, but the planning document is neither the journey nor the adventure.[13]

He goes on to say that a technology plan is more than a document; it is the action to maintain a technology-rich environment.

Because it is easy to let the technology dictate, it is important to focus on the curricular outcomes, to remember that student learning and achievement are the driving force. Because collaboration is essential to the learning process, it is the key component of the technology plan. Some questions to consider before beginning to write a technology plan are found in Appendix A. Discussed below in more detail are some components to consider for the technology plan.

Online Database Searching

A wide range of subscription online databases are available to provide additional resources for students, teachers, and administrators. Online databases are often superior sources of Internet-based information because they are more likely to be authoritative, relevant, accurate, and usually available from the school library, classroom, and home. They exponentially expand the school library media center's resources. For teaching purposes, the reference information from databases is at least as accurate as print resources for research projects, and in many cases they are more current.

The speed and ease of access to information found online offer quick answers to cataloging information and reference searches. For those who do not purchase materials preprocessed, bibliographic databases provide citations and access to cataloging data. They may also provide location information for resources that can be secured through interlibrary loan and may even offer the opportunity to order the resource through a telecommunication network.

Databases also provide access to periodicals, newspapers, encyclopedias, and other quick answer reference books such as *Famous First Facts* and *Books in Print.* Vendors such as EBSCO, Gale, NewsBank, and UMI provide increasing numbers of current references and a wide variety of retrospective holdings. The library media specialist must use care in choosing which database will offer what is needed in the school for the best price. The databases offer a variety of formats for abstracts, full text, graphics, and photographs. Online databases have the added advantage that they are updated immediately.

Many states now purchase licenses to commercial vendors' databases. The license may allow access to all users in the state who have access granted. In Pennsylvania, anyone with a public library card has access to the state's database. Schools also may use this database, and students who do not have their own library cards are given access while they are at school. This serves as an excellent model of providing access to information for all citizens within the state.

Online Public Access Catalogs and Circulation Systems

Library media specialists attracted positive administrative attention when they demonstrated the value of automated circulation systems. Now, almost all media centers are automated, and book vendors provide electronic records for materials purchased when they send the books. School library media specialists still using a manual system should seek suggestions from others who have automated systems in their media centers when they plan a conversion. Careful selection is important because the time and effort of library staff as well as adaptations that are often necessary are costly.

Communications Links

The numbers of communications links grow in almost unbelievable numbers daily. E-mail accounts are established in homes, schools, and businesses in almost inconceivable quantities. Beyond the use by adults in their automobiles and other locations, the numbers of mobile telephones, hand-held communication devices, MP3 players, and mobile game systems in the hands of youth under 18 grow as parents capitulate and provide these icons of sophistication. Blogs and wikis also grow at phenomenal rates. Library media specialists must help teachers understand and accept these phenomena so they can make use of blogs and wikis in their classes.

School library media specialists need to work with their advisory committees and teachers to help establish guidelines for the use of MySpace, Facebook, and other social network sites in the library. Controlling communication links with the ease of texting is virtually an impossibility, so to meet the challenge, perhaps if you can't beat them, join them.

Telefacsimile Transmission (Fax) and Internet Access

Those who have access to fax machines and the Internet find it difficult to understand how communication and transmission of documents was accomplished before these technologies existed. International conferences can be planned totally online. Registrations are sent, papers submitted, and travel plans confirmed literally in seconds. The fax machine and Internet have opened up the world of information to everyone in a school because the information is accessible from many locations. To send information using either of these requires a copy machine (if the material is in a format that cannot be placed directly into a fax machine), a scanner if it is to be transmitted by the Internet, and the fax itself or the electronic record in the computer. When a record is needed, cost is minimal compared to an unrecorded telephone conversation. Speed of delivery makes it preferable to "snail mail."

The Internet provides a very rapid format for communication, and it is available to many students in their homes. Library media specialists use the Internet for administrative functions such as interlibrary loan through e-mail and also for access to 24/7 reference services now available in addition to the

World Wide Web. Costs involved with this technology are tied with cost of telephone lines into the school and long-distance charges so that most schools are modernizing away from the use of traditional phone lines to using broadband solutions such as cable, where long distance costs are generally not as great a concern.

One of the newest entries into a broadband solution is Skype. Skype allows free calls to be made to other people on Skype; calls to landlines and cell phones around the world are inexpensive. Founded in 2003, Skype is based in Luxembourg, making global communication easy. According to Skype's Web site, it is available in 28 languages. Users must have a broadband Internet connection.

Because so many homes are connected to the Internet, information about library media center holdings are available to teachers and students at home. Access to the school's databases may also be available from classrooms and homes via electronic transmission.

Access to the World Wide Web opens media center users to an endless variety of sites both local and global. Locating links from one Web page to another can occupy a great deal of professional time as one traces each link. However, the results can be very useful for teachers and student researchers. Many school library media specialists create library home pages where they provide links to quality Web sites. Providing lists of links to credible information helps students to navigate through vast amounts of information on the World Wide Web and decreases time wasted on fruitless searches.

Home pages developed by library media specialists provide information about media center holdings and links to resources available from other libraries. The site may also provide links to other classrooms and experts from around the world. Caution must be taken to protect the privacy of individual students at all times. Individual student pictures, addresses, or personal e-mail addresses should not be given. However, valuable information can be shared without compromising student safety when addressing national and international topics such as similarities and differences between cultures and countries in matters of geography, occupation, holidays, religion, education, and science. Students today live in a global world, and understanding that world is essential to their success.

Some library media specialists help students develop their own Web pages using great care that access to these pages does not provide information about where students live or what they look like. Internet predators are searching for vulnerable children to exploit. Although there are inherent risks to allowing students to create and maintain their own Web presence, individual Web pages allow students to express themselves and assert their independence. Many youngsters are able to find an electronic community in which they have a natural affinity and can connect with peers when they have trouble making friends at their own school.

Filtering

School districts may, for a variety of reasons, choose to filter online resources coming into the school. Some of this filtering is a product of the Children's

Internet Protection Act (CIPA), a federal law that halted schools from receiving discounts offered by the E-Rate program to reduce their telecommunications costs. Administrators had to certify that they had an Internet safety policy that blocked or filtered Internet access to obscene pictures, child pornography, and pictures that are harmful to minors. The policy also had to block access by minors to inappropriate materials on the Internet, keep them from harm while using e-mail and chat rooms, and halt them from hacking or being hacked and from giving away their personal information.

Parents should always give written permission for their child to use technology. One such policy is shown in chapter 3. Most technology acceptable use policies allow parents to decide whether the child (or teacher) can

- access the Internet at school
- post work on the school's or teacher's Web site
- use digital photos of the child on the school's or teacher's Web site
- detail the responsibilities of the student in using school equipment

Parents are legitimately concerned about what their children may find while surfing the Internet. For this reason, as well as compliance with CIPA, school districts may choose to filter online resources coming into the school. Although filters do not guarantee that the clever student cannot get access to the sites that parents fear, effective policies are in place to apply when it happens and act on those instances to prevent it from occurring again.

Local and Wide Area Networks to Wireless

Earlier, school library media specialists established their system of microcomputers into a local area network (LAN). These connections allowed sharing of word processing programs, CD-ROM references, and other electronic resources. Advances in technology have made these networks obsolete.

Wide area networks (WANs) expanded the holdings of one library to access another site with the transfer of information from multiple locations. That is, LAN to WAN interconnections provided users with greater access to a wider range of information resources.

Public access catalog workstations were a primary focus for WANs, thereby expanding access to collections in many libraries. Librarians moved from placing information concerning their collections onto a mainframe with dumb terminals attached, a relatively easy-maintenance environment in the hands of experts in a central location often away from the library or media center. Use of the online public access catalog has changed to connecting microcomputers whose performance has become the responsibility of the librarian.

Adding connections to other networks adds a further concern for security. Some library media specialists install firewalls to keep others from entering the system. As discussed earlier, others may install filters to keep users from inappropriate sites.

The costs and the benefits of participating in a WAN should be examined carefully. Media specialists will need to train other students to help, or they must make a strong case for additional technical and clerical positions;

otherwise, time to collaborate with teachers may be lost in the maintenance of technology. Again, it is not a choice of whether to accept responsibility for an evolving technology. That is essential. What must be decided is the degree of time commitment that is possible and advisable given the important role of instructional collaborator and leader that must be maintained.

Wireless technology is available in coffee shops and airports, and entire cities are beginning to provide this access for their citizens. It provides some benefits, and it also has some negative elements. The negative is that hackers can, while sitting near you while you use your wireless connection, hack into your system and get information about you that you would not wish them to have, and they would do so without your knowledge. This tends to cause red flags to go up when that information and the information from your students' access might lead the hacker into the greater school system. That being said, the benefits of 24/7 access to information with a wireless connection is extremely valuable to teachers and students as they prepare their lessons and students work on their responses to assignments. It is imperative to help both groups understand the problems with wireless technology and how to use it.

TELECONFERENCING AND DISTANCE EDUCATION

Bringing a teacher or speaker to students electronically and allowing them to interact is an education innovation that is being expanded in the United States and many countries. Students sharing in broadcasts started with transmission of instruction from airplanes circling above the reception area. As communication satellites are launched and satellite dishes become more common, schools can subscribe to a variety of programs. An instructor in Japan can teach Japanese to students all over the United States. The possibilities are limitless. The first responsibility of the media specialist is to make administrators and teachers aware of the potentialities as well as the costs of equipment and other resources. The next responsibility is to demonstrate how this technology can be useful to students—teleconferencing and distance education are available at several levels.

A first level is to connect classrooms with audio capability through regular telephone lines or an option such as Skype. This allows two-way transmission and permits a limited number of students to participate in a learning situation that would be too costly to be offered at their school. It is the responsibility of the media specialist to research the opportunities for this type of instruction and help administrators and teachers find helpful information to use. Some popular uses have been to have students interview a children's book author or illustrator or speak to an expert in an area of research interest.

Interactive video classrooms increase student participation and decrease the sense of isolation from the instructor. Students at multiple sites may see the classroom at each location. However, this technology is costly, and it requires technicians, equipments, and dedicated transmission lines.

Another method of distance education involves using e-mail to present content, monitor student interaction, and test student progress. Teachers are developing courses that link these electronic modules to other sites on the

World Wide Web for students to gather additional information. This may be a totally stand-alone process, or it may be expanded from regular or interactive classroom instruction.

Many classroom management systems are available such as Blackboard and Web CT. It may be that it becomes the library media specialist's responsibility to conduct in-service sessions to prepare teachers to use these systems or any other system the district might provide.

At no time in the brief history of school library media professionals has it been more challenging or more satisfying to be an information professional. Technology advances have made it possible to find information for all from inside and outside the media center. We live in a virtual world. The possibilities are limitless.

THE ROLE OF LIBRARY MEDIA SPECIALISTS AND CRITICAL THINKING SKILLS

In recent years, more and more emphasis has been placed on critical thinking skills. According to Richard Paul, "Good thinking is thinking that does the job we set for it."

> For the most part we are "naturals" at aimless thinking. Where we have trouble is in purposeful thinking, especially purposeful thinking that involves figuring things out, thinking, in other words, that poses problems to be solved and intricacies to reason through. "Criticality" and "creativity" have an intimate relationship to the ability to figure things out.[14]

Critical thinking skills are designed to teach children to use their minds; this skill is and has always been part of teaching library media skills. Teaching critical thinking skills through an information literacy program establishes the role of librarians as leaders in their schools.

Choosing which terms to seek before searching the card catalog or the OPAC requires critical decisions. Information literacy requires the use of critical thinking skills as exhibited when students read materials and make choices among items for inclusion in research reports. At a very basic level, school library media specialists need to use the terminology of critical thinking when they develop objectives for activities in the media center. In Figure 2.1, Frank Smith gives a cookbook list of verbs that are synonymous with thinking:

It is not difficult to take each verb and match it with an activity in the school library media center. School library media specialists stress the elements of critical thinking that relate specifically to information literacy, such as analyze, verify, problem solve, infer, transfer, find evidence, and synthesize.

In a discussion of the relationship of media center activities to critical thinking skills, Craver states

> As new information technologies are substituted for previous industrial operations, many workers . . . will be forced to leave manufacturing and

analyze	conjecture	fabricate	organize
anticipate	consider	fantasize	plan
apprehend	contemplate	foresee	plot
argue	create	guess	ponder
assert	deduce	hypothesize	postulate
assume	deem	imagine	predict
attend	deliberate	induce	premeditate
believe	determine	infer	presume
calculate	devise	intend	presuppose
categorize	discover	introspect	project
classify	divine	invent	propose
cogitate	emphasize	judge	rationalize
comprehend	estimate	know	reason

Figure 2.1 Cookbook List of Verbs

Source: Frank Smith, *To Think* (New York: Teachers College Press, 1990), 1–2.

enter the "thinking business." Such a society will require individuals with the ability to think, to reason, to solve problems, to analyze, to make comparisons, to generalize, to digest existing information, and to create new information. Library science researchers will need to know how to improve the ability of students to find, synthesize, and correctly apply information to everyday situations.[15]

King places critical thinking needs into more personal terms directly applicable to the lives of students after they have completed basic education:

which career to pursue, how to use their leisure time, which consumer products to purchase, what political causes and candidates to support, how to manage their financial resources, and what to do in their personal relationships.[16]

It is the role of the school library media specialist to help build these critical thinking skills into the curriculum, one described by Violet H. Harada as "built on thinking and problem solving." "Effective thinkers are disposed to explore, to question, to probe new areas, to seek clarity, and to be open to different perspectives." She tells us to help educate students who "are not only problem solvers, but problem posers." These students don't just recite or regurgitate, but they listen and learn, question, collaborate, support others, and they also teach others as well as learn.[17]

When media specialists, working with teachers, plan instruction that will both interest students and expand their critical thinking skills, the next generation of graduates will be well prepared to find, synthesize, and correctly apply information to everyday situations. As they face decisions about career changes, consumer goods, political candidates, financial resources, and personal relationships, their choices should improve.

A DAY IN THE LIFE OF A HIGH SCHOOL MEDIA SPECIALIST

With so many new roles and technologies to handle, what is it like to be a library media specialist at the beginning of the twenty-first century? A look at a typical day might help.

The director of the media center opens the door and glances at the bulletin boards to see if they have been finished for the week. Three announcements of contests are in the media center mailbox: the first from the state school library media association announcing this year's online searching contest for students, the second from the state Friends of Libraries announcing their essay contest, "Libraries Make a Difference," and the third about a photography contest sponsored by a local service organization. Another item in the mailbox is a reminder for the evening's parent-teacher open house.

Before the school day begins, a small group of students arrive to create a PowerPoint™ presentation for their reports. A second group uses the reference collection of print and electronic sources. Two students carefully wheel out the cart holding 20 laptop computers to take to their classroom.

The director stops at the administrative microcomputer to read the latest e-mail messages. Next an e-mail message is sent to the student council to thank them for providing funds for free copies on the photocopy machine and to remind the officers that continuation of funding for this project next year would be appreciated. Also, two requests must be sent to recall materials checked out by students or teachers that are needed by others. This recall process has saved time because the circulation period for everyone is one semester. Recalling a few items needed by others during the semester is simpler than sending overdue notices for materials at the end of a two-week circulation period.

The need to check wikis and blogs has increased the time spent in front of the computer screen. Learning to scan for what is important, making rapid comments when necessary, and answering questions posed are essential. The director feels less anxious because some of this has been done quickly at home yesterday.

Because the director is responsible for several technologies, a quick check confirms that all systems are functioning before picking up a questionnaire for a research study being conducted by a student at a local college. The needed statistics are available on a spreadsheet on the administrative computer, and the director moves to that computer program to generate the information before bringing up the day's calendar.

Looking at the calendar, the director notes that the programming schedule for the media transmission system, prepared by a second media specialist, shows a two-hour segment to project *Romeo and Juliet* in the auditorium for the English literature classes. A group of students will arrive soon to locate materials for their research reports. This group must be reminded to develop a sound search strategy before going to the computer terminals. A 20-minute segment must be scheduled for a teacher and the director to evaluate the team-taught unit that has just been completed. They will review their scoring of the research papers and the final grades that have been output from the computer used for the final test as well as the products to be placed in student portfolios. Results of short student surveys show that materials were heavily used at one point because a second teacher had made a similar research assignment.

A brief time is available to discuss the probable change in the U.S. history curriculum with the principal and the chair of the social studies department. The bibliography generated on the proposed topic may not be adequate, and additional funds will be requested.

When the warning bell rings five minutes before the first class, students check out materials at the circulation desk. The clerk confirms the status of materials already in each student's possession by running a bar code wand over the student's identification card.

Students entering for the first period go to the OPAC, which also shows the holdings of all libraries in the vicinity of the school. Students have access not only to materials in the school but also the local public library, the community college, and a nearby university. In addition, an online modem connects them through the Internet to databases listing the holdings of other libraries throughout the United States. Because one of their first library lessons in elementary school was how to complete an interlibrary loan transaction, requesting items is an automatic process.

Students use print, electronic data bases on the Internet, and the World Wide Web to select information sources. They send messages via e-mail and use electronic lists to locate additional facts or information about holdings of other libraries. E-mail is used to request fax transfer of print documents. Other students use an Internet transmission for full-text retrieval. Still others send e-mail messages to classrooms and students at other sites all around the world.

At the end of each period, the director makes note of both successes and failures. At the end of the day, the director, the other media specialist, and the staff analyze the day's activities. Then they place suggestions for future orders on the acquisitions database, draft memos to teachers, and outline activities for library staff for the remainder of the week or semester.

The final note on the calendar is a reminder to call the local supplier of trophies to confirm delivery of the Debate Club plaques. The director cosponsors the Debate Club this year.

It has been a busy day, and the director of the media center thinks briefly of university courses in which the activities of the media center that were just accomplished in seven hours were described in lectures given over 15 weeks. These activities are repeated and rearranged daily, weekly, and monthly. It has been a particularly tiring day, and the director begins to review the reasons for choosing this career. On tomorrow's calendar is a note to respond to an e-mail message from one of last year's students. The message reads as follows:

> My new school seems to be OK. The media center isn't as big, doesn't have any good books at all, and there aren't as many computers or electronic databases to use. I'm back to writing notes with my pencil because they have a line to get to the word-processing programs, but I'm still thinking about being a media specialist when I go to college next year.

Exercises

1. Visit a library media center and observe the media specialist for one or more days. Note especially the number of students given individual assistance, the interactions with teachers, and the content of any classes taught in the media center.
2. Create a time line showing the development of school library media centers in such a way that it would interest middle school students in an introduction to their library media center.
3. Research the development of the school library program in your area. Match this to the time line suggested in the historical background given in this section.
4. Review the current education literature to determine the newest trends or concepts in education improvement. Create a plan to coordinate the media center program with one of these trends.
5. Draft a note to your principal detailing a new trend and include a bibliography. Be sure to ask the principal whether any of the citations should be sent to the office for him or her to read or if a presentation would be appropriate for a teachers' meeting.
6. Using the terminology of Frank Smith's critical thinking skills, write a list of objectives for activities in the media center that help develop these skills.

NOTES

1. Barbara K. Stripling and Sandra Hughes-Hassell, *Curriculum Connections through the Library* (Westport, CT: Libraries Unlimited, 2003).

2. Ibid., xviii.

3. Sandra Hughes-Hassell and A. Wheelock, *The Information Powered School* (Chicago: American Library Association, 2005).

4. Eric M. Meyers, "The Complex Character of Collaboration: Current Practice and Future Challenges, in *Into the Center of the Curriculum: Papers of the Treasure Mountain Research Retreat #14, Reno, Nevada, October 24–25, 2007,* eds. David V. Loertscher and Marcia Mardis (Salt Lake City, UT: Hi Willow Research and Publishing, 2007), 112.

5. Paul G. Zurkowski, *The Information Service Environment Relationships and Priorities* (Washington, DC: National Commission on Libraries and Information Science, 1974), 6.

6. David V. Loertscher and Blanche Woolls, *Information Literacy: A Review of the Research: A Guide for Practitioners and Researchers,* 2nd ed. (San Jose, CA: Hi Willow Research and Publishing, 2002), 2.

7. American Association of School Librarians and Association for Educational Communications and Technology, *Information Power: Building Partnerships for Learning* (Chicago: American Library Association, 1998), 1.

8. Ibid.

9. Joie Taylor, *Information Literacy and the School Library Media Center* (Westport, CT: Libraries Unlimited, 2006), 28–30.

10. Sharon Coatney, "Assessment for Learning," in *Curriculum Connections through the Library,* eds. Barbara K. Stripling and Sandra Hughes-Hassell (Westport, CT: Libraries Unlimited, 2003), 157.

11. David V. Loertscher and Blanche Woolls, *Information Literacy: A Review of the Research: A Guide for Practitioners and Researchers,* 2nd ed. (San Jose, CA: Hi Willow Research and Publishing, 2002), 8.

12. W. Bernard Lukenbill and Barbara Froling Immroth, *Health Information for Youth: The Public Library and School Library Media Center Role* (Westport, CT: Libraries Unlimited, 2007), viii.

13. Larry Anderson, *Guidebook for Developing an Effective Instructional Technology Plan, Version 2,* http://www.nctp.com/downloads/guidebook.pdf.

14. Richard W. Paul, *Critical Thinking: What Every Person Needs to Survive in a Rapidly Changing World* (Sonoma, CA: Foundation for Critical Thinking, 1992), 17.

15. K. W. Craver, "Critical Thinking: Implications for Library Research," in *The Research of School Library Media Centers: Papers of the Treasure Mountain Research Retreat, Park City, Utah, October 17–18, 1989,* ed. B. Woolls (Castle Rock, CO: Hi Willow Research and Publishing, 1990), 129–30.

16. A. King, "Inquiry as a Tool in Critical Thinking," in *Changing College Classrooms: New Teaching and Learning Strategies for an Increasingly Complex World* ed. Diane F. Halpern. (San Francisco, CA: Jossey-Bass, 1994), 13.

17. Violet H. Harada, "Empowered Learning: Fostering Thinking across the Curriculum," in *Curriculum Connections through the Library,* eds. Barbara K. Stripling and Sandra Hughes-Hassell (Westport, CT: Libraries Unlimited, 2003), 41–42.

Chapter 3

Becoming a School Library Media Specialist

People decide to become school library media specialists for a variety of reasons, examples of which are listed below. Some reasons might be perceived as more likely to produce a dedicated library media specialist than others.

1. Dedicated educators choose to serve all the children in a school rather than a single classroom; they not only love books but appreciate the opportunity to take a leadership role in the teaching and learning process of all students in one building.

2. Some librarians prefer the opportunity to work 9 or 10 months a year rather than 12.

3. Some teachers may elect to manage the library one or two hours a day rather than teach another section of a subject area.

4. Some teachers are "drafted" in times of media specialist shortages.

5. Furloughed teachers seek a permanent position when a school library media specialist's position becomes vacant.

6. Persons who have served in a paraprofessional position choose to continue their education and become a certified media specialist.

An excellent school library media specialist should possess outstanding teaching skills and enthusiasm for learning and the continued accomplishment of students. A service orientation is necessary so that information flows steadily from the media center to the teachers and students, and a helpful attitude must be maintained at all times. Creativity is essential for implementing the most effective methods and making the program exciting, ever changing, and ever challenging to students. Finally, practice in leadership is essential if the media program is going to continue to serve the school. If teachers and the media specialist are to collaborate in providing instruction, the media specialist must take the lead.

Before choosing the school library media center as their preferred "classroom" assignment, interested persons should decide whether they are willing to accept a leadership role in effecting positive change for all students and to practice flexibility in methods to help students achieve success. The media center has grown far beyond the book collection to include information in a wide variety of formats and an ever-changing array of technologies. The media specialist's role is constantly changing. An interest in trying new things is essential because the necessary skills to manage these diverse collections are constantly evolving.

Changes in the role of the school library media specialist coupled with new trends in technology have radically changed the competencies needed for persons managing and working in information centers today. Programs to prepare new library media specialists and update the veterans are available through institutions offering college credit. Continuing education programs offer experiences with new materials, curriculum innovation, use of new technologies, resource-based teaching, and other subjects.

PREPARING SCHOOL LIBRARY MEDIA SPECIALISTS

Programs to prepare school library media specialists are offered in schools of education and of library and information science at universities and colleges at both undergraduate and graduate levels. Courses are selected by or assigned to students to help them meet the certification, sometimes referred to as credential, requirements for the state where they plan to teach. State and local certification requirements are developed for and approved by each state's board of education. State board members usually delegate the responsibility for confirmation of appropriate certification to specific teacher education units in a state's department of education.

State departments of education may grant certificates to persons with bachelor's degrees. The number of semester hours required at the undergraduate or graduate level varies greatly. While some states might require as little as 18 to 20 hours in library science at no specific level of instruction, others specify a master's degree. The Web sites of state departments of education are shown in Figure 3.1. URLs change, so this information, although accurate at publication, should be verified. Log onto the state's department of education, locate certification or credential, and find school library certification, and be flexible about names. The new title for California is teacher-librarian.

In the past, certification for elementary schools had fewer requirements than secondary, but, presently, the requirements are the same in most states. Requirements vary at different times. When positions are available and candidates for positions are not, requirements are sometimes lowered.

One major change in certification has been the requirement for a competency test. Some of these tests are administered at the state level, such as the California Basic Skills Test. Other states use the NTE Core Battery. Information about competency testing is available on each state's Web site.

Alabama
  http://www.alsde.edu/html/sections/section_detail.asp?section=66&
    footer=sections

Alaska
  http://www.eed.state.ak.us/TeacherCertification/

Arizona
  http://www.ade.state.az.us/certification/

Arkansas
  http://arkedu.state.ar.us/teachers/teachers_licensure.html

California
  http://www.ctc.ca.gov/credentials/CREDS/library-media.html

Colorado
  http://www.cde.state.co.us/index_license.htm

Connecticut
  http://www.sde.ct.gov/sde/site/default.asp

Delaware
  http://www.doe.state.de.us/info/certification/

District of Columbia
  http://www.k12.dc.us/dcsea/certification/licensing/
    licensing.html

Florida
  http://www.fldoe.org/edcert/

Georgia
  http://www.gapsc.com/TeacherCertification.asp

Hawaii
  http://www.htsb.org/

Idaho
  http://www.sde.idaho.gov/TeacherCertification/default.asp

Illinois
  http://www.isbe.state.il.us/certification/default.htm

Indiana
  http://www.doe.state.in.us/dps/licensing/welcome.html

Iowa
  http://www.state.ia.us/boee/

Kansas
  http://www.ksde.org/default.aspx?tabid=123

Kentucky
  http://www.kyepsb.net/certification/certFAQ.asp

Figure 3.1 Web Sites of State Departments of Education

Louisiana
http://www.doe.state.la.us/lde/index.html

Maine
http://www.maine.gov/education/forms/fingerprint/letter_1.htm

Maryland
http://www.marylandpublicschools.org/MSDE/divisions/
certification/certification_branch/

Massachusetts
http://www.doe.mass.edu/educators/e_license.html

Michigan
http://www.michigan.gov/mde

Minnesota
http://education.state.mn.us/MDE/Teacher_Support/Educator_
Licensing/index.html

Mississippi
http://www.mde.k12.ms.us/ed_licensure/index.html

Missouri
http://www.dese.mo.gov/divcareered/certifications.htm

Nebraska
http://www.nde.state.ne.us/TCERT/index.html

Nevada
http://www.doe.nv.gov/licensing.html

New Hampshire
http://www.ed.state.nh.us/education/beEd.htm

New Jersey
http://www.state.nj.us/education/educators/license/

New Mexico
http://www.ped.state.nm.us/div/ais/lic/index.html

New York
http://usny.nysed.gov/professionals/lpny.html

North Carolina
http://www.ncpublicschools.org/

North Dakota
http://www.nd.gov/espb/licensure/

Ohio
http://www.ode.state.oh.us/GD/Templates/Pages/ODE/ODE
Primary.aspx?page=2&TopicRelationID=513

Oklahoma
http://www.sde.state.ok.us/home/defaultns.html

Figure 3.1 *Continued*

Oregon
http://www.tspc.state.or.us/

Pennsylvania
http://www.pde.state.pa.us/teaching/cwp/view.asp?a=90&Q=32511&
    g=140&teachingNav=|93|94|&teachingNav=|1904|1911|

Rhode Island
http://www.ridoe.net/EducatorQuality/Certification/default.aspx

South Carolina
http://ed.sc.gov/topics/certification/

South Dakota
http://doe.sd.gov/oatq/teachercert/index.asp

Tennessee
http://www.state.tn.us/education/lic/

Texas
http://www.sbec.state.tx.us/SBEConline/certinfo/routescertif.asp?
    width=1280&height=800

Utah
http://www.schools.utah.gov/cert/require/reqs.htm

Vermont
http://education.vermont.gov/new/html/maincert.html

Virginia
http://www.pen.k12.va.us/VDOE/newvdoe/teached.html

Washington
http://www.k12.wa.us/certification/teacher/teacherinformation.
    aspx

West Virginia
http://wvde.state.wv.us/certification/

Wisconsin
http://dpi.state.wi.us/tepdl/tm-license.html

Wyoming
http://ptsb.state.wy.us/certification/applications.cfm

Figure 3.1 *Continued*

Three types of credentials may be awarded: emergency, temporary, or permanent. When the supply of candidates is much fewer than the positions available, persons may be able to begin working in a school library on an emergency credential. Graduates of undergraduate programs may receive a temporary certificate. Persons who begin their careers with a temporary certificate must replace it with permanent certification within a specified time. The requirements for permanent certification also vary. Some states require teaching experience but no further education beyond a bachelor's degree, and others demand a master's degree.

Because persons attending institutions of higher education expect to be eligible for certification in a state upon graduation, university and college education programs respond to the certification requirements of their state and, whenever possible, meet requirements for adjoining states. State requirements, therefore, dictate the components of programs that certify school library media specialists. For many states, the certification program remains competency based; for others, specific courses are described. Many states require a practicum, which varies from 200 hours divided between elementary and secondary schools to three hours. Some states require both a classroom teaching credential and the school library credential; others require successful teaching experience before granting certification.

Granting certification is accomplished by one of the following means:

1. Department of education staff review the transcript of an applicant to determine whether the applicant's record meets state requirements.
2. Program approval is awarded to the school or department in the college or university, based on a visit by a team of selected educators reporting to the department of education.
3. An independent group or agency confirms eligibility of the school or department.

CHOOSING A LIBRARY MEDIA SPECIALIST EDUCATION PROGRAM

Deciding where to go to earn a library media specialist certificate is usually based on the student's ability to attend classes. As certification moved into a master's program, many who wished to pursue this profession already held full-time positions or had family responsibilities or both. Their choices were limited by the proximity of the institution. Older adults planning a career change with family responsibilities in one location found it difficult to move to a new location to take classes. Many colleges and universities offered full programs during the summer, when teachers who wished to become media specialists could move from home to campus to take classes.

Through technology and the possibilities opened by distance education, options for obtaining certification have changed. Many colleges and universities offer full degrees through a combination of possibilities such as televised sessions in the immediate area followed by short sessions on campus. Interactions between teachers and students in a distant location are possible with a camera that shows students and teachers in one location to students who are off-campus. Faculty members travel among the various locations to teach one or more classes each semester; in this way they meet in person all students taking the course.

In other programs, students come to campus one or more times each semester and complete courses via the Internet. Many institutions offer complete master's programs online so that students never need to leave their homes. As more institutions undertake this type of instruction, it will become increasingly easy to pursue both advanced degrees and continuing education experiences without leaving home.

When choosing a certification program, one must consider the curriculum proposed at any site. A major concern is that media specialists not be taught away from other students pursing another teaching credential or another type of library position, in schools of education or in library schools. Media specialists are teachers and they are librarians. To be isolated from others means that media specialists lose valuable opportunities to learn what they have in common with both teachers and other types of librarians. One should also make sure that the curriculum includes philosophy and psychology of youth, methods of teaching, selection of materials for youth and the curriculum, knowledge of the curriculum offered in schools, and current technology. Knowledge of library management and reference materials is essential.

Those who work with children and young adults must understand the learning processes and learning styles of their clientele. This is taught in educational philosophy and psychology courses and in classes on special-needs children, whether gifted or learning disabled. Understanding the growth of children from age six through the teen years helps the media specialist recognize different behaviors. These courses should provide ideas for maintaining discipline in the media center.

Because the media specialist is a teacher, it is essential to study teaching methods. Some colleges and universities may require teaching certification before admitting a student to the media specialist program. Others offer teaching methods during the media specialist program. A program should allow the media specialist-in-training to teach in an actual school for no fewer than eight weeks.

Most library science programs offer courses in children's and young adults' materials; these courses are mandatory for media specialists who will work in a school. The program should offer at least one such course at each level. The volume of materials published each year makes it difficult to combine both levels in one course. Further, the types of materials published for children and young adults must be reviewed, including new technologies for management and the database program available.

Knowledge of the curriculum taught in schools with instruction in fitting the media center into the curriculum is another required course. Choosing materials is only one part of the process of integrating the library media center into the school's curriculum. Media specialists must understand how to work with curricula and teachers and how to blend materials in the media center with materials in the classroom.

One of the most important elements to consider in selecting a program is the kind of laboratory experiences and the types of technologies offered. It would be unthinkable for any library media specialist program in the beginning years of the twenty-first century to reject new technologies. To promote new technology applications as they arrive to school administrators, the library media specialist not only must be familiar with the technology but also must have tested the technology and found it essential in the lives of students and teachers.

OBTAINING CERTIFICATION

Once upon a time, a student called the author to discuss obtaining certification. This student had graduated but had neglected to apply for certification immediately. The reason given was that no one had ever made it clear that an application process existed. This person assumed that the college granting the degree automatically sent an application for certification when a student graduated. This seems a little like assuming one would receive a driver's license after taking a driver's education course. Because most certification applications require a fee for processing, it is unlikely that such a process occurs automatically.

Each state handles the certification process differently, as stated earlier. The requirements are established in each state; the actual application forms and processing fees all vary. Many states have both their student expectations and their certification processes under review and subject to change.

With the changes in performance criteria for students, it is inevitable that expectations for teacher performance and the consequent preparation of teachers should be reviewed. The prospective school library media specialist who has recently completed a program for certification should have met the requirements for the area where the university is located. Few states have reciprocity. That is, they seldom recognize certification in another state. The most usual missing requirement is a course in state history, although it may also be completion of a degree. As stated earlier, some states require only a bachelor's degree and others require a master's. Those who completed certification in the past or who plan to apply for positions in a different state should confirm certification requirements before applying. It would be embarrassing to apply for a position for which one is qualified but not eligible because of certification requirements.

Finally, some states require police checks on arrests. In one state, a student who has a conviction for driving under the influence of alcohol or a drug-related arrest will not be granted a teaching credential. Such a check will also indicate whether an applicant for a credential has a record of child abuse or other crimes against children.

It is the responsibility of media specialists completing their programs of instruction to learn the requirements for certification and to apply for and receive their certificates as soon as those requirements have been met. Penalties may apply if this process is not completed in a timely fashion. In some states, one must complete the competency program in place when applying for the certificate. If certificate requirements change, it might be necessary to take more coursework or complete more requirements at a later date. Although these additional courses may be considered continuing professional education, it is preferable to choose continuing education experiences based on one's own needs rather than on making up some deficiency dictated by the state department of education.

Toward the end of formal education or when considering a job change, the school library media specialist begins to look for an appropriate location. This job seeking requires some preparation.

HOW TO FIND A JOB

Sometimes, finding a job is a matter of luck, being in the right spot at the right time. Declining enrollments resulting in school closures and decreases in funding play havoc on hiring teachers and other school staff. Often reduced funding for education means school library media specialists are furloughed or returned to classrooms and the library media center is turned over to clerical staff or volunteers.

The creation of media centers beginning in 1965 provided opportunities for graduates to choose the job of school library media specialist as a career. Positions were made full-time, increased from part-time classroom teaching with part-time responsibility for management of the media center. Now, more than 50 years later, teachers who transferred from the classroom to the media center are retiring. Others take early retirements as states make such options attractive. Vacancies caused by these early retirements cannot be filled unless large numbers of teachers and education students earn school library certification. Although the economy during the period after September 11, 2001, and other national and international situations has shown some decline in new positions, this will change.

Technology advances are redefining the competencies and expectations for school library media specialists, some of whom are retiring rather than accepting the responsibility for implementing constant changes in technology. Competency in new technologies greatly increases the opportunities for those seeking library media specialist positions. As library media specialists gain experience in their new positions, they may begin to plan to achieve National Board Certification for Library Media Educators, which will be discussed later in this chapter.

Jobs will be available, but matching preferences to positions will require attention to the process. The student should ask the practicum or field experience supervisor to write a detailed letter about the experiences of the student in school so that potential employers understand the applicant's capabilities. Care must be taken to include reference letters from professors who can attest to the competencies of their students to manage a school library media center, especially if their education prepares them for all levels from kindergarten through high school. It is usually preferable to ask for letters of reference before graduating. Writing such a letter 10 years later may be difficult for any professor who has taught many students in the intervening years.

Next, the student should prepare a résumé and cover letter. These must be kept up to date, because they contain the date the résumé was prepared, name, address, telephone number, educational background, schools attended after high school, and courses taken relevant to the job under consideration. Degrees received and specialization are followed by work experience, both full- and part-time, with emphasis on positions related to school library media services. Examples include library page or aide during high school, summer work at the public library, and experience in the college library. A brief description of related jobs and responsibilities should be included.

Finally, most administrators want to know a little about the applicant's interests and hobbies. One applicant might be chosen over another because of an ability to sponsor an extracurricular activity such as the tennis or debate team.

Résumés should be well formatted, using a word-processing program to allow easy updating. Printed on a laser printer, they must be eye-catching in case they are one of many submitted for the job.

The cover letter is addressed to the prospective employer, states the information understood about the position, and cites the reasons why the applicant is interested in the job and well suited for it. This letter must be carefully proofread to assure the reader that the applicant is articulate, accurate, and acceptable. A sample letter is found in Appendix B.

After the résumé is prepared and the placement file is complete, the student may begin the job search. Professors in the school library media training program often have information about openings because school officials check with the training programs when they have jobs to fill. If the college or university provides a placement service, it will post job openings sent to the placement office.

Many state library associations provide job hotlines in their states. Although these may list more job openings for other types of libraries than school libraries, they are a good first place to seek information. The professional literature also provides information about openings in school districts.

Another job-search method used by some students is to request that their field experience or practicum experience be assigned in a school district where they might like to find a position. This is positive for both sides. The prospective school library media specialist can assess the school district at the same time school district personnel are reviewing the competencies of the student.

The network of school library media professionals is another source of information. These persons have immediate knowledge of resignations, transfers, and retirements in the school district and may have information about neighboring districts.

State department of education personnel usually are aware of openings in school districts in their state and can be called for help. Job seekers also can talk with persons in federal agencies responsible for library programs. These persons talk regularly with state department of education personnel, library school educators, and supervisors in large school districts and are aware of openings.

Professional association conferences are a source of information about job openings. Many students attend a state or national conference before they graduate to talk with media professionals about situations in various school districts. These experiences may aid the decision process by helping match skills to preferences.

Finally, openings for temporary positions occur when library media specialists take sabbaticals or leaves of absence. Accepting a temporary position may lead to a permanent position in the district. When interviewing for these positions, it is wise to find out one's options. What is the possibility that this position will be permanent in the immediate future? Do others in the district wish to have a permanent library media position? Will the school district accept your resignation if a permanent position opens in another location? The responses to these questions will help the job seeker to determine the possibility for permanent employment after a temporary position closes.

Thorough preparation for an interview will help the applicant remain calm during the process. After reviewing the situation, the applicant can formulate a list of intelligent questions to ask about the school district. It is wise to research the district in much the same way the administrators will be checking the applicant. Just as the administrators attempt to determine whether the applicant will fit the district, applicants will want to know if the situation will suit them. Some managerial questions are discussed at the beginning of chapter 4.

Applicants should always be on time for an interview. This means making sure of the location of the building, the amount of time it takes to arrive, and how difficult it will be to locate parking. An attempt to be calm and relaxed will fail if unexpected traffic rerouting, missed turns, or lack of parking space delay arrival.

The interview process is designed to find out as much about the applicant as possible. One or more persons will be asking questions. The applicant should listen carefully to the questions and reply to the person who directs the question, not to the entire review panel. Questions should be answered as positively as possible, with mention of personal skills that are appropriate. Although an applicant should appear interested and enthusiastic about the position, it is important to act naturally. Acknowledge when unsure about a response rather than attempting a clever guess.

Many books have been written about clothes making the person. This may not be true all the time, but it certainly is true in the job interview. If an applicant really wants the job, this is, perhaps, not the time to try out the latest high-fashion attire. It is a time to look professional.

The interviewers will learn a great deal about applicants—what kind of persons they are, their skills, their thoughts on education issues, and perhaps a little of their philosophy of education. Practicing how to interview can help prospective media specialists formulate careful answers quickly.

The interview also gives the interviewee a chance to ask questions about the position, the school district, and the organization of the educational and media center programs. An applicant who asks pertinent questions can learn much about a position during the interview.

After an interview, it is appropriate to send a letter of thanks. At this time, interest in the position can be restated.

CONTINUING PROFESSIONAL EDUCATION

The school library media specialist's education should not be over when permanent certification is received. In some states and in many school districts, continuing education is required of all teachers who wish to renew their teaching contracts. Such requirements as number of credits, college or workshop credit, and time allowed to complete courses are specified by the governing body. School library media specialists must learn not only state certification requirements as they relate to permanent certification, but also continuing education requirements in effect for their school district.

Regardless of whether additional education is required, school library media specialists must remain on the cutting edge of education, and this can only happen through reading the literature and taking part in new learning experiences. The school district or intermediate or regional service unit may offer programs carrying continuing education credits. Often professional associations plan workshops and offer these experiences for college credit or continuing education credit. Many colleges and universities offer short courses or summer sessions designed to attract school library media specialists who wish to upgrade their skills.

A new approach to confirming skills in teachers and school library media specialists has been the National Board for Professional Teaching Standards (NBPTS). The NBPTS, an independent nonprofit group governed by a national board, was created in 1987 with its mission

- Maintaining high and rigorous standards for what accomplished teachers should have and be able to do
- Providing a national voluntary system certifying teachers who meet these standards
- Advocating related education reforms to integrate National Board Certification in American education and to capitalize on the expertise of National Board Certified Teachers.[1]

The professional standards in each certifying area were developed by expert teachers in that field, reflecting the five core propositions endorsed by the NBPTS:

Teachers are committed to students and their learning.

Teachers know the subjects they teach and how to teach those subjects to students.

Teachers are responsible for managing and monitoring student learning.

Teachers think systematically about their practice and learn from experience.

Teachers are members of learning communities.[2]

Designed by a select group of school library media specialists and educators, the National Board standards take an unusual approach: They examine school library media performance irrespective of resources. To achieve accomplished teachers status, a school library media specialist must meet the same rigorous standards as classroom teachers, standards that have become the basis for the performance-based certifying assessment that enables library media specialists to become nationally certified. The NBPTS Web site (http://www.nbpts.org/for_candidates/certificate_areas1?ID=19&x=55&y=6) identifies the school library media specialist as someone with "extensive knowledge about the field of information." It is suggested that library media specialists "apply technology to instruction in ways that strengthen information-based programs, enhance communication and instruction, help teachers expand the subject matter content of their instruction and extend the availability of information to all students." They are responsible for demonstrating outstanding competence at collaborating with classroom teachers to teach information skills; integrating technology; and encouraging reading and love of literature while demonstrating further their personal knowledge of management practices, technology basics, children's and young adult literature, collection development, ethical and legal tenets, and information literacy.

According to Dickinson, library media as a certification area first became available in 2002, with the first class of 435 library media-certified teacher candidates.[3] While this is not available to students preparing to be school library media specialists, they should be aware of opportunities to undertake NBPTS in the future. In some states, this is subsidized by the state and carries a salary increase upon successful completion.

RECRUITING FOR THE PROFESSION

Professional school library media specialists who began their careers in the 1970s are retiring. Early retirement plans have encouraged others to leave school districts before the normal retirement age. The need for qualified persons to fill these positions is becoming critical. School library media specialists need to encourage their brightest students to consider pursuing this profession. Further, they should observe their fellow teachers to determine which ones have the skills for managing media centers and encourage them to begin programs to prepare for these vacancies.

Exercises

1. Compare the regulations and competencies for certification in your state with an adjoining state or a state in which you might like to apply for certification. Estimate the amount of time it will take to complete those requirements and determine whether you could complete some of them in your present program.
2. Request an application for certification from your state department of education. Carefully read the instructions and confirm the requirements for certification. What information needs to be included? For example, is a physical examination required? What clearances are needed? What fees are assessed, and what method of payment is suggested? Are college transcripts necessary? To whom is the form to be submitted? What is the probable length of time between submission and return of the certificate?
3. Generate a list of questions you might ask about a school district during an interview.

NOTES

1. National Board for Professional Teaching Standards, http://www.nbpts.org/about_us/mission_and_history/the_five_core_propositio.

2. National Board for Professional Teaching Standards, http://www.nbpts.org/UserFiles/File/what_teachers.pdf.

3. Gail Dickinson, "National Board Effects on School Library Media Education," *Knowledge Quest* 32, no. 2 (November/December 2003): 18–21.

4

Choosing and Beginning the Job

Graduation diploma and certification credential in hand, the new school library media specialist has located several positions that seem interesting, has submitted job applications and résumés, and has visited for a preliminary interview. If qualifications match needs in the school district and the applicant has interviewed well, a job offer should be forthcoming.

However, some questions must be answered before accepting a position and signing the contract. Although it may be tempting to launch into the daily routine of the media center, a wiser approach would be to learn first about the organizational and political structure of the school district. The more one knows about the situation, the easier it is to fit the media program into its environment. To attempt to manage a media program without understanding administrative practices may cause the media specialist to make unintentional errors.

When a school district has a coordinator or director of library media programs, the school district administration believes in the importance of the media program, and the building-level practitioner has a specialist in administration to query with specific questions related to the media center and its operation. When no such person exists, it is less likely that school library media specialists will meet as a group for in-service sessions or that an advocate is available to speak for media programs to higher administration.

DETERMINING DISTRICT ADMINISTRATIVE PRACTICE

Managers of the school district, members of the board of education, and district-level administrators are the first group to research. School boards are either appointed or elected. Appointed members are often selected by a public official such as the mayor; these members maintain their position as long as the appointing politician wishes them to do so. When elected, members appear on the ballot in bipartisan elections or on a special ballot. Elected school board members serve at the pleasure of the voters of their community, and their decisions may be greatly influenced by community reactions. Individuals sometimes run for office to correct what they perceive as a problem, such as the actions of the current superintendent, the addition of a program to the curriculum, or the withdrawal of a program considered unnecessary or less necessary. The latter category may include programs begun with outside funds and discontinued when the funds are withdrawn or depleted.

School boards are legally responsible for setting policy for the school district. Because state sunshine laws mandate open meetings of public officials, school board meetings are open to the public. The school library media specialist should plan to attend meetings to observe the actions taken, the sides chosen by individual members, and the general attitudes toward certain issues. School board members are powerful individuals in the public education of children.

School board members review graduation requirements for high school students. Although state boards of education establish criteria for curricula within the state, a local school board may increase the requirements. That is, the state may require two semesters of physical education, and the local school board may include the requirement of swimming a prescribed distance.

School boards approve all budget allocations and confirm that monies are being spent as requested and approved. School boards are also responsible for purchasing and selling property owned by the school district. They must agree to the purchase of additional property and the construction of new buildings in places where the school population is growing. In some locations, school board members place a tax on construction of new homes and apartments to ensure funding for the building of schools. It is the school board who must hire architects, approve plans, award jobs to contractors, and see that the building is built as specified.

Board members must also agree to the closing of school buildings when enrollments decline or other circumstances require relocation of students. In western Pennsylvania, a region heavily mined for coal, mine subsidence (the caving in of old mine shafts) can cause a school building to crack. Other schools may be plagued by the discovery of asbestos in the walls or ceilings. School boards must find alternative locations until buildings can be repaired or new buildings constructed.

Finally, the school board is responsible for interviewing and selecting the superintendent and approving the hiring of all administrators, teachers, and staff. School board members must ensure that state regulations are carried out with regard to certification of employees. This may include ensuring that proper health tests are conducted, that police checks are made (some states now require confirmation that a prospective teacher has no arrest record), and that all teachers have the appropriate degrees and certificates.

As stated earlier, the superintendent is usually chosen by the school board, although in some locations this person is elected by community vote. State law may govern the superintendent's length of appointment. Such mandatory contracts provide the superintendent some protection from the whims of the community. Superintendents are responsible for the day-to-day management of the district program, the selection of administrators and teaching staff, the development and implementation of curriculum, and the continuation of the school district program, including maintenance of buildings. Management of the school program requires, among other things, creating, refining, and presenting the school budget for the approval of the school board.

Superintendents choose administrators to work with them. These administrators are assigned to the central office staff and to the building-level programs. Central office staff is responsible for special areas of the school program and assume districtwide responsibility in a particular function (e.g., art coordinator, elementary supervisor, athletic director). Teachers in those functions are first responsible to their building principals and second to the coordinator of the specialized program.

Another position has been added to many school districts, that of technology coordinator. This person's assignment includes maintaining external communication links, servers, and microcomputer-related hardware and software in buildings throughout the district. In some cases, additional staff will be assigned to individual buildings reporting to this administrator the status of equipment in their buildings. Often the building-level assignment belongs to the library media specialist, and anyone applying for a position would need to have appropriate education, training, and experience.

When technology is not necessarily the library media specialist's responsibility, learning how many staff members are available to assist from a district level helps determine the speed with which assistance will be given to any single school. Because it is difficult for school boards to fund technology staffs with sufficient personnel to serve individual schools, a library media specialist with the knowledge and willingness to help may perform an unassigned technology specialist role in the school.

In the restructuring movement of the 1990s, many central office staff positions were reassigned to a broader area of responsibility encompassing many functions or returned to a building-level position. The removal of the central staff person responsible for the school library media program or the reassignment of someone who knows little about this area means that the new library media specialist will rely on another media specialist in the district to answer questions. This process will be discussed more fully in the later section on Human Factors.

Building administrators include the principal, assistant principal, department heads, and lead teachers. Filling any of these positions may be solely the responsibility of the superintendent. Or, in the case of a department head, the person may be appointed by the principal or elected by the department teachers. Administrators at all levels manage their programs. Who reports to whom is a system worked out in the central office by the superintendent and staff, and the school library media specialist should be aware of this process to be successful in effecting change. In many high schools, it is important for the school librarian to be the head of the department in order to be considered for inclusion on curriculum committees and for other leadership roles.

An organizational chart of the school district shows the relationship of the assistant superintendents to the superintendent and the reporting sequence of coordinators and their relationship to the principals. A chart of one school district before restructuring is shown in Figure 4.1. Figure 4.2 displays this same district after restructuring.

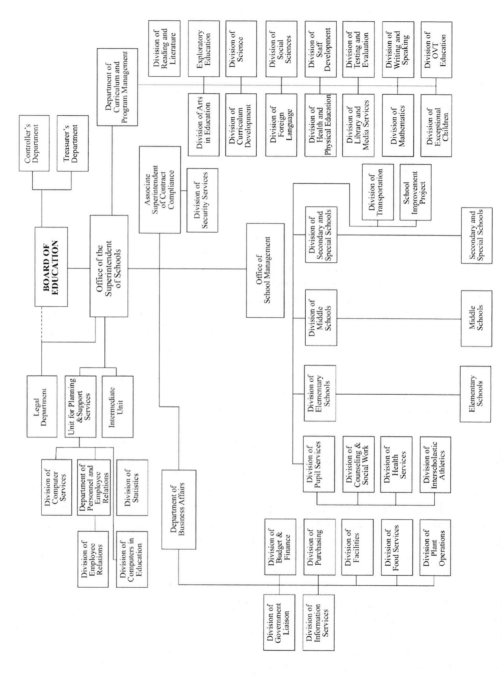

Figure 4.1 School District before Restructuring

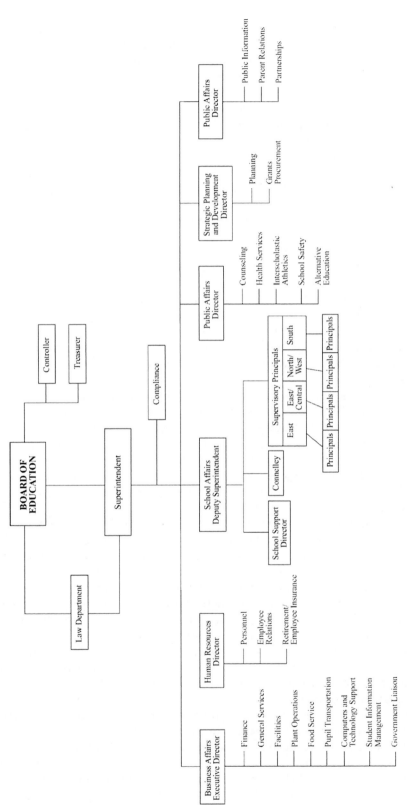

Figure 4.2 School District after Restructuring

In both charts, the board of education is responsible for the school district, and the superintendent serves as liaison between the board and the administrators and teachers in the district. The superintendent in the first chart had several associate superintendents, one for curriculum and program management, another for contract compliance, a third for school management. Among the division directors, the division of library and media services reports directly to the associate superintendent for curriculum and program management. Originally, principals reported to the associate superintendent in charge of school management. This meant that the director of the division of library and media services would bring a building-level problem and its suggested solution to the associate superintendent for curriculum and program management, who would transmit the request to the office of school management. That associate superintendent would bring the matter to the attention of the school principal.

With restructuring, the central office staff has been greatly reduced. Rather than a department of curriculum and program management, a school affairs deputy superintendent oversees supervisory principals in four geographic locations of the city. Rather than having a unit for planning and support services with computer services, computers in education, and statistics, these are disbanded or placed under the human resources director, who handles employment and personnel exclusively. This is a large school district, and smaller districts would have more tasks assigned to even fewer individuals.

In school districts teachers may be selected by a district personnel office, the building principal, or the superintendent. Teaching areas may be determined by certification, and curriculum is specified by the state with local modifications. Choices of textbooks may be dictated by a state or local list, but the classroom teacher determines methods of teaching, choice of primary use of one textbook from the prescribed list, or the use of alternate materials. Nevertheless, assigned the authority by the school board, superintendents are ultimately responsible for the total curriculum.

Superintendents must assure the school board that state requirements are met. They must respond to teacher and administrator suggestions for improvements or requirements beyond state requirements. That is, teachers may consider it important for students to have additional writing experiences or insist that students pass a basic computer literacy test. These activities will then be required by the school district with the approval of the school board. The superintendent must be aware of trends in education so that the district can offer the best possible education to all students.

Another responsibility of the superintendent is to see that facilities are maintained. Daily tasks in individual school buildings are the responsibility of the principal, but any major changes must be approved by the superintendent, who makes recommendations to the school board. If a media center is too small to provide services, the principal must bring proposals for renovation or new construction to the attention of the superintendent.

The superintendent also develops and presents the school budget in such a way that the school board will accept it. Some superintendents divide the budget into a per-pupil allocation, with additional money given to special areas. That is, instructional funds are allocated with a certain number of dollars provided for each student in a given grade or subject area for newly adopted textbooks (if they are provided by the district) and a supplemental amount awarded for additional instructional materials. Art departments and school library media programs receive an amount based on the number of pupils in the building.

With restructuring and site-based management, buildings receive a lump sum to be allocated by the principal or building committee or by whatever mechanism the restructuring or site-based management committee has chosen. When a district employs site-based management, the library media specialist investigates thoroughly the funding devoted to library media services to confirm that the program will be supported and can grow.

After weighing the positive and negative points of the district administrative practice, the candidate will decide whether to accept a position. If the candidate is hired, a formal contract is signed and the media specialist is ready to begin the job.

BEGINNING THE JOB

School library media specialists bring to any new position all their background experiences, their observations of other school library media specialists, their reading and learning in their educational program, and their perception of what makes a good media program. Sometimes many of the elements are in place in the selected position. At other times the specialist may accept a position that is less desirable because of other circumstances, such as family needs or preferred location. In any case, the media specialist's own goals and objectives should be initiated the first week. These goals and objectives may be refined in the first months on the job, but the initial projects to be planned will be evident from the first visit to the school, and objectives must be set if any plans are to succeed.

School library media specialists just beginning in a new job should try to learn as much about the system as possible to choose the best strategy for implementing a plan. One way to do this is to study the school Web site and any school library Web sites.

It is also important to find out as much as possible about what has gone before. This is not to propose that all that has gone before has been done in the most efficient, effective, or successful manner, but a new position may provide a media specialist with a unique opportunity to decide exactly what changes to make and in what order. Ignorance of past procedures might innocently create problems that would impede the progress of other program changes. An understanding of past procedures can help in analyzing present problems. In fact, some procedures may not be problems at all. Remember the proverb "If it isn't broken, don't try to fix it." The review helps to determine whether something is, in fact, broken or more broken than another procedure.

Beginning the job requires as much knowledge as possible about the facility itself, the human factors, and the collection factors. Each of these will be discussed in the context of what a media specialist who is new to a building should try to accomplish in the first few days on the job.

FACILITY FACTORS

Although human factors are more important than facility factors, it is more likely that library media specialists beginning the job will be shown the facility before meeting any of the staff or patrons. A review of the facility will include finding out how traffic flows through the library media center and locating essentials such as the circulation desk, the reference collection and other materials, and the division of spaces.

First, the new media specialist should locate the library media center within the school. Is it near the classrooms or in another wing of a huge building? One school library media center with which the author is familiar is in a separate building at the center of a campus. Its location means that it must accommodate not just students but their outer garments in cold weather, raincoats and umbrellas on rainy days, and their lunches when they come to the media center the period before lunch. This creates a certain type of isolation that the media specialist must, in the first week at the school, determine how to overcome.

Second, the media specialist should count the tables and chairs in the center to determine how many students and teachers can use the center at one time. Next, review the placement of tables and chairs. Tables and chairs grouped together increase opportunities for social interaction, but natural dividers can disseminate noise. If the media center has no separate classroom, can a classroom setting be created and still leave room for other students to come in as independent users?

Next, the media specialist should analyze the traffic pattern. The circulation desk should be placed near the entrance so that students see it immediately when they enter and are reminded to check out materials before they leave. The circulation desk in one library visited by the author was located in a far corner. When the bell ending the period rang, students gathered their materials and left. Anxious to get to their next class, many left with materials that were not checked out.

With the addition of online technology to the responsibility of the school library media specialist, the library media classroom may have been transformed into a computer laboratory. The allocation of spaces to computer use has increased the need for electrical outlets in the library. The location of computers and file servers is a priority in reviewing space in the media center. Are they located where their use can be monitored? When a school population is large and numbers of computer stations is small, space for students to wait becomes a consideration that needs careful planning.

Although many new school library media specialists fear making changes in the facility, relocating furniture and shelving can generate a new perception of the facility for users. Changing the layout to provide for different activities may reverse negative attitudes of students and teachers or change their perception of behaviors that are acceptable in the room. Those most likely to resist change will be the building custodians, sometimes titled building superintendents, who are responsible for the wax buildup on tile floors or the fading colors in carpet. Few bookshelves are bolted to floors, and moving requires only the removal of books and rearrangement of shelves. It is usually well worth the effort to make the move.

Before moving any furnishings, the media specialist should make sure the furniture, technologies, and shelving will fit their new locations. A tape measure may not be necessary; stepping off space one foot at a time can give a fairly accurate measure. Counting the tiles on a tile floor or ceiling can also give a quick measure. Once the appropriate traffic flow is determined, a move can be made.

To assist in a simple review of the layout, a graph sheet and corresponding scale drawing of tables and chairs is found in chapter 6, Figure 6.1. This may be used to draw a rough layout of the present library media center so that it may be viewed from above and decisions can be made about the floor plan before actually moving the furnishings. Should the furniture be moved immediately? This depends on how tolerable any problem might be versus how a bad situation might influence the first weeks on the job. Time is a factor. If a single day is available before students arrive, there might not be time to rearrange. Conversely, changing a media center can modify the attitudes of those who used the facility in the past. If the media specialist feels that an attitude adjustment is needed, then by all means a rearrangement should be carried out to see if it will help solve some of the problems.

The new media specialist should locate not only the computers, servers, and other equipment located in the media center as soon as possible, but also must learn if this responsibility extends beyond the media center. Media center responsibility for equipment may include items stored in locations away from the media center, and an inventory of equipment and its probable location should be available in the school office, if not in the media specialist's desk or file. When this equipment expands to the computers located in classrooms and connected to the media center for access, this record becomes crucial. Teachers will be using equipment as soon as classes begin. Some may need to preview materials before school officially opens. Locating the equipment and assessing its state of repair are essential.

A quick review of the media available is also necessary. Many library media specialists save media when they should be discarded. They may feel that the original cost warrants saving, or the small size of items such as CDs makes them easier to store. Weeding to make room for new items seems less necessary. However, ease of storage is no excuse for keeping irrelevant materials.

The media specialist should review the periodicals collection. If no serials holdings list is available, one should be generated as soon as possible. Students need to know what is available in hard copy, online, or available at another nearby library when they begin their research papers. In the past, most students preferred hard copy to microforms, but the speed of computer searching leads students to an online database with full text. Is a list of periodicals and online databases available, including the holdings of nearby libraries with directions for accessing? What are their borrowing policies for hard copy, and what about the delivery system for exchange of materials? Is a fax machine available? What are the guidelines for requesting copies of periodicals from neighboring libraries?

Become familiar with the operation of online databases available in your library and in other libraries to which you have access. You need to locate the documentation if you are unfamiliar with the system and practice searching so you can help users immediately. You will also need to know the policy for making copies of information located on databases.

Many states now have statewide licenses for access to commercial databases. You need to find out which databases are available to your students. If no records of this are in your desk, you should call another library media specialist in the district or your local public library. These persons can provide telephone numbers to call in the state agency funding the license. You will need not only information about the resources available, but you will learn the passwords and other access information so that students and teachers will be able to access information immediately.

When libraries and media centers are connected to the Internet, policies for access by students may be in place. Look to see what guidelines have been written for the use of this resource. If none seems to be in place in the school, check immediately for policies in other schools in the district or neighboring districts and the local public library to write a first draft as quickly as possible.

Of most importance is the operation of the circulation system if it is on a database. Online public access catalogs (OPACs) must be ready when the first patron arrives.

In reviewing the reference collection, make a quick analysis of the age and coverage, and give warning if encyclopedias are more than three years old. Many administrators consider the presence of an online encyclopedia evidence of fulfilling the need for this reference. However, the numbers of computers available in the library and classrooms and the connectivity or lack of both means that hard copy remains an important need. The vertical file is another reference tool that should be reviewed. Often dated materials remain in file drawers; this is one of the reference sources less likely to receive the attention it deserves.

Whatever the past excuse for leaving dated, irrelevant material in the library media center, it is not valid today. Useless materials and equipment should be removed as soon as possible. If in doubt about any item, remove it from the shelves and hold it until the appropriate teacher has an opportunity to review and recommend. Or hold it for one year to see if anyone requests to use it. It is inappropriate and unethical to offer inaccurate information. Students learn little except frustration when they sift through information only to find that it has little value except as historical record.

HUMAN FACTORS

Reviewing human factors requires a first look at staff in the media center, then administrators, teachers, and students. During the job interview, the media specialist should discuss the numbers of professional and clerical staff. When job descriptions for these persons are not available during the initial interview, the media specialist should attempt to locate them as soon as possible. If no descriptions are available, these must be developed in a way that covers the services and tasks, maximizes staff activities, and permits each person to feel self-worth. This can be accomplished only when library media specialists can match tasks to human competencies.

Finding Out About Staff

Many school library media centers are one-person operations. In others, a newly hired media specialist may find there are two professionals. Ideally, one is designated director and is not expected to share management responsibility. An argument has been made that two persons can share equal administration of the media center, but this is seldom efficient. Someone must be responsible for policy decisions, final selection of materials, division of the budget, discipline of students, assignment of tasks, and other routine functions. It takes two unusually cooperative persons to share such responsibility equally and consistently.

When the tasks of the library media center are divided, the division may be made in one of several ways. Perhaps the most common is to divide the readers' advisory and technical and technology services functions, as is often done in academic and public libraries. With this division of duties, one person works closely with teachers, students, and the curriculum, and the other is responsible for ordering and processing materials and keeping up with new technologies. A second type of division is by grade level; that is, one person works with primary and another with intermediate grades, or one with 9th and 10th and the other with grades 11 and 12. A last type of division is by subject area. Similar to subject bibliographers in an academic library, one person works with English and literature teachers, another with science and math teachers, and the third with social studies and history teachers. A fourth takes responsibility for art, music, physical education, and any remaining departments, such as guidance.

In the age of new technologies, one staff member takes this as a major responsibility. This is becoming one of the more important roles for the school library media specialist in the new century.

Division of clerical and professional tasks is accomplished following an analysis of program needs in relation to professional staff. Clerical staff may be assigned to work with individual media specialists, or they may be given more independent roles such as maintaining the circulation desk and reserve books, reporting only to the director. In some situations, clerical staff members have assumed managerial roles, and they may jealously guard their seeming positions of authority. It is wise to discover this early.

With a larger staff, the new library media specialist should meet with other professionals at first opportunity to discuss the tasks and procedures in place. If no other professionals are assigned, the clerical staff should be queried about procedures. In all cases, the media specialist should assess the strengths of each person in order to choose the best one to accomplish a task. Initial meetings can help determine the perceptions of duties of professionals and staff, so that plans for changes can be made and reassignments can occur smoothly.

Finding Out About Building Administrators

Certainly the school library media specialist needs to assess the principal's perception of media programs in general as well as the program offered in the school. An easy way to discover some things about administrators is to listen in the teachers' lounge. Knowing a principal's interests can be useful when you need to get this administrator's attention. The media specialist can discover all principals' perceptions of media programs by asking them to complete a questionnaire revised from one published in the National Association of Secondary School Principals (NASSP) *Bulletin* (see Appendix C). This simple questionnaire can be completed by other school personnel as well, and reviewing the responses will help the media specialist learn which perceptions must be modified or overcome.

Finding Out About Teachers

The modified NASSP *Bulletin* questionnaire can also be used to determine attitudes of teachers. Perceptions of principals may be compared with those of teachers to check similarities and differences.

A second method for finding out about teachers is to discover ways you can participate in the curriculum of the school. Begin with a review of the textbooks. Many school library media centers house single copies of textbooks and curriculum guides. In fact, in California many high school library media specialists are assigned responsibility for maintaining the textbook collection for the school. If your media center does not have copies, collecting them for future use is imperative. Although not all teachers use these guides and textbooks, certainly a large number do. A review of the curriculum guides will provide an outline of the topics to be covered each semester. Ask teachers how long they spend on each unit, what research assignments they give as part of the unit, and what information they feel the media center should provide.

At this point, files should be searched to see whether bibliographies are available. If not, the media center should develop bibliographies on each major area of instruction, using a word processor for easy update. With an OPAC, generating such lists is quite simple. Bibliographies developed from the OPAC are one method to confirm the currency of information in the media center.

Records may be in place to show collaborative units that have been used in the past. These will make the job of working with teachers much easier because you will have instant allies. Knowing the resources used, the plan for presenting the unit of instruction, the roles and responsibilities of the teacher and media specialist, and the method of evaluating the unit outline of previous work can be used as a model for working with other teachers.

To respond to teachers' needs, the media specialist must learn about their teaching methods as well as the curriculum. Some teachers may use media frequently, and some may use them incorrectly. If this is known, changes can be tactfully suggested. If teachers never use media, the media specialist can suggest appropriate media to use with a unit. Library media specialists must learn about teachers, but they must help teachers learn about the media center and the services offered. When teachers are unaware of how the media center collection can support teaching and learning, the media specialist must change this as quickly as possible.

What type of assignments do teachers make? Do they make assignments that are busy work and boring to their students? This will not be easy to discover immediately, but it will become apparent as you talk with students when they visit the media center. Helping teachers improve their assignments is the beginning of collaboration. This is not the perception that most teachers have of the role of the media specialist.

Teachers often have an incorrect perception of the role of the library media specialist. If student time in the media center is seen as the teachers' preparation period or an extension of study hall rather than an extension of the classroom, the media specialist must plan a sales program to develop a completely new image. An in-depth presentation of marketing strategies is provided in chapter 11. However, the school library media specialist should begin developing an advocacy plan including a sales program the first week. Determine what services the faculty may perceive they need and wish to have available. Prepare a checklist of services, present and projected, and ask teachers to rank or prioritize those services most useful to them. A sample checklist follows in Figure 4.3:

Teachers: Using no more than 100 points, please "buy" the following services that you expect from your library media center. We will discuss your rankings at the next teachers' meeting.

Extended hours of service should be available to students
_____after classes end and until 4:30 P.M. (or later)
_____on week nights

More online databases should be provided
_____in the media center
_____available to teachers and students 24/7
_____available in classrooms with a wireless network cart
_____100 Total

Figure 4.3 Checklist of Services

Source: Model adapted from Mary Virginia Gaver, _Services of Secondary School Library Media Centers: Evaluation and Development_ (Chicago: American Library Association, 1971).

In devising such a checklist, school library media specialists should suggest only services that can be offered, unless they are trying to build support for a new service. Allowing teachers to choose "wireless network cart" from a list of services would be pointless unless plans were being made to add the equipment, the telecommunications link, and other necessary and costly items to the library media center budget. Teachers may need clarification of "additional online databases" when a statewide license is already available in the school. This process of analyzing services will be covered more fully in chapter 10.

Finally, the novice school library media manager must try to locate the "gatekeepers." A gatekeeper, in this sense, is that person—teacher, administrator, school secretary, or custodian—who holds information and shares it with an inside group. Gatekeepers often can analyze situations and, based on their experiences, solve problems. The gatekeeper in a school may be able to suggest alternative plans to satisfy teachers when one course of action does not appear to achieve what is desired.

Finding Out About Students

The first step in finding out about students is determining the methods used to admit students to the library media center. In some situations, admission is by library pass signed by one or more teachers and countersigned by the library media specialist. Very few obstacles are placed before student access and use of the media center, or most students simply will not bother. Some may argue that a relaxed pass system will fill the media center with loafers or escapees from study hall, but this premise should be tested. An analysis of media center use for one week will reveal whether students are using the facility for study or recreational reading, whether they are coming from a classroom or study hall, and the types of behavior (e.g., if study hall students tend to misbehave).

The second step in finding out about students is checking when they are allowed to come to the media center. Rigid scheduling of the library media center may mean that access is severely limited, and students can only attend once a week for 45 minutes. Suggestions for moving from a totally scheduled program to partial scheduling to free access will be given in chapter 5.

Rules and regulations for the library media center should be printed. Regulations may state that only 10 students may come from each study hall, no more than 6 students can be sent for small group study, and other requirements. These rules may also state the disciplinary action that will be taken in case of misuse of the library media center or the materials there. Library media specialists should remember that all rules require a response for any infringement of the rule. Often the monitoring of the penalty is more troublesome than the action that prompted it.

After determining the method of access for students, scheduling, and rules and regulations, the media specialist should find out whether students are assigned to the library media center as aides or work study helpers or in any other function that might secure student support of the media program. This author opposes assigning students to do dull tasks such as shelving books, reading shelves, or replacing magazines. Many students enjoy planning bulletin boards, helping at the circulation desk, moving media equipment to and from classrooms and monitoring the microcomputer lab or helping students navigate through new databases. They are very able to prepare new books and other media for the shelf. By assisting in the library media center, students expand their reference skills, conduct online database searches, participate in the selection of materials by reading reviews, matching materials available to topics needed, and help other students learn how to conduct electronic searches as well as help them choose from the available resources those that are most pertinent to their needs. A very able and trustworthy student or two can help keep the library media center Web site up to date. This will help computer-adept students build experiences and prepare for their lives after school.

Finding Out About Parents

In many schools, parents take a great deal of interest in their children. They help children with homework, monitor their progress carefully, and support decisions by teachers and administrators. They observe their children in special events at the school. If they are not working during the day, they may volunteer to help in the school.

If a school has an active parent association, the media specialist may be able to call on parents to assist in the media center. The first week on the job, the media specialist finds out whether parents have assisted in the media center in past years and, if so, how to communicate with these parents. Although working with volunteers is covered more thoroughly in chapter 7, the media specialist should find out as soon as possible whether parent or other adult volunteers are available.

In schools where parents are less able to participate in the education of their children, the library media center becomes a center for tutors from a local high school or college. Special attention is needed to help these students reach their full potential.

COLLECTION FACTORS

The new school library media specialist needs to find out as much as possible about the holdings for the collection of materials to match various curriculum units. While finding out about teachers and their subject areas, the media specialist should seek information about their teaching methods and curriculum units. By matching teachers' needs to the materials available in support of the curriculum, gaps in the collection can be determined. These gaps may be in the age, relevance, or interest of the materials for the students who will be using them. These are all factors in building a collection.

Locating Curricular Resources

A first question should be, "Does the library media center have a Web site?" As strange as it may seem as a source of curricular resources, the media center Web site may have links to databases, outside resources, and a variety of information to help the school library media specialist understand what students expect to find when they are searching. While you are looking, jot a note to find out as soon as possible who helps maintain the Web site.

A school library media specialist has usually developed a collection of bibliographies to match both curricular needs (e.g., community helpers or Civil War) and recreational reading (e.g., sports stories, mystery novels). During the first week in the media center, it will be helpful to locate any existing bibliographies. Each bibliography should be reviewed for when it was created as well as the age of materials listed and their availability—that is, whether lost, incorrectly shelved, or discarded. If these bibliographies have URLs to electronic sources, these URLs should be checked to see whether they are still live.

If no bibliographies can be found, teacher units for the first six weeks are quickly reviewed and resources should be located for these units. This will help the media specialist quickly become familiar with the collection and be more helpful when students and teachers inquire about available resources. Also, when teachers request assistance in locating materials, a bibliography should be created for media center holdings under that topic.

When the collection is computerized, determining the holdings in particular areas is greatly eased. Depending on the program used to input the media center's holdings, materials on various subjects can be located and a bibliography prepared with a minimum of searching. When students have access to the holdings of nearby libraries through an interlibrary loan program, appropriate holdings of these libraries should be added to the bibliography with the location noted. If the card catalog is the only record of the media center's holdings, a more tedious search may be needed.

As media specialists access the Internet and the World Wide Web for resources, the addresses for resources are added to the bibliographies in existence to expand this resource as quickly as possible. Care is taken to review URLs each semester to delete those no longer available. When the actual units are being taught, links to these URLs are placed on the library media Web site to speed student access. While it is important that students learn how to make use of computer access to resources, their searches may take more time than a search of print resources. Lengthy searches will seriously limit the numbers of students who can search when the period of time the student is in the media center is set and the numbers of computers available for searching are limited. When links are placed on the Web site, students are quickly able to find appropriate sites rather than trying to navigate the chaos of commercial search engines.

Once concerns about the materials have been analyzed, decisions must be made about their distribution to patrons. If a written policy exists, the circulation procedures should be reviewed. When no policy exists, the media specialist develops rules for circulation.

Rules for Circulation and for Use of Computers

Two major areas of circulation are of primary interest for print materials: the circulation period and the policy for overdue materials and fines. The two-week circulation period has long been a standard. However, just because it has always been done that way does not mean that the policy should be continued. A great deal of time is usually spent reminding students that a book is overdue after two weeks. Some of this effort might be saved if the loan period were lengthened to three or four weeks or even a semester. A newly arrived media specialist might make this transition. Placing materials to be used by entire classes on reserve to limit circulation is more appropriate than using a two-week loan period.

Fines are always controversial. This author feels that fines are one of the worst possible public relations devices for any school library media specialist. The image of the library media center becomes punitive. Rather than teaching responsibility, a prime excuse for collecting fines, it promotes clipping pages or sneaking items through the detection system. In some instances, the library media specialist cannot use the funds collected; rather, they go into the district's general fund and are used for other purposes. Even if the money collected from overdue charges is used for the library media center, the cost to the center's image outweighs any advantage. To keep materials past deadline when other students need them is poor citizenship, and this behavior is not absolved by payment of a fine. Again, a school library media specialist new to the building may be able to reassess the process and begin the school year with a new, less restrictive and punitive policy.

Use of computers in media centers includes word processing and information searches, which may include access to an OPAC or access to the Internet and the World Wide Web. Often a computer station may be restricted to one or two of these functions rather than each station providing all. Users who wish to word process may need the computer for a longer period of time if they are writing papers. On the other hand, students who are searching for information may lack the skills for rapid searches. The numbers of computers available in the media center and the numbers of students and teachers who need to use them will set the framework for regulations for which type of use and the length of time students may use any computer. As wireless systems are installed and the cost of computers—especially laptop computers—gets lower and lower, many of these problems will be overcome. However, until that time, policies for the use of computers as well as policies and procedures for students who have access to the Internet, whether or not filters are in place, are needed. An example of an acceptable use policy is available on Joyce Valenza's Springfield Township High School Virtual Library (http://www.sdst.org/students/acceptableuse.php) located in Erdenheim, Pennsylvania.

WHEN THE STUDENTS ARRIVE

First impressions are critical. The novice media specialist must dress as a professional. For a time, it was difficult to distinguish between teachers and students. One of the author's favorite educators, a principal in Minnesota, insists that teachers adhere to a dress code. The teachers in that building are to be role models for the students, not peers, and they are there to teach rather than be pals. The professional appearance of the media specialist lends an air of competence and importance to the activities of the media center. Another caution comes with the awareness of the types of students in the building. A principal visiting a large school district remarked to this author that the teachers in the inner city schools seemed to wear drab, "serviceable" clothing, as if the students were somehow less deserving of better clothing on their teachers. As she visited schools more distant from the center, the clothing of teachers changed noticeably as they wore "business" dress. The following additional suggestions should be helpful to the new media specialist as students arrive.

Be visible when students first enter the media center. Learn students' names as quickly as possible. This shows an interest in and respect for the students' presence in the media center.

Avoid at all costs being intimidated by students. A positive posture, use of guidelines of expected behavior, and a genuine regard for students as sincere researchers will bring a positive reaction.

Students must understand the expected behavior in the media center. These expectations may be written on a handout or bookmarks and distributed or prominently displayed at the charge-out desk or elsewhere. Explaining behaviors is as important as explaining location of books, magazines, media, and equipment.

Whenever possible, avoid using voice commands. A strident voice in the media center will disturb everyone there. Students quickly learn to read messages in body language and eye contact. These silent signals are far preferable to other means of attracting attention.

Address discipline problems immediately. Ignoring a problem will encourage other students to create similar problems. Quickly respond to students when they misbehave so they understand that the consequences for bad behavior are immediate, fair, and positive. Sarcasm or ridicule is as harmful to the giver as to the recipient. Unkind behavior is often returned later, and the media specialist will be the recipient.

Establish a reputation for being positive, fair, caring, understanding, and flexible. Students should be the focus of attention. It is not fair to them if the media specialist's personal problems become part of the media center attitude. It is difficult to hide personal stress and strain, but students may not understand that a curt response is the result of something that happened elsewhere.

Beware of physical contact with students. Most states have laws against physical punishment of students. The media specialist should intervene physically only in a situation in which physical harm might come to another pupil. Again, eye contact and a soft voice are far more effective than aggression.

Take care not to punish the whole group for the behavior of some. A private reprimand or a more public but personal acknowledgment of the misbehavior will be as effective. Depriving a group will only make the group angry and may, in fact, draw the group into support of the poor behavior of the few.

Do not return a student to the teacher for misbehavior. By the same token, teachers should not be allowed to send students to the media center for misbehavior. If the media center is not to be looked upon as a jail, the media specialist should show the same courtesy to the concept of the classroom. The author took a class in educational psychology in which the instructor pointed out that students misbehave because they want to leave the classroom. To send them to the principal or back to the teacher is, in a sense, rewarding them just as the Fox rewarded Brer Rabbit by throwing him into the brier patch.

Finally, be prepared for the students when they enter. "Flying by the seat of your pants" may work occasionally for the veteran media specialist, but it is not likely to work for the beginner. Well-developed plans with more activities than could possibly be carried out are preferable to the embarrassment of running out of things to do. As the media specialist becomes familiar with the pace, it will be possible to conduct activities with less detailed plans, but in the beginning your calendar or plan book should be carefully developed.

Having survived the first week on the job, the school library media specialist must begin to plan for the immediate future, for the remainder of the school year, and for the long-term future of the school library media program. The following chapters expand the responsibilities.

Exercises

1. If unfamiliar with school district organization charts, visit the administration offices of a nearby school district and ask to see the organization chart. Determine who is responsible for the school library media program. How many bosses does the school library media specialist have?
2. If possible, interview a new school library media specialist after the first week on the job. Compare this person's experiences with those of someone returning to a familiar situation.
3. Review the school library media center Web sites in at least five schools and compare them for their ease of access, their clarity, and their links to resources as well as the information given there.
4. Create a generic Web site for a school library media center. Establish links to resources you have found that would be useful to students.

On the Job: Managing the Media Center Program

The management of the media center is an assignment based more in the realm of business than in teaching and education. Although school library media specialists are educators, responsible for all parts of the school's curriculum and for the learning of all students in their building, they must also manage a many-faceted operation that involves staff, materials, equipment, facility, and furnishings. The inventory of the media center has a very big price tag, as many districts learn when they are opening new schools or when they must rebuild after a disaster. Managing this inventory requires special skills.

The exemplary management of a successful library program requires both the expertise of a gifted educator adept with pedagogy, curricula, and behavior management and the skill of an administrator. This is a great deal more complex than managing a single classroom and its students. This complexity is often overlooked by administrators who may wonder why a clerk or a volunteer can't replace a school library media specialist in their school.

School districts and state boards of education give classroom teachers uniform goals and objectives to reach during the year for their grade level or subject. Teachers adapt these general goals and objectives as they plan their year's activities. This process changes slightly with new textbook adoptions and more when implementing new educational strategies. Matching teaching and learning to the No Child Left Behind regulations and matching curriculum to the content area standards causes even more changes for teaching. Although these changes affect the role of school library media specialists, their tasks are usually not a part of the general goals and objectives for the school year.

When a district has a director of media programs, a vision, mission, goals, and objectives for the program may be in place; if a district does not have a director of media programs, school library media specialists must create their own mission, goals, and objectives after they have created the vision. This

73

planning process can easily follow a business model, with the first objective at the beginning of the year to establish an advisory committee.

Because the media center affects the entire school, few media specialists would feel comfortable with or capable of planning the entire program without input from the users: teachers, students, administrators, and parents. An efficient way to get appropriate comments from users is to form an advisory group that meets regularly, as frequently as is practical but seldom more than once per semester. This group not only will act as advocate of the media program but will also be directly involved in setting goals and objectives and planning or revising programs in the media center.

THE LIBRARY MEDIA ADVISORY COMMITTEE

Classroom teachers sometimes forget that the media center serves the entire school, not just the media staff. When they help develop the mission, policies, goals, and objectives, they begin to understand the media specialist's challenges. Requests for funding for the media program may be interpreted as support for the media specialist only. As advocates of the library media program, the advisory committee members are most helpful because their efforts can in no way be construed as serving a vested interest.

Effective advisory committee members have a clear purpose or charge, and all members understand their roles. They will want to have an active assignment so they consider their membership worthwhile. Library media specialists, in consultation with the principal, set the parameters for the group. Advisory committee members should help establish the purpose of the group. All of this is much easier accomplished when the principal is an active part of the advisory group.

The advisory committee might be interested in many areas of the media program. Members could help with reviewing the mission statement and in establishing the year's objectives after analyzing the information needs of media center users. When these objectives have a relationship to financial support, they should help plan for budgetary expenditures. This takes some pressure off the media specialist when requests far exceed resources. Once an advisory committee has been formed, you can begin the strategic planning process.

STRATEGIC PLANNING

Management of a school library media program is based on a planning process. According to Robert Stueart and Barbara Moran,

> Strategic planning, then, is the systematic outcome of a thinking process that enables libraries and information centers to organize efforts necessary to carry out major decisions and to measure the results of these decisions against the expectations through organized systematic feedback and adjustments.[1]

The library media program is the shared vision of the library media specialist and staff of the media center. This is the direction the media center program will take for the future, where the media program should be going, and, as such, it guides the development of the mission statement.

The vision should be translated into a mission statement—a "short, succinct statement focusing on the purpose of the organization, its reason for existence, and what it hopes to accomplish."[2] The media center staff and the advisory committee members first discuss the mission statement for the district and their school if it has its own mission statement. They then develop the media center's mission as it relates to the school's mission and agree upon this statement. In the best of all possible worlds, the entire school will agree on the mission. Identifying the mission allows the formulation of objectives, policies, and, finally, the procedures and methods to provide services to meet needs. With this basic introduction to the library media center, the planning process can continue.

Planning is the process of deciding what work must be done and who should do it. Principle 5 of the American Association of School Librarians' (AASL) 1998 guidelines states: "Comprehensive and collaborative long-range, strategic planning is essential to the effectiveness of the library media program."[3] In the planning process, the library mission and goals can be established and a policy statement developed. During the planning process, school library media specialists work directly with those who will carry out the plans. This includes all members of the media center staff who should be involved in goals and objectives for the media center. The advisory committee reviews the plans.

Developing policy statements, goals, and objectives is the next step in the planning process. The sound media policy statement, if missing at the district level, is developed at the building level. This statement need not be redone each year, but it and the mission statement should be reviewed yearly.

Policy Statements and Needs Assessment

At the theoretical level, planning begins with a policy statement to describe library media services. Before the advisory committee can participate in developing policies, it may be interested in two books that can help in developing a school library media policy. *School Media Policy Development,* by Helen Adams,[4] describes the argument for developing policies, the policy development process, and the political process for ensuring acceptance of established policies. In *Policymaking for School Library Media Programs,* Marian Karpisek[5] cites the following eight steps of policy writing:

1. Research: written manual, district and school policies, climate of the school
2. First draft: philosophy
3. Advisory committee consideration
4. Final draft: rewriting to incorporate advisory committee considerations
5. Advisory committee review of revisions
6. Administrative approval

7. Distribution to faculty and parents

8. Dissemination to students

As an example, access to the media center may have problems with media center scheduling. The first step is to find any manual in existence, any school policy, and the climate of the school. If principals use the library as the teacher preparation period in elementary school or for large numbers of students coming from study hall to the library in secondary school, the climate of the school will be different than if there are policies of flexible scheduling in elementary or open access in the secondary school. A philosophy can be established for a different schedule, and the rewriting—incorporating the advisory committee's considerations—may help modify the schedule with some flexible scheduling in elementary and limited numbers of students from study hall in high school.

Once the basic policy has been determined, planning becomes the identification of problems to be corrected. In this phase, objectives, policies, procedures, and methods are developed based on the needs of students and teachers. During this part of the planning process, school library media specialists also work directly with those who will carry out the plans. This includes all members of the media center staff who should be involved in developing and reviewing goals and objectives for the media center. Their suggestions are also shared with the advisory committee.

At this point, the advisory committee has another essential role. As an advocacy group, it can speak for additional resources from its awareness of needs. The media specialist also uses the advisory committee to test new ideas and interpret the results of any evaluation exercise to the appropriate audience. Because the advisory committee can be extremely helpful in establishing needs, it is critical to the development of a needs assessment. In a sense, the committee becomes an extension of media center staff in recognizing needs. For example, a committee member reports that a new world history textbook is being adopted. As a part of the needs assessment process, the textbook is analyzed to find which topics, when matched to the collection, have print and electronic resources available in the media center and then what new materials need to be added to the media center collection. If new materials are to be ordered, world history teachers are queried about suggestions for additions to the collection and to prioritize the order of purchase to meet budget limitations while allowing some materials to be ordered immediately.

After the needs assessment is conducted, courses of action are reviewed and prioritized for adoptions. Needs might be small, such as a change in the placement of furniture in the media center to make it easier to handle technology use. Needs may be great if the addition of new technologies requires remodeling the facility to add space for more students to come into the center or to implement new technologies. Alternate strategies are determined in case the first course of action is not possible, and the results of each alternative are discussed.

Example 1 (see page 77) describes a need for more materials in world history. Because students are quick to use the Internet to find information, the most effective strategy to meet the world history need would be the use of databases and resources on the Internet. Using Internet access as a substitute for any print resources requires consideration of the following:

1. Parental concern for open use of the Internet
2. Filtering problems if schools are required to filter the Internet
3. Costs of the purchase of databases
4. Number of online connections available for use by students and teachers
5. Number of computers available for searching
6. Need to teach students how to make careful, relevant selections
7. Ease of downloading that leads to plagiarizing
8. Lack of teacher and student awareness of resources on the Internet
9. Teaching teachers and students how to use the various databases

---

Example 1

One objective determined during the planning process, upon adopting a new world history curriculum, is to provide each student with at least six in-house sources for research papers. The teachers recommend the type of materials that should be added to the collection or make suggestions for specific materials needed to support this curriculum unit. The media staff prepares a list of materials and their cost. If the media specialist plans to bookmark Web sites for use, teachers are shown the Web sites so they are familiar with their content and are prepared to help students navigate through the information.

The media specialist keeps a record of the process of making choices and ordering new materials. Teachers are scheduled to preview materials and make selections. Finally, orders are initiated, and the media staff processes the items and shares them with teachers and students. Because of the uncertainty of any Web site address used in a previous semester, all must be tested to see whether they remain active resources. The usefulness of every related item, both new and existing, should be assessed and recorded so that future plans are made to reuse those which worked well. The media specialist and teachers will want to know whether the materials have been adequate, relevant, and recent enough for research, and whether students were able to complete their assignments.

Use of Internet resources in the media center may require facility modification and equipment planning as well. Acquiring the computers as well as a number of connections with adequate bandwidth requires a larger budget for technology. Decisions must be made about the placement of the Internet stations or the introduction of mobile wireless. Both software and hardware will require almost constant upgrading, and a well-drawn plan to ensure proper safety and reliability of equipment is vital. When new technology is introduced, the media specialist must plan to conduct computer literacy instruction for teachers and students.

With the changes in curriculum related to restructuring the schools, the media specialist becomes even more important to help plan strategies for teaching and learning that go far beyond the current classroom and the school. Standards-based curriculum and balanced literacy, among others, present challenges to managing the selection of materials, the expansion of services, the provision of equipment, scheduling, and, most important, managing staff to allow planning time with teachers.

At each step of solving a problem, alternatives may be reviewed in terms of cost accountability. This will be discussed in more depth in chapter 9. In the case of a new curriculum adoption, the media specialist is directly involved in setting objectives for classroom activities and then modifying programming in the media center to meet the newly determined needs.

Objectives

Objectives written after a needs assessment process define the media center role in the new curriculum. The objectives should be clear, and the reasons (basis for their choice) should be recorded. The activities or strategies to meet the objectives will depend on the media specialist's level of participation in curriculum planning. It is essential that the media specialist accept leadership responsibility in this process, becoming an integral part of classroom planning, participating in the development of all strategies and alternatives and the reasons for final choices. This planning will make it easier to adjust the strategies later if they appear to be failing. The media specialist should record this process, perhaps in a log, to help recall successful activities as well as the outcomes of revisions. These successes can be reported to the advisory committee, teachers, or administrators in monthly or yearly status reports. Recording changes or planning to use a previously successful strategy will help anyone who wishes to implement similar plans.

ORGANIZING

In the process of strategic planning, school library media specialists organize the efforts that are necessary to carry out major decisions. In the organizing process, collaborating with teachers (see chapter 10, Managing Services) is logical because school library media specialists have full knowledge of the curriculum, the way teachers teach, the assignments they give and the activities they plan in classrooms, and the media center support teachers will require. These activities—whether conducted in the media center or elsewhere—impact management because the different forms of instruction and the assignments requiring resources used both in the media center and through its online resources require much more planning and organizing than in the past. School library media specialists perform a variety of roles, from consulting to collaborating fully with the design and implementation of classroom units. Organizing teaching and learning units that go across the curriculum involves the entire school. This type of teaching, particularly when it involves many teachers and many curriculum areas, requires the particular organizational skills of the library media specialist.

While organizing, decisions are made about who should do what work, what activities the work entails, and what facilities are available to accomplish the task. What is the nature of the media center's involvement in the teaching activities? The media specialist and the teachers must agree on work division and work assignment, and activities should be allocated between classrooms and the media center in the organizing process. In the example of the world history project, a first activity is selection of new materials, and teachers are asked to review materials for purchase. The media specialist sets up a system of preview, and receipt of items and their subsequent distribution to and return from teachers should be automatic. Clerical and professional staff should carry out the process. Again, Web sites are reviewed for their availability, continued relevance, and usefulness.

A next step in organizing is to review the unit to see what activities will involve media center staff. When production of materials is a requirement, necessary supplies must be purchased if they aren't available. Then the media specialist must decide what materials to place on reserve or have the students (as a part of the unit objectives, particularly in elementary schools) choose material for reserve, which materials to send to the classroom, and which to circulate to students. A search of database resources and information available on the World Wide Web will result in links being placed on the library media center Web site. If additional materials must be obtained outside the school, the media specialist must assign a staff member to locate them. Then policies and procedures related to these new materials must be reviewed, because policies for the use of materials in alternate locations might differ from policies for school-owned materials (see Example 2).

Example 2

Examine "pure" administrative sequence. A major goal of many school library media specialists is ensuring the availability of a wireless connection to databases for access from classrooms as well as the media center. At the planning stage, those involved write objectives and investigate the cost and installation of such a system. If the project requires selling to school administrators, cost benefits should be determined. This can be done by examining the price of an online database versus the cost of all materials in print, ease of access, search time saved, and clerical time saved in reshelving print materials. Justifying search time saved acknowledges that student and teacher time is real time with a cost factor, even if students are not paid and teachers are "paid for their time, anyway." Many forget that time spent looking for items is time lost from teaching and learning activities.

At the organizing level, the media specialist will need to decide whether additional databases are needed even if a statewide system exists and who is responsible for training in use of a new database or bookmarked Web site. Who will maintain the network once the system is in place, and how will access to terminals be managed? Do staff members have priority to conduct searches? If electronic resources are available, how will access to workstations be scheduled? Will users be timed at terminals to control long waiting lines? In overseeing the search process, databases are monitored to see which are used most often and if users are choosing the best databases to answer their questions. Finally, during feedback, the media specialist completes an analysis to evaluate real time and cost savings in relation to anticipated time and cost savings.

Finally, those involved must decide how to divide the teaching of the unit, what research skills are required, and what reference sources and materials will be used, so that the media center and the services of the media staff can be scheduled. A review of the unit as it progresses can determine the appropriate time for media staff involvement.

Some decisions will be needed to determine why and how group members perform their tasks. To relate this directly to media center activities, some questions must be answered. When will the assignment be introduced, how many sessions will students need in the library, and when will the assignment be due? What media are shown to the entire class in the classroom, to a small group in the media center, or to individual students? Teachers and media center staff will again need to assign tasks. They must decide whose task it is to start, continue, or complete activities related to the unit. For example, the teacher and the media specialists choose a film to show. A clerk will be responsible for showing a video or DVD in the media center after it has been introduced by the teacher in the classroom or in the media center. Any discussion during and at the end of the showing will be the joint responsibility of the teacher and the media specialist.

Responsibility for each activity is assigned to the appropriate person or persons. Care is taken to ensure that the activities continue as planned, and that the appropriate materials and equipment are available. This stage involves matching the plan books of the teacher and media specialist with the media center schedule.

SYSTEMATIC FEEDBACK AND ADJUSTMENTS

To meet the guidelines of Stueart's and Moran's planning definition, school library media specialists must constantly evaluate the process, particularly as it applies to student learning. Did the unit work as planned? When, where, and how were the activities performed? Were they performed in accordance with the plans? To answer these questions, those involved will check progress during the unit and hold follow-up sessions. How well did students perform on evaluation exercises? Were sufficient resources available? What activities did teachers and students consider the most successful? Any final reports, comparisons with other units, costs, and projected budget needs are a part of planning process. Finally, the media specialist and teachers ask whether the activity met the program goals.

GRAPHIC REPRESENTATIONS OF THE PLANNING PROCESS

Often, implementation of the planning process can be shown graphically. Two ways to do this are described below. The first, a flowchart, is for shorter-term projects; the second, a Gantt chart, is for extended projects.

FLOW CHARTS

When the author asked a colleague what was missing from this text, the immediate response was "how to flowchart." Programmers building computerized systems describe each step with symbols that act as a code for the type of operation. These symbols are described in Figure 5.1.

The process of flowcharting places each step of any operation in jeopardy. The next step in the process must be examined in terms of what has gone before and the best way to move forward. Any problems to be encountered should have solutions offered. An operation in selecting materials that uses these symbols to plan is shown in Figure 5.2.

EXTENDED PROJECTS

Planning for one week at a time is better than no planning at all. However, a school library media program can continue to succeed and improve only if

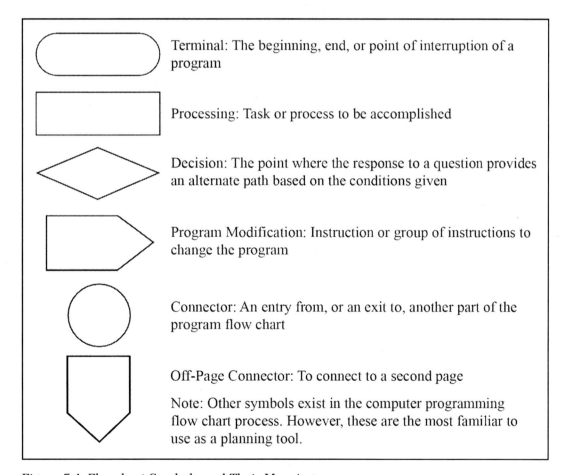

Figure 5.1 Flowchart Symbols and Their Meaning

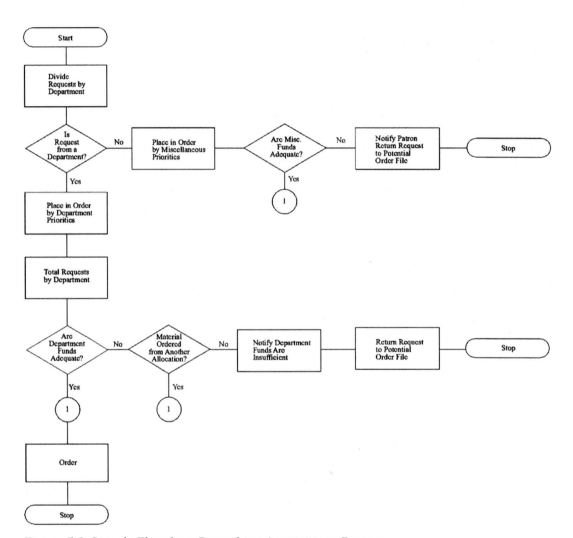

Figure 5.2 Sample Flowchart Describing Acquisitions Process

planning extends beyond one school year. For too long, media specialists have neglected to set goals and objectives beyond a single semester. However, this short-term planning limits the ability to set priorities for major purchases that will continue the progress of the media program beyond a single school year.

School library media specialists should develop a 3-, 5-, or even 10-year plan for media center operation. In this plan all components of the media program should be listed with an indication of "what is" and "what should be," taking into account all necessary additions to the program—whether staff, equipment, materials, or facilities. Additions or modifications to the present situation should be proposed somewhere in the 1st, 2nd, 3rd, 5th, or 10th year, with a budget analysis for each activity. A sample 5-year plan is shown in Appendix D.

For planning large projects, school library media specialists can learn from project planners who develop a time line. One simple time line is the Gantt chart, which displays tasks on the left side with the time line across the top or bottom. The time line is flexible, depending on the time allocated for completion of the project. The chart shown in Figure 5.3 was developed as a planning chart for a new elementary school's library.

The Gantt chart is helpful because one can see immediately where a project stands in relation to the schedule. When deadlines are not met, additional resources may be allocated if the opening date appears to be in jeopardy.

The final step of the chart is the turnkey date. At this time, "keys" should be turned over and the project completed. The purpose of such an exercise is to establish a time line for a long-term project. However, the school ibrary media specialist must also be able to manage time on a day-to-day basis.

SCHEDULING THE MEDIA CENTER

The facility must be scheduled for maximum use by students and teachers—as individuals, as small groups, and as entire classes. Scheduling and monitoring access to the media center is a major task requiring careful management of time.

Time management is a particularly difficult skill to acquire in any school, where interruptions are commonplace. The school library media specialist, just as any other teacher, must plan carefully to allow for these interruptions. In fact, media specialists come to expect the unexpected. On any day, a student or small group from a classroom needs information immediately. At the same time, a teacher needs additional time for research because of an event that has just occurred. They enter the media center enthusiastically, only to find the library media specialist conducting a story time with the kindergarten, an activity that should not be interrupted. Working this special need into the day is possible with a little advance notice.

Capturing the "teachable" moment involves the library media center as much as or more often than any other area of the school. Perhaps this is one of the most compelling reasons to provide free access to the media center rather than limiting access because of a rigid schedule of classes. Students and teachers with information needs must have these needs met at the earliest possible moment. Most high schools have full-time staff and large enough centers to

	Oct	Nov	Dec	Jan	Feb	Mar	Apr	May	Jun	Jul	Aug
Hire librarian and clerk	■										
Prepare budget	■										
Choose OPAC system		■	■	■							
Order print collection		■	■	■	■	■					
Order nonprint collection		■	■	■	■	■					
Order administrative software		■	■	■	■						
Order educational software		■	■	■	■	■					
Choose technology network		■	■	■							
Plan media center layout		■									
Plan shelving arrangement			■								
Plan equipment storage			■								
Plan production area			■								
Select furniture and shelving				■							
Select audiovisual equipment				■							
Order supplies		■	■	■	■	■					
Process new materials					■	■	■	■	■	■	■
Accept furniture & equip. delivery						■	■	■	■		
Connect and test all technologies									■	■	■
Arrange materials										■	■
Set up displays											■
Send out publicity											■
In-service for teachers											■
Open house for parents											■
Open house for community											■
Welcome students											■

Figure 5.3 Planning Chart for Opening a New Elementary School Library Developed Using the Gantt Chart Technique

accommodate both full classes and small groups. This is not as often true in elementary schools, and schedules sometimes present a problem.

Many school library media specialists will argue that, unless elementary teachers are scheduled to bring their classes to the media center, they will not do so. If this seems to be the attitude of teachers, a regular book exchange time can be scheduled. As shown in Figure 5.4 (page 87), for kindergarten and first grade, book exchange should be a daily event. With the other model found in many school districts, the elementary teachers' planning time is built around "special" subjects, such as music, art, physical education, computer literacy, and library media center. When this occurs, an administrator arranges scheduling, and the school library media specialist can only hope to find additional time slots for spontaneous use of the media center and its resources. As discussed earlier in planning use of the facility, the advisory committee can be helpful in suggesting an appropriate schedule for the media center that allows for teachable moments to occur.

When a rigid schedule is in place, the media specialist must plan activities to help break this use of the media center. It will take the endorsement of the advisory committee and detailed, careful, curriculum-related planning with one or more teachers. If a class activity has been planned for a full semester, it may be possible to exclude other classes from the media center for their regular schedule for a special culminating event for one class. For example, students in a class focusing on the study of early settlers in the Northeast may build one or two houses in the media center for a week's activities, sharing this project with the entire school. This will not be easy to achieve, but if such an event is successful with one class, other teachers will want their students to have a similar opportunity. This can create the attitude among teachers that the media center is a research center rather than a free period.

At the secondary level, many students who have no study hall scheduled can come to the media center only when their teachers bring an entire class. Other students have so many study halls scheduled that they use the library media center as a change of scene or social gathering spot. Both situations must be addressed. Students need opportunities to use the media center during the day. Homeroom might provide access for those with no study hall scheduled. With the help of teachers, media specialists might plan alternative activities for students using the media center during study hall. The time it takes to plan such activities would be well spent, especially if the activities could be repeated with other students at other times.

For all students from elementary through high school who come to the media center with no apparent reason or assignment, this presents an excellent opportunity to encourage reading because, in this instance, it will allow the students to choose and read whatever interests them. Stephen Krashen reports that

> Free voluntary reading (FVR) is one of the most powerful tools we have in language education, and . . . FVR is the missing ingredient in first language "language arts" as well as in intermediate second and foreign language instruction. It will not, by itself, produce the highest levels of competence; rather, it provides a foundation so that higher levels of proficiency may be reached. When FVR is missing, these advanced levels are extremely difficult to attain.[6]

When free reading and direct, or traditional, instruction are compared directly in method comparison studies, free reading nearly always proves superior on tests of reading comprehension, vocabulary, writing, and grammar.[7] A variety of reading materials—from catalogs from department stores and specialty shops, graphic novels, comic books, paperback light reading, and magazines—can be placed near these reluctant refugees from study halls. The daily newspaper also provides many possibilities (perhaps multiple day-old copies could be obtained): a contest to discover the best price for bananas in grocery ads or a tracking of stock market prices for a month, for example. Some library media specialists have developed reference questions for contests. Developing a series of activities that can be used from one year to the next may lessen student boredom and increase the value of the media center in their education.

The media specialist takes every opportunity to plan classes around the curriculum and queries teachers often to discover their unit plans so that media center visits can be built into the unit at appropriate times. Library media specialists who collaborate with teachers find their media centers heavily used by students who need the resources of the media center to complete their class assignments.

During the past decade, there has been a movement to develop local, state, and national standards in the various subject areas. Teachers use the standards as a framework to develop curriculum, pace their instruction, evaluate student learning, and compare against benchmarks. These standards set uniform goals and objectives for classroom teachers to reach during the year for their grade level or subject. Teachers adapt these general goals and objectives as they plan the year's activities.

ELECTRONIC CALENDARS AND DAILY PLAN BOOKS

Classroom teachers are expected to maintain a daily plan book to post the goals and objectives of the lessons, activities, and evaluations of progress through the units. The school library media specialist, also a teacher, maintains a similar record, although the daily plans cover several classrooms rather than one. This plan book is a log of activities being planned, in progress, and being evaluated. It is a record of alternatives when the original plan is being revised. If timing of a unit is off, the plan book shows the new schedule. In this book the library media specialist states goals, objectives, and activities and, finally, records progress. Keeping the plans as an electronic calendar makes it easy to record revisions to the daily schedule. When this calendar becomes available on a school's electronic communication system, its list service, teachers have immediate knowledge of open periods in the media center and can make their preliminary plans with an e-mail message.

A sample page printed from a media specialist's electronic calendar is shown in Figure 5.4.

LEADERSHIP AND THE LIBRARY MEDIA SPECIALIST

Library media specialists must move beyond the management role of overseeing a collection of materials and providing reading guidance to a

Tuesday, October ___, 20___

8:00 A.M.–8:30 A.M.
Meeting with fourth-grade teachers to discuss reading project.

9:00 A.M.–9:30 A.M.
Begin fall holidays unit with three students. Introduce *Brewton's Poetry Index*. Review OPAC searching.

9:30 A.M.–10:00 A.M.
Weekly book exchange, all kindergarten; book sharing grade five; art teacher shares pictures of fall by famous artists.

10:00 A.M.–10:30 A.M.
Collect work from grade three as they leave.

10:30 A.M.–11:00 A.M.
In the lab: grade four to work on their reports on insects; grade six researching U.S. government officials. Introduce *Statistical Abstract*.

11:00 A.M.–Noon
Confirm Internet addresses for grade five election/candidates unit.

Noon–12:30 P.M.
Lunch: Remind clerk to fill two book trucks with first-grade books. Take list of new picture books list to share with kindergarten teachers.

12:30 P.M.–1:00 P.M.
Music teacher needs info on Grofe's Grand Canyon Suite. Students in media center or music room?

1:00 P.M.–1:30 P.M.
Book exchange, all grade one with silent sustained reading after selection until 1:45 P.M.

1:30 P.M.–2:00 P.M.
Last 15 minutes of grade one, read two or three new acquisitions.

2:00 P.M.–2:30 P.M.
Book exchange, all kindergarten; book talk biographies for grade two.

2:30 P.M.–3:00 P.M.
Book exchange for all grade two; prepare tasks for Library Club.

3:00 P.M.–3:30 P.M.
Library Club, grades three through five.

3:30 P.M.–4:00 P.M.
Meet with parent to suggest books to encourage her child's reading.

Figure 5.4 Electronic Calendar

Wednesday, October ____, 20____

8:00 A.M.–8:30 A.M.
Meeting with all-grade curriculum team to discuss next semester's across-the-school major project.

9:00 A.M.–9:30 A.M.
Curriculum meeting continued.

9:30 A.M.–10:00 A.M.
Grade three students share their work from yesterday; review Internet search strategies; complete work sheet to specific topics.

10:00 A.M.–10:30 A.M.
Book exchange for all grade three.

10:30 A.M.–11:00 A.M.
Go to grade five classroom to meet with teachers and students to help introduce new unit.

11:00 A.M.–Noon
Fourth-graders finish research on insects.

Noon–12:30 P.M.
Meet with grade four teachers to discuss progress of research unit.

12:30 P.M.–1:00 P.M.
Lunch: Take new science fair project book to share with teachers.

1:00 P.M.–1:30 P.M.
Book exchange for all grade five; Great Books discussion with small group, grade five.

1:30 P.M.–2:00 P.M.
Book exchange for all kindergarten. Small group grade four with additional research on insects.

2:00 P.M.–2:30 P.M.
Book exchange for all grade one.

2:30 P.M.–3:00 P.M.
Book exchange for all grade two. Prepare tasks for Library Club.

3:00 P.M.–3:30 P.M.
Library Club, grades three through five; particular attention to condition of media center.

3:30 P.M.–4:00 P.M.
Teachers meet in library

Please note that, in this schedule, kindergarten and grade one have daily book exchange.

Figure 5.4 *Continued*

much broader role of collaborating with teachers to match teaching needs to learning requirements. This leadership role is described in AASL's *Information Power:*

> The library media specialist strengthens the program's connections by working as a curriculum and instructional leader on the school's leadership team. The library media specialist also acts as a leader in organizing learning opportunities within and beyond the school.[8]

A key element of this role is convincing teachers to use the best teaching strategies while helping students adapt their learning styles to the classroom environment. To this point, this chapter has covered the details of translating the vision of the program into the mission statement. The advisory committee and the media center staff have developed goals or positive statements that detail what should be accomplished over time to achieve the purposes outlined in the mission statement. These short-range, specific, measurable objectives become statements of accountability for the library media specialist. The completion of these objectives will lead to achievement of the goal or goals for the media center program. However, the library media specialist who wishes to meet the goals and objectives must take a leading role in the planning process with teachers.

Leading the Planning Process

The planning process is where the media specialist needs true leadership skills. This step requires the participating in units of instruction from the beginning. Suggestions for activities to be accomplished are broken down into steps. Some of these may be tasks to be performed by teachers, and others are the responsibility of one or more of the media center staff. Some may depend on others outside the media center. In a simple example, if an author is invited to the school, the arrival of the author depends on the author and not on any individual in the media center. The skillful media specialist approves the steps to accomplish objectives, making sure that each step furthers the process. Also, the media specialist must point out any missing steps in the process or activities that should be modified. Leadership is being able to anticipate success and seeing that as few unexpected problems surface as possible. The ability to foresee probable faults in the planning is a measure of a good leader.

In planning a unit of instruction, the media specialist helps identify the activities to be carried out by students, who presents what, and determines whether sufficient resources are available to support the planned activities. Objectives that cannot be met with existing resources should be scaled down at the beginning to minimize frustration. Otherwise, the necessary resources must be secured.

Another important aspect of planning is the assignment of time. Allocating enough time to complete an activity is necessary. Deadlines are established so that more human as well as material resources can be assigned if a project appears to be in jeopardy. A good leader manages time wisely.

It is difficult to predict what teachers and administrators expect of the media specialist. However, the following suggestions may increase your effectiveness through time management:

- Begin or end your day with a quiet time for planning. This may have to occur before you leave home, because every minute in the media center you are likely to be surrounded by teachers and students.
- Start the day with one task that can be performed quickly. This provides a sense of accomplishment and means the day ends with at least one task completed. This is perhaps one of the more frustrating aspects of media center management and the reason library media specialists undertake clerical tasks. The end product can be seen, while other tasks, such as curriculum integration, may appear to be never-ending.
- Keep your electronic calendar or plan book up to date. Recording the times of activities and what they involve will aid in keeping projects on track and confirming that nothing is unintentionally omitted.
- Try to focus on one project at a time. Continuity is preferable to reviewing the status of any project each time work is resumed. This is a difficult approach for a one-person staff, when interruptions are constant and work on one longer-term project comes to a halt with an emergency situation in a short-term project.
- Meet all deadlines, whether imposed by administration or personally established. It is difficult to expect others to meet deadlines for the media center if the media staff does not do so.
- Delegate well, but delegate. Although it is often faster to do a task oneself, it is wise to delegate as often as possible.
- Avoid trying to do everything perfectly. Most teachers and students will not recognize perfection when it exists.
- Assign priorities to tasks. That is, do the most important task first. Often, a more important task is set aside because it does not seem quickly accomplished; this means that priority activities may never be completed.

Managing the media center is the assignment that expands the role of the library media specialist beyond that of the classroom teacher. Media specialists manage inventories worth many thousands of dollars. This part of the media specialist's job assignment demands leadership skills. The media specialist as an effective manager will ensure that teachers and students have the information they need in a timely fashion.

Exercises

1. Review the daily plan book of a library media specialist. Estimate the percentage of time spent (1) working with students, (2) planning with teachers, (3) performing administrative tasks, and (4) doing clerical tasks.

2. Using information from a school library media center, create a five-year plan for improvement in chosen aspects of the entire program.

3. Outline an acquisition program for choosing an online database program using the flowchart symbols found in Figure 5.1 (page 81).

4. Review the literature published by the National Association of Secondary School Principals or the Association for Supervision and Curriculum Development to see what trends are being proposed there. Make an appointment to discuss these trends with a principal to see what information is needed to help with understanding or implementation.

5. Given the outline below, draw a Gantt chart (see Figure 5.3 [page 84]) for closing a school library in two months and transferring the holdings to two other libraries. A suggested procedure is:

Step 1. Weed the collection.

Step 2. Review contents for integration into the other two collections.

Step 3. Pull items from shelves, sorting for the two locations.

Step 4. Create electronic records to match sorted items.

Step 5. Pack items.

Step 6. Unpack items at new locations and shelve.

Step 7. Check electronic records against items placed on shelves.

Step 8. Add electronic records into existing online public access catalog, noting duplications.

6. Prepare an in-service program for teachers in one particular grade level or curriculum topic to share a bibliography of new materials for them showing how you could collaborate to make a research project interesting for students.

7. Find a school that has implemented the Professional Learning Community (PLC) model. Does it have minimum day schedules to provide for collaborative planning time? What is the role of the media specialist? How has the PLC encouraged the media specialist to take a leadership role?

NOTES

1. Robert D. Stueart and Barbara B. Moran, *Library and Information Center Management*, 7th ed. (Westport, CT: Libraries Unlimited, 2007), 96.

2. Ibid., 109.

3. American Association of School Librarians and Association for Educational Communications and Technology, *Information Power: Building Partnerships for Learning* (Chicago: American Library Association, 1998), 106.

4. Helen R. Adams, *School Media Policy Development: A Practical Process for Small Districts* (Littleton, CO: Libraries Unlimited, 1986).

5. Marian Karpisek, *Policymaking for School Library Media Programs* (Chicago: American Library Association, 1989).

6. Stephen Krashen, *The Power of Reading* (Englewood, CO: Libraries Unlimited, 1993), 1.

7. Ibid., 19.

8. AASL and AECT, *Information Power*, 125.

On the Job: Managing the Facility

Managing the facility may seem to have less priority than other aspects of administering a school library media program. Indeed, this topic is totally missing from AASL's *Information Power: Building Partnerships for Learning.* Few school library media specialists have the opportunity to design a new media center during their professional careers. Most inherit their space and have little opportunity to make major changes in the facility. This sense of accepting what is provided may be the reason that, although the 1988 *Information Power* devotes an entire chapter and an appendix to facilities,[1] a major part of the chapter outlines facilities at the district level. Nonetheless, assessing library media facilities to improve them is as important as other components of media center management.

The school library media center should make a positive first impression on all visitors, but especially the primary users—students and teachers. A visual welcome encourages patrons to move into the room with a pleasant attitude. If the view when the door opens is not inviting, they will resist using the facility.

Obviously, more exciting activities can go on in spaces that lend themselves to such activities. Spaces that are too small and too crowded limit action and people. The research on school library media facilities shows that people who liked their libraries gave such reasons as attractiveness and plenty of space. Dissatisfaction came from lack of space and the feeling that staff had had no say in planning new or expanded buildings. This often results in a "fixed nature of unattractive wall graphics or inconvenient structural features which staff could not change."[2]

One might question why staff members feel that they have no say in planning new or expanded buildings or that they cannot suggest that inconvenient structural features be excluded from construction or renovation. One reason may be that not enough attention is paid to facilities planning courses in library schools; thus, graduates are not comfortable with the responsibility for such action. Another may be that school library media specialists are unaware of the process of planning new buildings in their districts. Without a director of the library media program, building-level media specialists may not know that new construction is being proposed until plans have reached a stage where modification is difficult, if not impossible.

Housing the collection and staff does make a difference. Any service offered to interest teachers in integrating the media center into their curriculum planning or to attract students to the center for reading and research has space considerations, and these vary from one program to another.

Planning for spaces and rearranging facilities also becomes an extremely important part of management as new technologies are added. The space configurations that house word-processing equipment and online resources as well as the online public access catalog (OPAC) are different from the configurations found in media centers constructed before 1980. If telecommunications links mean cutting through walls in older buildings, it is time to prepare for wireless installations. Although rearranging to accommodate new technologies is mandatory, all this is done in the context of the goals and objectives of the school's educational program.

> Since differences exist in the goals and patterns of educational programs, facilities within the school are designed to reflect its curriculum and the particular instructional requirements of its students and teachers. The size and characteristics of school populations and the rapidly changing technologies for instruction demand alternatives and maximum flexibility in the design and relationship of functional spaces within the library media program facilities.[3]

Because of these differences in educational programs, planning for facilities takes into consideration:

- Size of the student body
- Attendance patterns of students
- Age and learning styles of students
- Teaching methods
- Number of staff in the media center
- Scheduling of students to the media center
- Size of the collection, materials, and equipment
- Technologies to be housed in and managed from the media center

The size of the student body is a major consideration. Often state agencies mandate building specifications. If the guidelines for schools state that the media center should seat 10 percent of the student body, this would require a larger facility for a school population of 2,000 students than 200. In addition, regional accrediting agencies often specify a ratio of building size to the size of the student body.

Students' school attendance patterns have a definite impact on the media center. For example, some students may attend classes in one building for part of the day and go to another school for the remainder of the day. In this case, a school population of 2,000 may have only 1,000 in attendance at any given time. Younger students usually attend school for fewer hours, and they tend to be voracious readers. Space must be available to allow teaching, reference, and group work to go on in one area, while, in another, students may come in for new reading materials. Thus, the need to accommodate more frequent use of the center must be taken into account.

Consideration must be given to the age of the students, particularly in terms of choosing furniture. Younger children need more areas for group work and storytelling, and high school students are independent learners with different seating requirements. Also, students with particular learning problems may need different spaces, such as quiet areas for emotionally disturbed students.

Although educators prefer to think that all teachers have moved beyond sole use of lecture and text, this is not yet true. It is unlikely that an entire staff is using this traditional teaching pattern; nevertheless, this pattern is a factor in planning media center spaces. That is, spaces are arranged to accommodate less reference and more recreational reading. In this situation, it is imperative that spaces be designed for ease of modification as teachers change their methods of teaching.

A large media center staff will allow, and even require, more enclosed spaces. A separate computer room for word processing and database searching limits distracting noise from the reading room area. Yet, a large media center with enclosed spaces for housing computers, production of materials, preview of items, and small group work will be difficult for a single person to oversee. Architects sometimes design media centers that are functionally impossible for one person to manage. Sunken circulation desks in the center of the facility, balconies, and multiple entrances and exits are examples of building flaws.

When students are regularly assigned to the media center on a weekly basis, additional space is needed to allow independent use of the facility while scheduled classes are there. The placement of tables and chairs to provide a classroom-like setting for teaching and away from the distractions of independent users presents a challenge.

Obviously, space is needed to accommodate the materials and equipment in the collection as well as the furniture. The amount of materials and size and amounts of equipment varies from school to school. When a television studio is connected to the media center, different heights are needed for the ceiling. Several factors affect the amount of equipment storage space needed. When sufficient equipment is available to place in individual classrooms, storage is needed only during vacation times. If equipment is heavily used by individuals and must be returned to the media center and reassigned, it must be stored between uses in the media center. This method of equipment distribution requires rolling carts for each piece of equipment, and these require much more storage space than bin shelving.

Planning for new technologies to be housed and managed from the media center dictates some rearrangement of furniture and electronic refitting. Proper wiring for new schools requires installation at the time of construction of adequate sources for both electricity and telecommunications links. When the building is older, rewiring is much more difficult. This is discussed in more depth under "Remodeling the Facility."

Few school library media specialists begin their jobs by opening a new facility. Rather, they must review the arrangement of their existing center to see that it is pleasant and that it can accommodate maximum use by students and teachers—as individuals, as small groups, and as classes. This begins with rearranging and remodeling—whether that is, as discussed in chapter 4, arranging signage and displays and rearranging furniture or reconstruction with removal and rebuilding of walls.

REARRANGING FACILITIES

Remodeling facilities can be an exciting challenge. The first step is to determine how much rearrangement can be done in the existing facility. In deciding how to rearrange furniture, it may be helpful to place the furniture and equipment into a grid (Figure 6.1). This will help preview the approximate spaces for the center.

Steps To Follow To Rearrange a Library

1. Measure the library. Use a tape measure or estimate by measuring one tile (floor or ceiling) and plotting from that estimate.

2. Using a grid, place tables and chairs, allowing sufficient space among all furnishings and the surrounding shelves. The second sheet provides you with furniture and shelves outlined to scale. Trace in shelves or cut them out and paste them down. Do not forget the circulation desk.

3. Indicate doors and partitions, and label the main entrance. If there is a fire escape rather than an exit, indicate that. These are all part of the facilities design.

4. Review the proposed changes. Do they improve the traffic flow and separate noisy areas from quiet study?

5. Determine costs associated with the rearrangement. Is furniture being added? Is equipment being moved away from rather than closer to electrical outlets? Are more electrical outlets required?

6. Analyze whether the rearrangement satisfies needs or is merely a temporary fix.

Review the proposed changes with the advisory committee to see that planned improvements will result in efficiency in all areas. Care should be taken that no new blind spots are created in rearranging furniture to correct an existing problem. Plan the rearrangement so that materials are moved only once. Then move those shelves if they require moving and begin to restock. If they do not require moving, merely restock the shelves with the books that will be there permanently. That way, materials will be moved from one space to their permanent location. When the last shelf has been cleared, it is a simple matter to replace those set aside at the beginning.

Most media centers installing equipment for new technologies have had to add spaces as well as rearrange. Removing the card catalog as a piece of

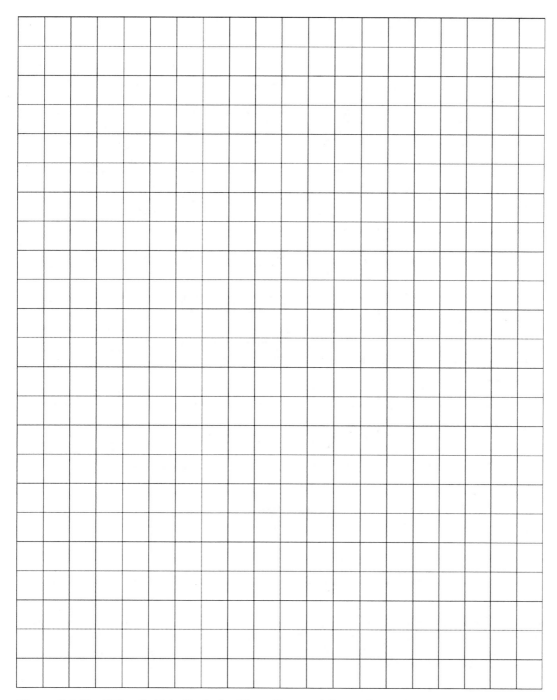

Figure 6.1 Facilities Grid to Scale for Floor Plan and Room Arrangement

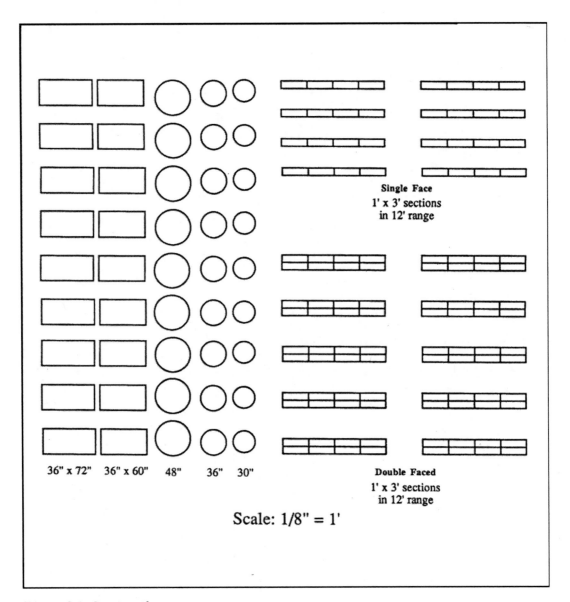

36" x 72" 36" x 60" 48" 36" 30"

Single Face
1' x 3' sections
in 12' range

Double Faced
1' x 3' sections
in 12' range

Scale: 1/8" = 1'

Figure 6.1 *Continued*

Note: Use this grid to outline the library facility. This will provide both a floor plan and a traffic pattern. The grid is to be filled in using a scale of 3/16 inch to two feet. That is, each square represents two feet. This need not be "architect correct," but it is important that furnishings be placed using approximate size relationships.

furniture does not provide enough space to house OPAC terminals. Although computer tables and chairs should be ergonomic, many library media specialists place both OPAC terminals and CD-ROM outlets on high tables so that students use them while standing to control extended usage. If printers are provided, these must be placed near the terminals. Allow for sheltering the connecting wires, so that they do not easily pull away from the equipment.

As computers are connected into networks, media specialists find their workrooms or offices transformed into telecommunications centers, and these need proper ventilation. Terminals for other uses such as connections to online databases or fax machines similarly occupy space that was not designed for this use, and adapting existing furniture for new uses is no better than the former method of using cafeteria tables and folding chairs in media centers. Although usually more costly, a media specialist should not overlook purchasing furniture designed for intended use in libraries. However, as discussed in the next section on remodeling, furniture designed for specific pieces of equipment will extend the life of any piece because it will be safely housed.

Media specialists should keep a record as new technologies are added and facilities arranged. Before-and-after photos will show an appealing and efficient media center. Teachers and students will forget how the media center looked before, and administrators may not even be aware of the alterations. Such modifications should be noted on reports to administrators, because they demonstrate this area of management expertise.

REMODELING THE FACILITY

Increased enrollment usually dictates a need for additional spaces throughout the school. If new areas are being created, the media center must be reviewed for changes. This is essential as new technologies evolve, and new equipment and new furniture to support the equipment are needed. Computer workstations require more space than carrels, where students sat with notebooks. Arranging the wiring for safety is a major consideration. Although some suggest that space can be saved by removing book shelves, this seldom yields enough space to accommodate tables and chairs for workstations and terminals.

More space is required for library media specialists responsible for the transmission of media programs to classrooms. Also, a wireless cart holding 20 or more microcomputers requires storage away from normal media center usage. The need to limit access to this type of storage area requires different kinds of media center spaces.

When remodeling is planned, the media specialist should look carefully at the building. It may be better to move the media center to a new location than to remodel the existing space. Far too often, the location of stairwells and rest rooms impedes expansion. Locate the best place in the building and help the administration understand how to rearrange what is there so that this space can be used for a new media center. This will not be easy, but it could make the difference between increasingly crowded spaces where the media center is presently located and a better area elsewhere.

The author is well aware of the transformation of one impossible situation. A high school had two media center locations. The fiction library near the office area in the original building had a reading room with a balcony housing back issues of periodicals. When an addition was placed on the building, a new area was devoted to the media center for housing nonfiction books. The media specialist walked between these two distant locations to meet students and teachers as they planned activities. Two sets of periodicals were purchased to have some research capability in both locations.

The media specialist learned that all walls in the new building were temporarily placed and could be easily moved. The next step was to get an estimate on partitioning the former fiction reading room into three classrooms. Within one year the materials collections had been consolidated in the new wing, an event the media coordinator had been striving for since the new building had been built. A situation of this kind requires only careful planning and justification for the change. The three teachers who moved into the three newly created classrooms from the old reading room were the only persons disrupted for the good of all teachers and students.

Remodeling need not always be costly. Walls can often be removed by building staff and do not always require the hiring of an architect and a construction crew. Such alterations can be carried out without major expense. However, necessary permits and inspections will still be required. Not all furnishings need to be expensive either. The author enlisted the school carpenters to build additional shelving when insufficient funds were available to purchase shelving for remodeled facilities. Shelving was built from less expensive wood, with runners for adjustments, and painted bright colors.

School carpenters should be reminded that all shelves must be adjustable, and no shelf must be more than three feet wide. The standard depth is 8 to 10 inches. Oversize shelves for reference books, picture books, and audiovisual media are 10 to 12 inches. Shelves should be at least $^{13}/_{16}$-inch thick. Cornices and trim are not needed and can be restrictive on the top or sides of shelves.

Elementary shelving should be no higher than five feet, junior high shelves no higher than six feet, and senior high school shelves no higher than seven feet. Adjustable runners allow variance in space between shelves to accommodate oversize books. Remodeling an existing facility may be more challenging than creating a new one. In either situation, potential improvements to the program will greatly outweigh the one-time effort to pack and unpack materials.

When more elaborate renovation is necessary, planning and justification are essential. In older schools, electrical outlets tend to be a major problem. Coinciding with the need for adequate outlets is the need for sufficient electricity to support equipment. In addition, networking throughout the school and telecommunications links outside the school have become commonplace. Rewiring older schools can be expensive. Conferring with someone who has renovated a media center to accommodate telecommunications access can help the media specialist plan such remodeling. The fact that the cost is high cost means the need must be documented and the process must be detailed enough to convince administrators.

Media specialists need to keep in mind the same considerations when choosing furniture for remodeled facilities. Choosing workstations to house equipment for distance education as well as workstations to house technology in the library media center helps turn an existing facility into something that looks like a more modern building. Furniture is being built by those who understand technology and the storage needs of library media specialists. Finding such a vendor helps with this important facet of remodeling.

New technologies and the new furniture to house them require increased space. When more space is needed, major renovations must be undertaken with care. Beware of load-bearing walls, which support the roof and the weight of the floors above the media center. Load-bearing walls cannot be removed, and cutting openings in them may be too expensive for the space gained. When walls are rebuilt, factors such as sufficient electrical current, surge controls, humidity controls, telephone lines, and advanced communication lines such as cable must be considered, because wires are best housed hidden inside the structure.

Renovation is often as costly as a new facility. If the renovation is major, an architect is hired and construction follows. Plans for a renovated high school library media center are shown in Figures 6.2, 6.3, and 6.4. Figure 6.2 is the pre-renovation plan, Figure 6.3 shows the shop drawing the library staff began with, and Figure 6.4 is the actual floor plan for the renovation. In Figure 6.3, the shop drawing, the school library director explained that the "pass area" is now a presentation area with a sound system, a projector, and a large screen that lowers electronically. The area can seat more than 32, as indicated by the tables there. The entire library provides wireless access and retained hard-wiring, too, in the technology lab, professional library, computer center areas, and pass/presentation area. The periodical storage is used for a variety of purposes. To plan such an extensive renovation, the media specialist follows the same pattern as in planning a new facility.

PLANNING NEW FACILITIES

As stated earlier, few media specialists will have the opportunity to plan a new facility. Guidelines for facilities, according to *Information Power*, are as follows:

> Library media center facilities within a district or a school provide the space for the materials, equipment and services needed to achieve the mission, goals, and objectives of the library media program. Since differences exist in the goals and patterns of educational programs, facilities within the school are designed to reflect its curriculum and the particular instructional requirements of its students and teachers.[4]

Although the media center, as a facility, provides the space for materials, equipment, and services, it exists to house the staff as well. Consideration of office spaces includes allowing a view of activities in the media center. Often, the media specialist's main station is a reference desk in the center of the room so that teachers and students can ask questions and solicit help quickly when needed. Few media specialists have the freedom to close themselves in an office to work on a project.

The main function of the media center is to provide an environment that will encourage and support teaching and learning within its spaces. Most media specialists inherit a location in the building, but sometimes the media specialist can choose the location for a new facility.

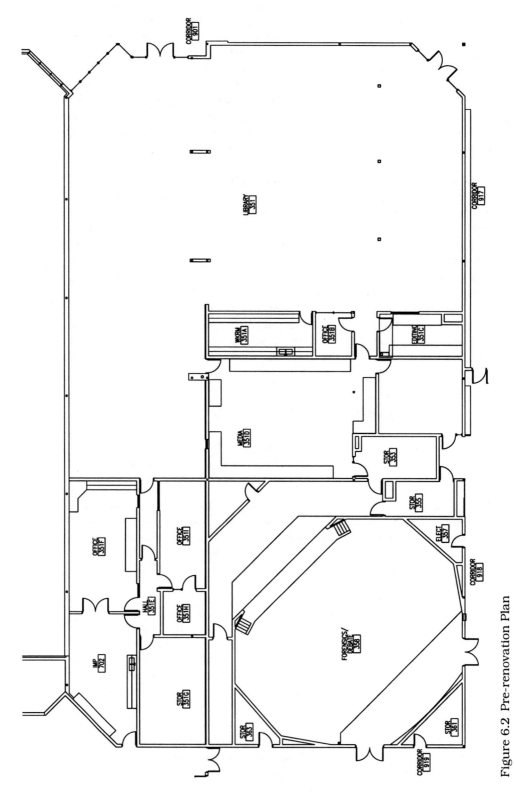

Figure 6.2 Pre-renovation Plan

Source: Courtesy of Kent Anderson, Architect, Design and Construction Manager, Blue Valley School District, Overland, Kansas.

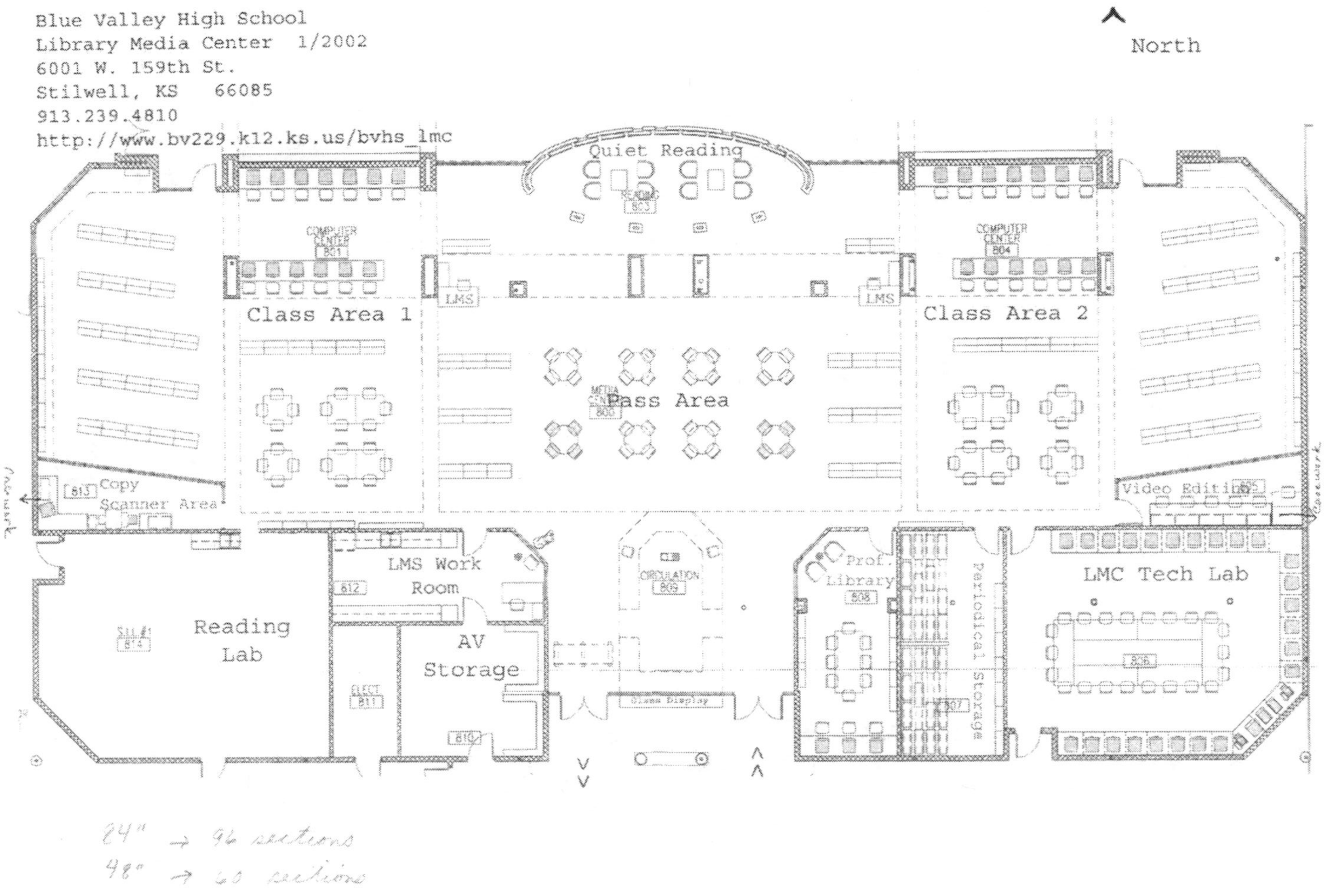

Blue Valley High School
Library Media Center 1/2002
6001 W. 159th St.
Stilwell, KS 66085
913.239.4810
http://www.bv229.k12.ks.us/bvhs_lmc

North

Class Area 2

COMPUTER CENTER 804

Video Editing

LMC Tech Lab

Periodical Storage

Prof. Library 803

Quiet Reading

Pass Area

CIRCULATION 802

New Display

Class Area 1

COMPUTER CENTER 801

LMS Work Room 812

AV Storage

Reading Lab

Copy Scanner Area 815

network

Figure 6.3 Shop Drawing

Source: Courtesy Linda Corey, Blue Valley School District, Overland, Kansas.

103

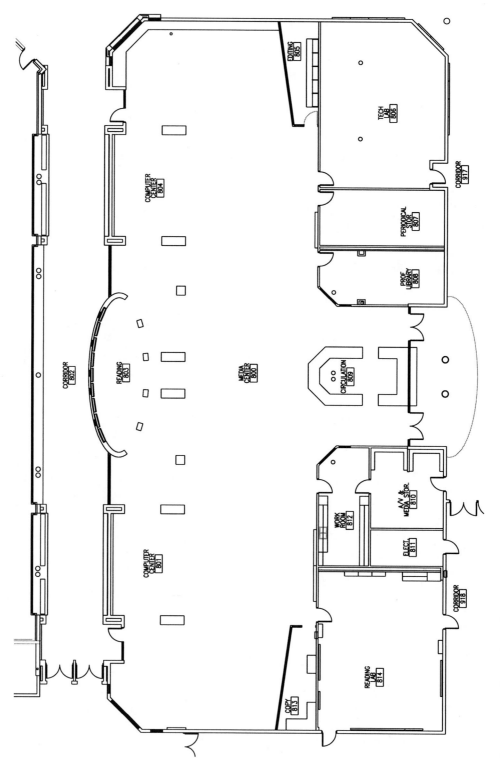

Figure 6.4 Floor Plan of the Renovation

Source: Courtesy Kent Anderson, Architect, Design and Construction Manager, Blue Valley School District, Overland, Kansas.

When library media specialists have the chance to build a new facility, they should visit several sites to review with other media specialists the strengths and weaknesses of their designs. What works well in one location may work well in another. What did not work in one location should be avoided if possible in new plans, although this is not necessarily an easy task. Architects tend to have limited opportunities to exercise creativity in designing classrooms, cafeterias, offices, gymnasiums, auditoriums, and band rooms. Thus, many architects see the media center as the place to make an artistic statement. Unfortunately, many of those statements create dysfunctional media centers.

Collecting ideas is always helpful, and a truly successful idea can be presented to the architect as a suggestion. Erickson and Markuson's book[5] on designing facilities is useful to the library media specialist who is helping to plan a new facility.

Building a new facility provides an excellent opportunity for the media specialist to remind teachers and administrators of educational trends that should be considered in planning the new school. Enlisting the assistance of teachers and students in planning creates advocates and supporters who may help deflect unworkable suggestions by architects. It also builds support for funding for new technologies both present and future.

Next, teachers and students should be reminded of the media center program philosophy and goals. They can then be asked to help define the areas of need in the media center. Reference areas—including the online public access catalog and access to online references and the Internet—should be near a media specialist so that students and teachers can be helped quickly. Proximity to a media specialist is particularly important because software changes so rapidly and also because staff can encourage students to choose a variety of sources rather than depending on a quick Google search.

Some areas may be designated for recreational reading, viewing, and listening, but other areas should be available for quiet study. Circulation of materials, borrowing and returning reserve materials, and requesting periodicals from closed stacks tend to be noisy activities and should be located near the entrance. Internet access points may also become noisy when students share computers for searching. Also, the need to observe Internet use means that these workstations need to be observed at all times for supervision and to offer help to users who need it.

When it is time to meet with the architects, they will be interested in the philosophy of service for the media center. This is the time to discuss the placement of the media center in the building. Although most teachers feel that their programs are central to the school, the media center should be quickly accessible from all classrooms.

Architects need to know the number of students and teachers to be served, the amounts of materials to be housed, and the areas needed for specific activities. That is, a separate classroom and spaces that can be darkened are requirements. Electrical outlets are needed for all equipment. Also needed are conference rooms for small group work, some magazine storage, work space, and other special spaces.

The seating areas, storage areas, shelving to house collections, and production room should be fully described. A computer room separate from the reading room may be a priority for computer access, especially when a monitor is available to oversee usage. Another school might prefer workstations in the reading room where computer screens are more visible. In addition, the architect may need to be reminded of such factors as climate control, acoustics, carpeting, moveable walls, moveable shelving, ceiling treatment, windows, doors, communication lines, and safety.

With the continuing development of information storage and retrieval in mechanized formats, the need to keep back issues of magazines and newspapers in paper form is decreasing steadily. Current information available online reduces the need for some storage areas, although it increases the need for more workstations to access the information. Moveable walls make it easier to rearrange areas of the media center as new uses are determined and former uses become obsolete.

Architects do not want detailed floor plans. Yet, they may wish to see the relationship of one area to another. That is, if the conference rooms need to be close to equipment storage, this must be specified. If there are noisy areas such as a circulation desk or reference area, their relationship to reading areas must be made clear. The architects must know of special needs such as sinks, cabinets, carpeting, electrical outlets, and plumbing. They must be apprised that cables should be run from the media center into the classrooms to carry electronic transmissions of data if wireless access is not being planned.

Architects design, draw blueprints, and return with the plans for further review. It is important to understand what is shown in the blueprint. A square in the middle of the plan probably indicates a load-bearing pillar. If it is placed directly in front of the circulation desk, rearrangement of the area may be necessary. Care must be taken to see that no blind spots are built into the furniture arrangement. Shelving arranged so students can hide may cause discipline problems. Architects often attempt to beautify with balconies or exotic entrances that are not workable in a center for students.

This author is well aware of strange lighting fixtures that did not emit enough light and melted when higher wattage was placed in them. Another architect built two bridges for middle school students to connect open classrooms to a second-floor "island." The reading room tables and chairs were directly under these two bridges. One can imagine how many objects were dropped onto heads below before these entrances were closed, forcing students into a corridor and down outside stairs to enter the front door of the media center.

It is sometimes impossible to convince an architect to make changes. If the situation is very bad, the media specialist should list the problems and the probable outcome if changes are not made. With logical justification, the superintendent should intervene with the school board.

The school board approves construction plans. When bids for building are far higher than anticipated, cuts must be made from the original design. It is imperative that the school library media specialist review the proposed alterations to make sure they are made in appropriate areas of the media center.

Some simple considerations for planning the new facility include the following:

1. Select shelving with backing, especially for elementary schools. It is all too easy to push books and boxes through double-faced shelving or down behind single-faced shelving that has no backing.

2. Select sufficient shelving to hold the present collection and anticipated additions for the next 10 to 15 years. It is difficult—often
   impossible—to match paint, wood, or even type of shelf with the
   same manufacturer after the initial order. If bids are let for new
   shelving and a different manufacturer is chosen, the problem is
   intensified.

   A three-foot shelf, when full, will hold approximately 30 books of average size,
   18 reference books, or 60 picture books (with dividers).

3. Select sufficient electrical voltages for present and anticipated use.
   Sufficient outlets in planning a new facility are mandatory, though
   state codes may not require enough. The new media center may
   resemble a renovated one if additional conduits must be strung outside walls.

4. Make sure communication links to the outside are available. This
   may mean including wiring for telecommunications links.

5. Check carefully the source of shelving and furnishings. Many times
   bids are let for educational rather than library furniture. The author
   remembers a slanting-top picture book table order for an elementary
   school that was custom-built by the company furnishing the entire
   building. The legs were too tall for six-year-olds, but the carpenters
   installing the furniture were reluctant to cut the legs to the proper size
   because this is difficult to do after the furniture has left the factory. Be
   sure to include furniture appropriate for the new technologies.

6. Confirm that partitions are temporary rather than permanent.

MOVING A MEDIA CENTER

When school populations decline or shift from one area to another or schools
close, school library media specialists are assigned the task of closing library
media centers. This involves sending collections, furniture, and equipment to
a central warehouse or distributing them among other schools.

If the contents are to go to other schools in the district, the media specialist plans the shift after taking a careful inventory at each media center. Equal
distribution may not be a case of "one for School A," "one for School B," "one
for School C." Redistribution should be made on the basis of need and existing
collections.

Collections, furniture, and equipment should be carefully scrutinized and
the old, irrelevant, and broken removed. Certainly the media specialist will
analyze the materials collection for duplication at other schools. It may be
preferable to keep materials in a central location where other media specialists
can pick only titles of use in their collections rather than to send cartons of
unneeded materials to another school.

When the administration in one school district asked each of the five librarians to work two weeks one summer to close one elementary school and move the
contents to the other schools in the district, the librarians calculated the time
it would take to remove each item from its place on the shelf, pull the shelf list

and catalog cards, pack the item into a box, unpack, reshelve, and refile cards (when moving electronic records, checking for duplication is still time consuming). When the administrators learned the estimated time the move would take, they increased the use of professional time and added clerical assistance.

If remodeling is in progress during the school year, much of the collection may be boxed and stored. Media specialists must decide the year before which important books and media will be needed while the collection is stored and move them to a classroom or another accessible area. The most used reference and other books should also be kept from storage. Equipment can be reassigned to storage areas or classrooms throughout the building. Again, this process takes careful needs assessment and planning.

If a new facility is projected, buying the new contents should be planned at least one year in advance, and the media specialist assigned to the new center should have release time and additional clerical assistance during this year. The amount of release time needed should be as carefully calculated as the collection—some of which is being transferred from another location and some of which will be added from new selections.

The success of any media program depends on the staff and the collection. Yet, the ambiance of the facility sets the stage.

Exercises

1. Using graph paper and furniture, draw the floor plan of an existing school library media center. See if this center can be easily rearranged to provide better access, quiet versus noisy areas, and any other improvements you would suggest. Take into consideration the addition of new technologies to the media center.
2. Review the location of a media center within an existing school. Make recommendations for ways to increase the size of the media center to accommodate new technologies and additional computer facilities such as a word-processing center. Are sufficient spaces allocated for the storage of such equipment as a carrier for a classroom collection of laptop computers?
3. Visit a media center and determine if the present furniture will meet the needs of new technologies that may be added later.

NOTES

1. American Association of School Librarians and Association for Educational Communications and Technology, *Information Power: Guidelines for School Library Media Programs* (Chicago: American Library Association, 1988), 85–101, 131–39.

2. Blanche Woolls, "Facilities," in *The Research of School Library Media Centers*, ed. Blanche Woolls (Castle Rock, CO: Hi Willow Research and Publishing, 1990), 261.

3. AASL and AECT, *Information Power*, 85.

4. Ibid.

5. Rolf Erickson and Carolyn Markuson, *Designing a School Library Media Center for the Future* (Chicago: American Library Association, 2001).

Chapter 7

On the Job: Managing Personnel

Many school library media specialists are single managers of their library media center; they have no paid staff to manage. Because of this prospect, education programs for media specialists often provide only skeletal instruction in management skills. The only personnel management skills taught are interpersonal skills for communication with administrators, teachers, and students. However, almost every media specialist has helpers in the media center. Whether it is directing paraprofessionals, student assistants, or volunteer parents, personnel management skills are needed. In fact, more management skills may be required with volunteers than paid staff:

- Volunteers are "paid" by receiving personal appreciation.
- Volunteer availability is generally erratic or sporadic.
- Volunteers require more training and direction.
- Correcting performance problems requires a great deal of tact.

In some media centers, a part-time or full-time paraprofessional is part of the media center staff. In very large schools, the school library media center may have two or more professionals and several paraprofessionals. Managing the people who perform the tasks that keep the media program running smoothly day by day requires more attention to personnel management.

Tasks to be performed in the library media center have been developed over time by practitioners who manage media programs on a daily basis. They share their expertise in supervision of practicum students from colleges, through articles they write and presentations at conferences, and in state and national standards and guidelines they create or task analyses they conduct. These task analyses are translated into education programs at colleges and universities and used in preparing articles, presentations, and standards. General practice focuses on selecting materials, organizing collections, and using new technologies, among others, rather than managing staff. Nevertheless, managing people is one of the most important factors in a successful media program. The media specialist must have the ability to manage and communicate with persons in the center and to assume responsibility for management of personnel and of those who use the center. The successful media specialist possesses the skills needed to interact with media center users and all others in the school.

Larger school districts have a human resources department with staff and director. In smaller districts, the hiring is assigned to a single person within another department of the district. These persons will be very knowledgeable with hiring teachers, but they may be much less familiar with the competencies of the various persons working in media centers. School library media specialists must be aware of the expectations of staff for supervising their work.

MANAGING MEDIA CENTER STAFF

In any situation, staff expects the immediate supervisor to direct their actions so they can complete their assigned tasks in a satisfactory manner. Such decisions may be group decisions. Nevertheless, staff members, students, and volunteers who can work independently should be allowed to establish how to do a job once the job has been defined. When improvement in task implementation is needed, the media specialist must help staff understand the problem and how to solve it.

The media specialist is also responsible for helping staff to prepare for advances in technology, learn about additions to the collection (especially reference sources), and implement new services and new relationships with agencies outside the school. Such changes may result in changes in the job descriptions for media specialists and staff.

Job Titles and Job Descriptions

Most jobs have titles and job descriptions. School library media specialists receive their titles and job descriptions from two professions: librarianship and education. As a part of librarianship, they are described by that profession as librarians. Asheim's 1970 manpower report prepared for the American Library Association described five levels of staff for the library: clerk, library media technician, library assistant, library associate, and librarian.[1] A master's degree was required for the library associate and the librarian.

As a part of the education community, the American Association of School Librarians and the Association for Educational Communications and Technology listed in their 1975 standards, media specialist, media technician, and media aide.[2] As a title, school library media specialist remains unchanged with *Information Power: Building Partnerships for Learning.* However, California has recently changed its job title to teacher librarian, a title that has been used in Canada.

Personnel Management Competencies

Because the role of the school library media specialist is somewhat different from the teaching staff or the other teachers in the special areas, writing job descriptions and participating in the hiring of personnel may be an assignment. This means the media specialist will have the responsibility for recruiting and terminating personnel when those situations occur.

Regardless of whether you have hiring responsibility, you are responsible for seeing that your staff is trained. Because of the rapid development of technologies, this may mean that you must help train the teachers. Being able to train is an important competency for a media specialist. The type of training that media specialists do is different from that of teachers who teach their students. You will be teaching your peers.

If the media center is to run smoothly, you must assign job responsibilities to specific personnel, and you will then need to supervise the staff to see that they carry out their duties efficiently and thoroughly. This is sometimes not a pleasant job. Supervising personnel means decisions must be made that may not be readily accepted by staff; at the same time, you have the responsibility of maintaining staff members' job satisfaction.

Finally, if you have been given these responsibilities, you will also be asked to evaluate staff performance. This is seldom pleasant unless the staff is unusually competent. It becomes even more difficult if merit raises are given for outstanding performance.

These competencies relate directly to the personnel working in the media center. The degree to which any library media specialist may participate in any of these functions is a product of the organization of the school district and the contracts binding on personnel in that school district. A building-level media specialist might be asked to create the job description for other professionals and the clerical staff, although this might be done at the district's central office.

Centralization of job descriptions at the district level eases uniformity in operation through all schools. When tasks in one media center are different from those in another, this must be taken into consideration. For instance, if a clerk is searching an online database, this becomes a part of the job description even though the service is limited to one school.

When staff leaves the school district, a job description should be provided for applicants for the replacement. Job descriptions are also necessary for any new positions that have been created.

Although there may seem to be little need to prepare a job description until funds have been allocated for the position, the school library media specialist described in *Information Power: Building Partnerships for Learning* repeats the 1996 ALA *Policy Manual* and holds that the following is necessary:

a master's degree in librarianship from a program accredited by the American Library Association or a master's degree with a specialty in school library media from an educational unit accredited by the National Council for the Accreditation of Teacher Education.[3]

It is the responsibility of the library media specialist to see that qualified staff and paraprofessionals "are appropriately prepared to perform clerical and technical duties."[4] The media specialist must clearly analyze those factors that dictate requirements for additional staff and prepare appropriate documentation to justify the positions. Administrators must be convinced of the need for a new or expanded position. The foundation established in the job description may become the justification for funding.

To approach an administrator with the need for additional staff or continuation of staff, the media specialist must present an analysis of the tasks currently being accomplished and those that cannot be accomplished because of lack of staff. The administrator must be convinced that a need is not being met. To state the request as, "I don't have time to write overdue notices," or "The books don't get shelved very fast," probably will not get an administrator's attention. Calculating actual costs of clerical tasks in relation to professional salary to establish cost accountability is presented in chapter 9.

Writing job descriptions for recruiting and hiring personnel is not an easy task. The 1988 *Information Power* has general descriptions of staff duties. For more specific tasks, review the 1975 *Media Programs District and School.* Although the 1975 standards are more than 30 years old, they serve as a good model. One need only modify their general descriptions for current positions. Duties of each library media center staff member are described and can be adapted to the local situation. If fewer staff is available, some duties can be moved from one or more position statements to describe a single job. Care should be taken to make sure administrators recognize the division between clerical tasks and professional tasks, particularly in relation to cost accountability.

The Role of the Media Specialist in Staffing

Staffing the library media program, according to *Information Power,* consists of

- defining personnel needs
- securing qualified personnel
- developing staff competencies to perform essential tasks
- establishing standards of performance
- evaluating personnel performance[5]

The school library media specialist is supported by both clerical and technical staff so that professional activities can be accomplished. To manage the program, the school library media specialist, if at all possible, participates in defining needs for personnel, choosing those, providing needed in-service training, setting expectations for accomplishing assignments, and evaluating staff. This is done in the context of the school setting. If hiring is the responsibility of a human resources department, the school library media specialist must use as much tact as possible to influence the job description and the evaluation of applications.

One of the most important tasks is to make sure staff members are working with a common goal and a common vision. Once the staff has established and accepted the goals and objectives, the media specialist works to build a common vision of information services with the other teachers in the building, defining the role of the media specialist as a part of the teaching staff.

The Media Specialist as Part of the Teaching Staff

Over time, school administrators and other educators have discussed differentiated staffing models. In the 1960s, divisions were proposed between master teacher and staff teacher, an expansion from department head and classroom teachers, with master teachers holding major responsibility for curriculum design and large group lectures. Staff teachers conducted small group discussions and worked with individual students. The media center became a center for research and teaching, and the media specialist became a part of the teaching staff.

As elementary schools were staffed in the late 1960s and early 1970s, the media specialist had dual responsibilities: as manager of the media center and as teacher of a subject area for one or more grades—for example, third- and fourth-grade math. One model for high schools with more than one media specialist had them teaching one subject area course each day and working in the media center the remainder of the time. Another comparison is to academic libraries with the technical services librarians and the collection development librarians acting as reference librarians not only to learn what users are requesting and what format, but also what level of information and what type of research patrons are conducting, and to provide bibliographic instruction. These roles earned them academic status. If media specialists teach part-time, teachers are more likely to view them as teachers as well as information professionals.

The present movement to outcomes-based education and curriculum across the school generates a new pattern of school staffing. The library media specialist leads curriculum planning teams as a part of the instructional staff. The perception of this person's role is changing. The role requires the assignment of additional media center staff and a reallocation of duties in the media center to provide the necessary time for consulting.

The Media Specialist as Leader

The role of the library media specialist in the new millennium is one of leadership. Information technologies at the beginning of the twentieth century seem tame compared to the present. Electricity, the typewriter, the telephone, phonograph, cameras and film, and motion pictures seemed to provide all that could ever be desired. One could read easily at night, and typing meant rapid preparation of records within the library. Mr. Bell gave us fast communication between sites, and Mr. Edison provided canned music. The development of the camera and film created the ability to store information on microfilm.

At the beginning of the twenty-first century, the rapidly expanding information resources and the communication links via computer generate new tasks and new challenges. Even the facility is under scrutiny. The suggestion that a media center is not necessary because students and teachers may find all their information on the Internet appears threatening to some, an opportunity to others.

Meeting the challenge presented by new technologies predicts a leadership role for library media specialists. They choose from the available technologies which ones will be most helpful and which will help teachers and students access the available information. It is the responsibility of the library media specialist to make the best choices from the vast array before them. They are also responsible for helping teachers and students learn how to narrow their queries, thus saving countless wasted hours in searching; but of more importance will be helping students discover misinformation they find in online resources. And so the media specialist becomes an information consultant.

> There is no doubt that the concept of the library is changing—some say it is in transition from "connection to connection." The extent to which this transition will actually occur and its impact on library services is yet to be fully determined. There is no doubt that libraries of the future will be looking for new skills and abilities among its employees and will be continually emphasizing retraining and continuing education as new technologies are introduced.[6]

The media specialist becomes curriculum leader, helping teachers understand what is being taught in every classroom and can lead in the development of cross-curriculum units of instruction that also span grade levels. Because media specialists have no assigned interest in a subject area or a grade level, they can help teachers move out of their assignment as responsible for particular content into merging that content with other disciplines and other grade levels. This will help students prepare for a world where disciplines merge or disappear, and where they will change jobs four or more times in their work life.

The newest leadership role requires the school library media specialist to work diligently to help students and teachers to use the Internet and World Wide Web wisely and well. This means both teaching effective use of information found on the Internet and also keeping the best possible Web sites linked from the library media center Web site to curriculum units to help students locate accurate and relevant information.

Securing Qualified Personnel

When positions in media centers become available, efforts are made to locate the best candidates. Personnel may be recruited at the district level through the district human resources office rather than by individual media center directors. Skills tests or assessments of credentials to meet employment standards are done centrally, and persons meeting qualifications may be assigned to a building, with the library media specialist having little or no control over selection. When selection occurs at the school, the advisory committee should be asked to help interview applicants to ensure selection of the best candidate.

Assigning Job Responsibilities and Motivating Staff

The assignment of individual staff to specific tasks must be undertaken with great care, because asking the appropriate person to do the job can make the difference between the program's success or failure. Dividing the program into discrete tasks and assigning each task to the most able person to accomplish it is the best way that the program will function efficiently, but this strategy requires the agreement of the staff to carry out the tasks.

When programs and staff are small, it is better if most tasks can be shared by all. Obviously, personnel must be assigned to tasks for which they are qualified and trained and that they are willing to perform, but all members of a staff as small as those assigned to most school library media centers should understand all basic operations. If only one person understood how to operate the circulation system, the media center would close if this person were absent.

Holding regular meetings to determine the work to be done and to share with staff what is happening is one way to keep staff motivated, and motivating staff is a major responsibility of the media specialist. At times, motivation is part of the perception of the staff member who is being asked to undertake a task. Once upon a time, the author's father suggested that she should never ask anyone to do something she was not willing to do herself. This is true of library media staff, professional and clerical. Media center managers and directors of media programs must not only say they are willing to do any task, but also demonstrate their willingness by doing the task. Media specialists, clerks, students, and volunteer parents are much more willing to shelve books and read the shelves if the media specialist is seen working at such tasks. That is not to say that clerical tasks are appropriate for professionals, but that professionals should not appear to be too important to do them. That attitude does not enhance the task or the self-image of the clerk, the student, or volunteer. The feeling of student helpers and volunteers that their assistance is critical—and it is—can only be enhanced if the media specialist demonstrates the importance of the tedious as well as the more exciting tasks.

Maintaining job satisfaction in the library media center should be easy. If staff members have been queried as to the best method to accomplish a task, and their suggestions implemented whenever possible, they feel worthwhile in the organization. They must also believe they have the opportunity to develop on the job.

Staff is further motivated when they are well informed about the tasks they are asked to perform. Fully understanding tasks and the relationships among tasks increases the possibility that staff members can offer useful suggestions.

In-Service Training

The library media specialist develops staff competencies. Conducting training for staff will be discussed in more detail in chapter 10 in the section concerning providing services for teachers and students. In-service training of staff, teachers, and students is considered in depth there. The focus of this section is on the preparation of staff in the media center.

The media specialist should see that all persons working in the media center understand their roles and are prepared to carry out the duties in the current job description, as well as any duties that may be added as media center services change. If staff needs to be trained, the media specialist conducts the training or arranges for a trainer to come to the media center. Seminars and workshops for continuing education and staff development are available, and the media specialist must see that time and funding can be arranged. Funding would include money for registration fees and travel to the site as well as for substitutes needed to keep the media center open during the staff's absence.

Media specialists should consider what happens when only one member is sent out to a training session. Although it seems much less expensive, the discussions that go on during training and the sharing of ideas based on the sessions later on are far more valuable when two or three staff members attend the training session. The concept of training the trainers becomes a better one when two or three have shared the original experience.

Standards of Performance

Setting standards of performance and monitoring staff as they perform their jobs becomes a supervision task for the media specialist. Supervision of personnel is the process of dealing with the persons who have been assigned the job responsibilities discussed above. Some supervisors view this role as one of a boss who must monitor behavior. At the other end of the continuum is the supervisor who is a colleague with the staff in accomplishing the task. These two concepts can be discussed in relation to Douglas McGregor's Theory X and Theory Y.[7] Despite the age of McGregor's theories, they are still applicable. In Theory X, management is responsible for organizing the work and directing the efforts of those involved to get the work accomplished. The Theory X manager believes that staff will work as little as possible because they lack ambition, that they dislike responsibility and are self-centered and indifferent to the needs of the organization. The Theory Y manager believes that staff can assume responsibility, and that it is the task of the manager to arrange the situation so that those working in the organization can direct their own efforts toward the objectives of the organization.

To be a Theory Y manager, the director of the media center must work with all staff to determine the tasks to be done and to solicit input on the best methods to accomplish the tasks. A regularly scheduled staff meeting can be used to discuss progress toward mutually set goals and objectives, to discuss the media center's weekly schedule, and to divide duties among the staff. Any items that may have been overlooked can be added, and any activity affecting another can be determined. For example, the media center classroom may be used by only one group at a time, and inadvertent double booking would be disturbing to all. Shout writes that

> Staff development depends upon two conditions. The first is *group relationships* that contribute to productivity and achievement of organizational goals. The second is *climate,* the work situation that helps individuals to grow, create, produce, and to give themselves enthusiastically to the work for which they are responsible.[8]

Job satisfaction exists in the library media center when (1) the facility is appealing, (2) staff appears to understand their jobs and they are doing them, (3) an efficient operation is in place, and (4) the library media center director is not a boss but a facilitator.

Evaluating Staff

In many school districts, state departments of education mandate personnel evaluation. For professional staff, the school district requirements may include evaluation of performance to determine reappointment or tenure. As suggested in chapter 3, the applicant should try to find out about evaluation steps to reappointment and tenure before accepting a position in a school district. Because many applicants do not always know exactly what questions to ask, after they begin the job, they need to research this process more fully. The principal, the district library media director, and the personnel office in the school district should be good sources of information about securing permanent certification and earning tenure. It is essential to obtain correct information. Although many teachers think they understand this process, they may not be aware of the latest policies or requirements in the state or district. Once teachers have been tenured, they are less interested in the process and may have incorrect concepts. It is better to get this information from the district office. In media centers with more than one professional, directors must keep current on tenure policy because they will be evaluating personnel. Evaluation may be required even after tenure is granted.

The state department of education provides forms to school districts to evaluate the teaching and clerical staff. These forms seldom cover the unique tasks of the school library media specialist. One of the more often heard complaints is that school library media specialists are judged with the same descriptors as classroom teachers when, in fact, their roles and tasks are very different. In some states, the evaluation form is developed by the state board of education for the evaluation of all education personnel. If this is the case, the library media specialist may help the principal by defining the evaluation criteria in library media terminology. With little specific evaluation criteria, administrators may not understand how to monitor the library media specialist's behavior and performance.

The author is reminded of a situation when a library media specialist requested release from a sabbatical commitment. Unfortunately for all concerned, the sabbatical replacement had been inadequate, but the administration had not given this person an inadequate evaluation. The substantial extra salary cost for the returning media specialist was borne by the school district. This demonstrates the problem when administrators do not understand how to define, monitor, and correct a bad situation in the media center. They may be well aware of how to improve the performance of a classroom teacher, but not a media specialist. This situation is also a problem because of standardized evaluation forms for all who teach.

Evaluation forms specific to school media specialists are usually available from the state library media organization. This group, often in cooperation with the state department of education's school library media director, may provide a better form for evaluating the performance of the building-level library media specialist.

The most efficient form of evaluation is direct observation. However, this method is usually uncomfortable for all concerned. Students are uneasy because the media staff person being observed is uneasy. It is difficult for the observer to be at ease because this is an evaluation situation. The performance is strained, and the process seems contrived. However, media professionals must be evaluated as they interact with students and teachers. If this is not to be an arbitrary judgment, it must be based on concrete facts. One way to get these facts is through direct observation.

As school administrators revise their expectations of performance, evaluation changes. In other words, as they recognize that the job of the media specialist is similar to, yet quite different from, that of the classroom teacher, they will better understand how evaluation criteria must also be different.

Unfortunately, media center directors may be asked to help with the review of a less efficient employee, and evaluation may involve keeping a detailed record of inefficiency to support dismissal. School library media specialists hope that they will not need to dismiss personnel, but when the situation occurs, the principal and the district library media director should be consulted to establish the appropriate procedures. Dismissal requires a carefully documented record of tasks done incorrectly or not done at all. It is not a pleasant assignment, yet it is irresponsible to allow inefficient, ineffective, and even harmful employees to remain when the education of students is at stake.

Because clerical and technical staff members are seldom tenured, evaluation determines salary increases and continuation of position. Records must be maintained at all levels. Efficient staff must be rewarded, and merit pay raises often must be documented as carefully as refusals to grant merit pay raises. The dismissal of inefficient clerical and technical staff requires careful and thorough documentation just as with professional staff. In our litigious society, many persons who are dismissed will sue.

Managing personnel may also be defined as getting along with the clientele. In the next four sections, suggestions are offered for managing with administrators, teachers, students, parents, and volunteers.

MANAGING WITH ADMINISTRATORS

This section might be subtitled "How to Get Along with Your Boss." Certainly, managing with administrators means getting along with those in authority in the school district. The focus here is on the building principal, but the methods and the suggestions for activities are equally applicable to the director of the library media program and the district superintendent. The first method is the planning phase. The school library media program will prosper if the media specialist learns to plan with the principal.

Planning with the principal does not mean discussing the titles of periodicals to which to subscribe. That is a professional task for which the media specialist has had training. Rather, planning with the principal should include such topics as the continuing costs of new online reference services and other reference materials—books and periodicals—needed to increase student potential in the school. This is a broad and somewhat different approach to the relationship between principal and library media specialist. Both touch the educational lives of every student through their interactions with students and teachers. However, the school library media specialist works with all the students, all the teachers, and all the curriculum all the time. While principals want to do this, they are often taken away to carry out other duties. This means the library media specialists are in a unique position to keep principals informed when they are away carrying out those other functions. The teaching needs of teachers and the learning needs of students as they are reflected in the library media collection should be continuing topics of discussion.

Successes, as well as needs, should be detailed in regular reports to the principal. This will help present the media center program in such a way that the principal can speak highly of it to other principals. Too often in life, the complaints outweigh the compliments, yet complaining is not the way to influence the principal. Regular monthly reports on the use of the media center and the positive experiences of students should outnumber the list of needs, great though they may be. Media specialists should also plan to submit a yearly report, which is a compilation of the monthly statistics. If the media specialist has developed a 3-, 5-, 10-, or 15-year plan with the principal, this yearly report will cite progress toward each of the goals, point out what has not occurred, and present the plan for fulfilling this objective in the next one or two years. The year-end report should be attractive and easily understood.

Another type of report presents trends in education. As professional periodicals are added to the media center collection, the media specialist may copy pertinent articles, highlighting the key passages, and forward them to the principal. Making copies of articles or information taken from the Internet and sharing them with the principal provides up-to-date information. Sending abstracts from the latest important books can also help the principal maintain a high level of expertise in educational trends as they develop. This makes you and your principal look good, an appealing perception under all circumstances.

The principal who participates in activity planning will better understand the role of the media specialist and the amount of responsibility involved in managing a media center. In evaluating performance, the principal must clearly recognize the dual role of the media specialist—as teacher and manager—and adjust the method of evaluation accordingly.

In some school districts, principals are administrators who are responsible for the day-to-day management of their building and also the discipline of students. They seldom have the opportunity to visit classrooms except to evaluate teacher performances. Inviting the principal to read to students, listen to final reports of research projects, and help to judge a storytelling contest gives this official the opportunity to share in media activities with children. The principal's participation also gives the library media specialist's project more importance and provides a positive experience for students, media center staff, and the principal.

Finally, the school library media specialist has full responsibility for accomplishing as much as possible in the education of each student. Testing, recording, and reporting the role of the media center in the educational progress of students will ultimately make the principal look good, the best of all possible results in managing with the administrator.

MANAGING WITH TEACHERS

Management with teachers is easily accomplished when the media specialist understands what teachers expect. Determining teachers' expectations was discussed in chapter 4. Success can often be defined as doing what teachers think should be done. Asking which services teachers want and then offering those services will build a positive image.

The media specialist must create the perception that the media center's priority is to be available for curriculum assistance. The media specialist will provide teachers with the help they need as they plan their classroom activities. Accessibility of resources when they are needed is essential. Media specialists should encourage teachers to plan ahead for their media needs, but instant help must be given willingly, not grudgingly.

Another proposed method of managing with teachers is to put as few restrictions as possible on media center access. Under this method, the media specialist allows access to the media center to as many students as possible and works with teachers to ensure the best possible experiences for their students while they are in the media center.

One way to help teachers understand the role of the media center in instruction is to provide in-service for teachers in information sources, research methods, research in the field of education, and additions to the media center. Also, the media specialist can provide in-service that will help teachers gain technological skills they may be lacking.

Helping teachers expand their skills, without implying that they do not have the skills, is a successful management method. Overcoming teacher resistance is easier when teachers are involved in planning the in-service activity. Then the program will be based on teacher-developed needs.

When helping teachers, it is always a good idea to be empathetic. When colleagues return from absences such as health leaves or sabbaticals, spending extra time to help them catch up on rules and regulations that have changed in their absence or curricular changes being discussed will contribute to a positive atmosphere for all.

Many teachers and media specialists complain that teachers who also coach sometimes misuse the media center on a game or contest day. Media specialists may consider it an imposition if coaches want to bring their classes to the library on those days. Coaches have enormous responsibility for the health and safety of their players, who are vulnerable in a way far exceeding that of other students. Working with teachers who have responsibilities such as the yearbook, the prom, or a field trip will ease their teaching burden for that period of time and can make the day more educational for that teacher's classes. This does not mean that the media center becomes a dumping ground, but that students are receiving the best possible education.

Finally, the media specialist should be willing to assist with extracurricular events. When the music teacher needs someone to attend the city choral festival with the school choir, the media specialist should volunteer rather than be drafted. The author spent many hours helping the music teacher with costumes, helping the drama coach backstage, and making hats for a physical education demonstration. As cheerleader sponsor for three years, she attended the athletic events. At intervals she also was responsible for publishing the school newspaper and helped the English and art teachers with the school magazine. These tasks were not in the job description of the media specialist but required a teacher-sponsor. Ignoring the opportunity to assist teachers would have made managing more difficult later when teachers used the media center.

MANAGING STUDENTS

Providing an orderly library media center is the first task of the media specialist in managing students. Letting them know what is expected behavior in the media center and other libraries they may use to gather research materials and in their care of the media center materials is a major responsibility of a media specialist. Few books exist to help teachers manage the classroom, and even fewer exist that treat the management of students in the media center.

Discipline is much easier if the traffic flow of the media center is under control. Locating the noisy areas near the entrance is one way to begin control. Rearranging furniture so that contact among students is reduced is another. Placing shelves for visibility is a third. Once the facility is arranged, attitudes toward students must be assessed. Frances Henne writes that,

> For some students, and in certain schools this may be many students, the only library skill that they should have to acquire is an awareness, imprinted indelibly and happily upon them, that the library is a friendly place where the librarians are eager to help.[9]

This friendly interest and demonstrated willingness to assist are often far beyond the attitude that a public librarian or an academic librarian is required to exhibit. When the author once told a class of aspiring media specialists that school library media specialists worked harder and happier than any other teacher, a student said, "I resent your implication that we must work harder. We aren't paid more." However, the freedom that should exist in the media center to allow students to explore their environment, to learn from one another, to read or view or listen to materials recommended by their fellow students poses a dilemma. Knowing when this interaction moves from exploration and encouragement into mischief is a skill that may take practice to acquire. The only suggestion is to continue to seek ways to allow students the freedom to explore.

The media center is the only room in the school where no student need fail. Students with reading or math problems find frustration in the classroom. If they ask the teacher for help, other students may perceive that as a lack of ability to accomplish a task they can do easily. For students who cannot sing or play an instrument, music class is uncomfortable. If students feel they have little aptitude for art, the art room may be a greater challenge than they wish to attempt. Certainly many students do not enjoy physical activities, especially if they are chosen last for team sports.

In contrast, the library media center has no specific curriculum area or grade level that might be found in a classroom. Rather, it should have information at all levels and to satisfy all interests. The media specialist should be available to give individual assistance to a student without drawing attention to the process. All students ask for help finding materials, and all students find something with which they can work.

Media specialists, when they assume the role of teacher, must follow the prescriptions for classroom management and effective teaching. For example, one principal suggests the following:

> A well-prepared lesson plan is your most important tool for effective teaching and classroom control. It will give your students a feeling that your class has structure and direction and it will give you confidence.[10]

He goes on to suggest that "good teaching is hard work, only bad teaching is easy." Good teaching happens when the media specialist plans and understands the units. It is impossible to fool an audience of strangers for long. Students are astute. They will be annoyed by busy work. Set objectives and share these objectives with students. It will not be busy work if they understand the reasons behind the exercise.

Units should be planned with a variety of activities: some lecture, some discussion, some viewing of media, some active exercises that allow them to move around. No one enjoys sitting for long periods of time, and the media center is one room in the school that truly invites browsing and moving from one place to another.

Not all students will earn affection, and in many it may be difficult to find redeeming qualities. However, it is the responsibility of media specialists to like students and to let them know it.

MANAGING PARENTS AND VOLUNTEERS

Much literature is available on the roles of parents and volunteers, especially on the role of parent as volunteer. Volunteers can be helpful, yet two cautions are in order:

1. The media specialist does not monitor the volunteer process.
2. Care must be taken to keep confidential information about students confidential in the presence of volunteers.

A volunteer coordinator is essential to maintain the regular service of volunteers. Because they are volunteers, other important events—a sick child, an unexpected errand—will cause them to miss their scheduled time. The media specialist cannot take time to make the telephone calls to get another volunteer for that day. This is more appropriately the task of a volunteer coordinator.

It is almost impossible to expect volunteers to remain silent about interesting events in the media center. However, for one parent to see the record of another child and report it to a third parent might leave the media center open to legal action.

Also, the media specialist must be very careful not to leave a volunteer in charge of a group of students. The legal responsibility for students in most states lies with a professional with teacher certification. A student injury while the professional is away from the media center could cause much difficulty and perhaps legal action.

Volunteers, who are of great help in the media center, can become excellent advocates. They must, however, be carefully managed. A form that may be helpful in the management of volunteers is found in Appendix E.

The parent as parent is a separate issue. Media specialists may think that they will see few parents because they are not classroom teachers, but this is not the case. The media specialist must be ready to listen to a parent who comes into the library media center to discuss a child. Situations may range from a complaint about a book to a concern that the child is not reading at grade level to a request that the child be permitted to take home the unabridged dictionary. The parent may also be interested in helping the media program and may be an advocate for the next budget request or the next effort to update materials or equipment.

FRIENDS OF THE LIBRARY

Library media specialists may be aware of and even members of the friends of the public library in their town. The national organization Friends of Libraries USA (FOLUSA) has been interested in encouraging friends of school libraries. A media center friends organization may extend beyond the local parent and teacher organization in the school to include other members of the community. In some schools, these friends help with programs such as Junior Great Books, and in other schools they act in the same fundraising capacity as they do in the public library domain. More information about FOLUSA is available from the American Library Association.

One media specialist recruits his friends group from students in the school. These students are his library helpers, for he has a very large school with a 12-month program and no clerical assistance.

Exercises

1. Discuss with media specialists the greatest problems and the greatest joys they have experienced in each of the following categories. Then see if you can plan practical solutions to the problems.

   Managing staff
   Evaluating personnel
   Managing with administrators
   Managing with teachers
   Managing students

2. Outline the topics you might cover in a meeting with your principal, including:

   Internet costs
   Upgrades to current computers in the media center

3. Create a list of tasks in the library and determine which could be carried out by students or volunteers, freeing the library media specialist to collaborate with teachers.

NOTES

1. Library Education and Manpower," *American Libraries* 1 (April 1970): 341–44.

2. American Association of School Librarians, American Library Association, and Association for Educational Communications and Technology, *Media Programs District and School* (Chicago: American Library Association, 1975).

3. American Association of School Librarians and Association for Educational Communications and Technology, *Information Power: Building Partnerships for Learning* (Chicago: American Library Association, 1998), 103.

4. Ibid., 104.

5. American Association of School Librarians and Association for Educational Communications and Technology, *Information Power: Guidelines for School Library Media Programs* (Chicago: American Library Association, 1988), 51.

6. Richard E. Rubin, *Foundations of Library and Information Science* (New York: Neal-Schuman, 1998), 90.

7. Douglas McGregor, *The Human Side of Enterprise: 25th Anniversary Printing* (New York: McGraw-Hill, 1985).

8. Howard F. Shout, "On-the-Job: Staff Development at the Detroit Edison Company," in *New Directions in Staff Development: Moving from Ideas to Action,* ed. Elizabeth W. Stone (Chicago: American Library Association, 1971), 58.

9. Frances Henne, "Learning to Learn in School Libraries," *School Libraries* 15 (May 1966): 17.

10. Norman Koslofsky, "Planning and Behavior: Two Factors that Determine Teacher Success," *NASSP Bulletin* 68 (September 1984): 101.

Chapter 8

On the Job: Managing Access to Information

Managing information was formerly managing the print and nonprint collections. The expansion of resources into technology formats available to users in libraries, schools, offices, and homes requires a new version for management of information. This moves beyond managing the on-site collection to providing access to information at all hours and over the entire week from many locations. These opportunities for access to information greatly increase the responsibility of library media specialists to make sure that library patrons have equal access. More collaboration with teachers is needed to make sure students have good grounding in the information, technology, and health literacy skills covered in chapter 10. Greater access to information also increases the likelihood that a student may succumb to the temptation to plagiarize, thereby violating copyright.

The first part of managing information involves the age-old problem of censorship and its limits to access to information as well as user rights to privacy. Technology resources have expanded these considerations from what is found on the media center shelves into what enters and exits the media center over communication lines and wireless networks.

RIGHT TO PRIVACY

Traditionally, users signed book cards or slips when they checked out materials from the library media center. Replacing the book card or destroying the slip when the material was returned completed the transaction. As collections expanded and use increased, students and teachers were issued identification cards to speed circulation. However, these methods permitted the recognition of persons who had checked out any items, and this has been interpreted as a violation of individual privacy. The American Library Association policy on confidentiality follows:

Policy 52.4 Confidentiality of Library Records

The ethical responsibilities of librarians, as well as statutes in most states and the District of Columbia, protect the privacy of library users. Confidentiality extends to "information sought or received, and materials consulted, borrowed, acquired," and includes database search records, reference interviews, circulation records, interlibrary loan records, and other personally identifiable uses of library materials, facilities, or services.[1]

The American Library Association recognizes that law enforcement agencies and officers may occasionally believe that library records contain information that may be helpful to the investigation of criminal activity. If there is a reasonable basis to believe such records are necessary to the progress of an investigation or prosecution, the U.S. judicial system provides a mechanism for seeking release of such confidential records: the issuance of a court order, following a showing of good cause based on specific facts, by a court of competent jurisdiction.

The Council of the American Library Association strongly recommends that the responsible officers of each library in the United States

1. Formally adopt a policy which specifically recognizes its circulation records and other records identifying the names of library users to be confidential in nature.*

2. Advise all librarians and library employees that such records shall not be made available to any agency of state, federal, or local government except pursuant to such process, order, or subpoena as may be authorized under the authority of, and pursuant to, federal, state or local law relating to civil, criminal, or administrative discovery procedures or legislative investigatory power.

3. Resist the issuance or enforcement of any such process, order, or subpoena until such time as a proper showing of good cause has been made in a court of competent jurisdiction.**

*Note: See also ALA Policy Manual 54.15, Code of Ethics, point 3: "Librarians must protect each user's right to privacy with respect to information sought or received, and materials consulted, borrowed, or acquired."

**This means that upon receipt of such process, order, or subpoena, the library's officers will consult with their legal counsel to determine if such process, order, or subpoena is in proper form and if there is a showing of good cause for its issuance; if the process, order, or subpoena is not in proper form or if good cause has not been shown, they will insist that such defects be cured.[2]

These policies were expanded with the following statement:

The members of the American Library Association, recognizing the right to privacy of library users, believe that records held in libraries which connect specific individuals with specific resources, programs, or services, are confidential and not to be used for purposes other than routine record keeping: to maintain access to resources, to assure that resources are available to users who need them, to arrange facilities, to provide resources for the comfort and safety of patrons, or to accomplish the purposes of the program or service. The library community recognizes that children and youth have the same rights to privacy as adults.[3]

Libraries whose record-keeping systems reveal the names of users would be in violation of the confidentiality of library record laws adopted in many states. However, the passage of the USA Patriot Act in 2001 has changed this landscape. School library media specialists must now seek the advice of counsel if in doubt about whether their record-keeping systems violate the specific laws in their states, and, if their school district receives federal funds, whether they follow the restrictions imposed by the Patriot Act. Efforts must be made within the reasonable constraints of budgets and school management procedures to eliminate records of use as soon as reasonably possible.

With or without specific legislation, school library media specialists are urged to respect the rights of children and youth by adhering to the tenets expressed in the Confidentiality of Library Records Interpretation of the Library Bill of Rights and the ALA Code of Ethics.[4]

Both Pennsylvania and California have passed legislation that prohibits access to library records. Pennsylvania Act 1984–90, Section 428, reads as follows:

> Library Circulation Records.—Records related to the circulation of library materials which contain the names or other personally identifying details regarding the users of the State Library or any local library which is established or maintained under any law of the Commonwealth or the library of any university, college, or educational institution chartered by the Commonwealth or the library of any public school or branch reading room, deposit station, or agency operated in connection therewith, shall be confidential and shall not be made available to anyone except by a court order in a criminal proceeding.

The California Government Code, Section 6267 reads:

> Registration and circulation records of libraries supported by public funds.
>
> All registration and circulation records of any library which is in whole or in part supported by public funds shall remain confidential and shall not be disclosed to any person, local agency, or state agency except as follows:
>
> (a) By a person acting within the scope of his or her duties with the administration of the library.
>
> (b) By a person authorized in writing, by the individual to whom the records pertain, to inspect the records.
>
> (c) By order of the appropriate superior court.
>
> As used in this section, the term "registration records" includes any information which a library requires a patron to provide in order to become

eligible to borrow books and other materials, and the term "circulation records" includes any information which identifies the patrons borrowing particular books and other material.

This section shall not apply to statistical reports of registration and circulation nor to records of fines collected by the library.

No patron record is to be released to any person, police, sheriff, FBI, or other law enforcement agency without a court subpoena to the library director of the appropriate jurisdiction or the library director's designate. This includes information concerning library staff and volunteers.

The need to maintain the privacy of administrators', teachers', and students' use of materials has been one strong justification for technology decisions such as automating the circulation system. All of these efforts have been called into question with the passage of the Patriot Act in October 2001. In the aftermath of the September 11 terrorist attacks, Congress passed this act, with its 10 separate titles and 150 sections covering 342 pages, with implications for many laws, including the powers of the Federal Bureau of Investigation to request access to private records. Section 215 "allows an FBI agent to obtain a search warrant for 'any tangible thing' which can include books, records, papers, floppy disks, data tapes, and computers with hard drives." While this act does not directly contradict most state confidentiality laws, it does change the need to get court orders to demand library records. It is unlikely that school library media specialists would be targeted by FBI agents requesting records unless students were attacked by other students within the school.

DEFENDING THE RIGHT TO ACCESS INFORMATION

A major problem for school library media specialists has been the necessity to try to filter information from the Internet, thus limiting access to information. Defending the collection—whether print, electronic, or transmitted—is a continuing obligation of the school library media specialist, but that role has changed with the introduction of electronic sources. On-site materials are carefully selected to meet the needs of teachers and students in the school. One, two, or more persons lodging complaints about items are not allowed to prohibit use by others in the school. Parents may request that their child not be allowed to read, listen to, or view materials on evolution or holidays, but the materials remain in the collection. With a selection policy in place and a procedure to follow in case of complaint, the media specialist's response to pressures is more organized and less stressful.

Teachers and students must learn how to make use of information found on the Internet if they are going to be informed members of present-day society. Prohibiting student use of the Internet, a valuable resource, is unthinkable. Although requirements of filtering software may appear to answer a major concern of some parents and others in local communities, they do not, and the installation of a filtering system does not solve the problem.

At first glance, filtering programs appear to be an easy solution; once installed, all troubles should disappear. Proponents of filtering programs miss the problems inherent in using such a solution. First, many vendors of filtering programs neglect to tell their prospective purchasers by whom and how the filter was created. Often this process is managed by clerks who pick out words that are on a list of possible offensive terms. They delete any text containing those terms, regardless of the context or content. This means that an article may be deleted with pertinent and important information that contains a word that was on a list of troublesome language. The most common example, *breast,* would delete articles on cooking a chicken and a knight's armor.

A second type of filter halts particular Web site access. This works for an acknowledged and recognized Web site but fails to stop access to any new Web site that appears, and new Web sites appear every minute. This means that filters do not ensure limited access. Clever students can find pornographic sites through their own ability to maneuver software. The best approach is to establish parent and student agreements for Internet use. Students are given a password for their privilege, and they understand and agree to the regulations that are in place so that they can keep their password.

All of these methods for finding information must be factored into the need to protect the copyright of the media center's collection. This often has unexpected challenges.

COPYRIGHT

Copyright is a legal concept that safeguards the intellectual work of a creator. Copyright law is difficult to understand for most people except copyright lawmakers, lawyers who defend creators and abusers, and judges who make the final decisions in court cases. It is very difficult for school library media specialists to have enough accurate information to convince administrators, teachers, and students, that, as a law, it must be obeyed. Principals want to save limited funds by encouraging mass copying of copyright-protected workbooks. Teachers want to use materials brought from a workshop or borrowed from another teacher, carefully ignoring the "copied with permission for x event" statement on the bottom of each sheet. Students who violate copyright may be caught under school rules for plagiarizing as well as for violating copyright.

Librarians in academic, public, and school libraries are the first line of defense for the free flow of information. To continue this flow, the creators, authors, illustrators, editors, publishers, and producers of that information must be protected so that they will be willing to continue writing, illustrating, editing, publishing, and producing. This will become more difficult as more information becomes available online.

The ease with which online information may be shared with a very large audience worldwide, downloaded, and reused makes it very vulnerable. For the school library media specialist to begin controlling this, it is imperative that one keep current about what is legal and what isn't. One-time use of material for classroom instruction is legal because schools are considered nonprofit users for educational purposes, the doctrine of fair use. Considering fair use also means considering loss of revenue for authors and producers, truly a never-ending circle. To have updated information means staying current on copyright changes and not getting lost outside the circle.

Because few educators and school library media specialists truly understand the copyright law, this is an opportunity for the library media specialist to take a leading role. Reading in the educational and library literature, attending conferences when copyright is a part of the programming, and making an effort to understand the law and any changes are just the beginning. Library media specialists must also explain any changes and point out any violations to colleagues, and this is never easy.

Working with teachers and administrators to keep them informed helps remind them of the correct use of materials. Reminding the administrator about the probability that lawsuits for copyright infringement will name the principal, the superintendent, and the school board—a situation most will not relish—may be an adequate warning. Post notices about copyright on all hardware that would enable copyright infringement. Finally, make sure that you are following correct procedures with the use of any material or information at your fingertips, that you yourself are not violating copyright.

New problems have surfaced with the Internet. This resource is so new that intellectual property laws to deal with it are just being written and tested. People can download Web sites onto their hard drives to be viewed at a later time. Using a downloaded Web site to show to teachers as a sample Web site before they create their own is questionable practice, because you haven't asked permission to use the Web site. Because it is no longer necessary to put a copyright notice on a Web site for it to be covered by the law, it must be assumed that this material is under copyright protection.

Another problem area may be in establishing links from the media center's Web site to other materials available online. School library media specialists need to be very cautious about what part, if any, of the information in that link is actually on the media center's Web site. You may be creating a derivative work, especially if it isn't identified as someone else's and appears to be your work.

TECHNOLOGY DECISIONS

Many school library media specialists have been able to renew or expand the interest of their administrators in the media program through the careful presentation of facts that lead to automation of library functions. To many administrators, implementation of high technology is desirable even if such implementation is little understood. Careful explanation of outcomes in relation to costs, with demonstrations of each application, often sells an administrator on the idea. The decision to implement new technologies brings with it the need to justify increased funding immediately and with knowledge that this will be a continuing cost. The amount needed is determined by the type and level of technology selected. Often, administrators respond to requests for equipment if such technology is available in a nearby school district or another school in the district.

When approval has been granted for technology expenditures, the questions then are what, how much, and which vendor to select. At this time, the school library media specialist learns as much as possible about information technology, which includes automated circulation systems, integrated library systems, CD-ROMS and online references, and the Internet.

The storage capability of microcomputers and auxiliary equipment is much larger than minicomputers and mainframes in earlier years, and that storage capacity, when combined with ZIP and flash drives, increases steadily. The storage capabilities are sufficient for most current activities, and one of the first priorities for most media specialists is an integrated library system to handle more than the circulation system and online public access catalog to help locate and circulate media center materials. The system must include the ability to provide access and store information gathered from outside the media center and to expand resource sharing among libraries.

Integrated Library Systems

Less than 15 years ago, the question facing media specialists was which circulation system to select. Choices were based on cost, scope, compatibility, choice of record, and method of retrospective conversion. Compatibility between systems was a consideration so that schools in a district could connect with each other, and the amount of training offered by the vendor was a selection factor. Now, the choice is the purchase of an integrated library system (ILS). A good place to find unbiased information is in copies of *Library Technology Reports,* a publication of the American Library Association. These reports may be available in the school district professional library or the local public library. Published both in print and online, they provide excellent details to help with selecting among the many different technologies.

Library Technology Reports offers this definition of an ILS: "A truly integrated online library system is a relational database, containing bibliographic records for each title. All library functions are processed from these records and updates appear in real time."[5] This system must not only handle materials on-site but must help locate and circulate materials available in other locations. The decision of which system becomes even more important when different vendors offer different options for upgrading and expanding the system as new applications surface. Adding a new application to an existing system can be more expensive than the original purchase. In making your selection, anticipate that the system will

- expedite current manual practices by streamlining them into an automated function
- provide access to a variety of information in a variety of formats
- provide connectivity to Internet and local data
- provide quick and powerful search options
- allow for the creation of databases
- connect users in a variety of shared resources[6]

As with the much simpler circulation systems of the past, the vendor is a key component. Media centers in most schools would consider the small library vendors unless the district is large and is purchasing a system for the district. Certain vendors specialize in a particular type of library, and school media centers are one of those specialties. An additional query includes the length of time the vendor has been offering the product. Often a new vendor will not be able to sell enough systems to remain in business. Also, a veteran vendor who has not been making a profit for a time may go out of business. Both of these situations mean that the media specialist will once again be looking for a new ILS.

Another consideration in selecting an ILS is the system's ability to talk with another system. Discussing your purchase with neighboring librarians will help determine the ability to communicate with these libraries to check holdings, reserve materials, or request them on interlibrary loan. Having their collections available through an ILS system is far easier than using the Internet to check holdings.

Additional queries must be made when selecting a system. As with any piece of technology, an important consideration is service. What happens when the system breaks down? Does the vendor have a hotline to answer telephone questions? Many vendors have 24-hour service representatives available to problem-solve. Certainly, swift service is a necessity.

Software providers are constantly revising their systems. If a major revision occurs, what is the responsibility of the vendor for the systems sold in the past? Will the new system accommodate the old records? Will the school library media specialist be given a free update or at least a chance to purchase at a reduced cost?

With this particular technology, training in the use of the system is extremely important. How many training sessions are provided free of charge with purchase of the system? Is additional training provided if additions are made to the system?

Some of these questions can be answered in the literature. Again, the American Library Association's *Library Technology Reports,* although published irregularly, provide excellent suggestions. These are dated almost as soon as they are published, but they do provide information useful to begin or update automated systems.

BUILDING AND MAINTAINING THE RESOURCE COLLECTION

Collection management of the on-site collection is presented in four segments: circulation of materials, selecting materials and equipment, acquiring materials, and cataloging them. Circulation of materials is a first consideration in adding to and maintaining the media center collection. The collection is provided for the school community, and the number of materials to circulate should not be limited if at all possible.

Circulation of Materials

In this new century, online access to information appears to alleviate the need for students to visit any library, even in the building where they attend classes. If they find limits on what they may remove from that center, it is even less likely that they will return. This is especially true with limits to books to help elementary children learn to read and for students in higher grades to read for pleasure. As students take part in more outside activities such as sports, clubs, and music classes, they have even less time for recreational reading. As many obstacles as possible must be removed, whether by eliminating fines or extending circulation periods. Further, the process for circulation should include minimum waits for patrons at the charge-out desk.

Selecting Materials and Equipment: Format Decisions

The second part of managing the collection is the selection of materials and equipment. The problems of censorship and some proposed solutions are described as well as methods for choosing functional equipment that will survive heavy use.

Between 1950 and 1990, format decisions were choices between print and nonprint. Students who preferred pictures to print were given filmstrips, slides, pictures, and 16mm films or videotapes. Periodical subscriptions and newspapers provided up-to-date information, and the nonfiction collection provided more historical records or fuller accounts of subjects under study. Today, a format decision has become much more complicated. Multimedia has taken on a much broader definition than a filmstrip or a tape. Reference books, magazines, and newspapers are no longer only paper and print, and decisions to buy the print copy, CD-ROM, or the online version also require determining the number of computers available in the media center or transmitted from the media center for use in classrooms.

Media centers and classrooms today offer many computers to access information. Once the selection of ILS has been made, license agreements for multiuse become pertinent. CD-ROMs have the advantage of being cost certain. That is, the price is established at purchase, and it is usually much less expensive than online services; however, CD-ROMs must be loaded into a computer. Although their storage capacity allows much information, they still contain far less than would be provided with access to a large online database.

Online references should have full-text and image files of current information. Full-text files and images can be downloaded, and users can manipulate these for research reports. This makes it very easy for a student to copy rather than create. Efforts to reduce plagiarism become a part of managing this resource. Helping teachers plan research assignments that build the research process for students to create products that reflect their work and to check papers for plagiarism becomes an important role for the media specialist.

Selecting Materials

Although the enthusiasm, willingness to help, and openness of the staff are the media center's keys to success, relevant information must be available to users. Adequate and carefully selected materials and equipment must be available for patrons, or the eagerness generated by the library media specialist will quickly wane.

All materials should meet the criteria of the library media center selection policy. If no selection policy exists, library media specialists, with help from their advisory committee, should write one that conforms to the American Library Association's (ALA) Intellectual Freedom Policy (no. 53.1–53.1.6), with the jointly developed Intellectual Freedom Committee and American Association of School Librarians interpretations. The ALA's intellectual freedom policy statements are found in Appendix F.

Selection policies are essential because they explain the process followed and the priorities established before any material is purchased or accepted as a gift and placed in the media center collection. The policy communicates the selection steps followed, which is useful when items in the collection are questioned by other teachers, parents, or community members.

School library media specialists who have had materials questioned will admit that the experience is frightening. In most media centers a single person is in charge, and that person feels very isolated when a parent, community member, or fellow teacher questions the availability of a certain item for students. Having a selection policy for the complaining person to read as well as a procedure should allow time to notify the principal. The principal may need to be reminded that the superintendent should also be told that any resource is being questioned and by whom.

The ALA's Office of Intellectual Freedom has staff trained to answer inquiries from school library media specialists who have censorship problems. This office will respond quickly to any question and will even accept collect calls when a library media specialist feels beleaguered. Further, state library and library media associations have intellectual freedom committees whose members can offer assistance both when selections are questioned and in developing a selection policy when none exists.

The selection policy is based on and guides actual selection practice. It includes a statement of the goals and objectives of the library media center, covers the needs of the clientele in the building, and describes any unique needs such as special programs of study.

People who read any selection policy should learn the grade levels and ages of students the collection will serve, the formats of materials to be included, and special geographic needs (e.g., schools on either coast will perhaps need more materials on the oceans than schools in the Midwest). A statement may be included regarding availability and use of materials in neighboring libraries.

A final section of the selection policy should contain procedures to be followed when a grievance is filed. This procedure must be carefully described and cover as many contingencies as can be predicted.

Selection policies should be reviewed by and approved by the school board. Although some states require that school districts have a written selection policy before state funds are distributed to school library media accounts, others do not. When school boards approve selection policies, they should cover all the schools in the district rather than a single building.

If no policy exists, school board members may decide that the process of approving a policy might create controversy, and they may be reluctant to discuss the issue. Regardless of whether the school board approves a statement, school library media specialists should prepare one to document their priorities and methods of selecting materials and to have available if questions arise.

The selection policy will cite the selection aids used in choosing materials. Current review periodicals such as *Booklist, Bulletin for the Center of Children's*

Books, and *School Library Journal* review new publications. Standard selection tools such as The H. W. Wilson lists—*Children's Catalog, Middle and Junior High School Catalog,* and *Senior High Core Collection*—are published in hardbound volumes with paperback updates. These volumes contain carefully selected entries of book titles and are helpful to media specialists in establishing a core collection and reviewing materials for retention or discard. These tools represent research and professional experience by experts in the school library media fields. However, they may not be as useful for selection because many of the materials listed are out of print.

Online resources are available to help make choices. Follett's *TitleWave* lists books with full bibliographic information, cost, and ISBN. This program also provides reviews from periodical sources. One can ask to have lists made by subject, grade level, and by places where the item is reviewed. Since all reviews in *Booklist* are for recommended titles, asking for resources that have been cited in that periodical gives a choice of only recommended resources.

Although selection of resources is a high-priority activity for the media center staff, it is not totally their responsibility. Rather, it belongs to library media users, including administrators, teachers, students, and, whenever possible, parents. Library media specialists who select a collection with little or no input from users may find that the resulting range of materials is too narrow.

Several methods are available to encourage teachers and others to make selections. Some of these will be discussed in chapter 10, because suggestions for purchases are made at the beginning and end of unit planning for teachers. At other times, teachers should be encouraged to make choices by sharing bibliographies of materials that might be of interest. Students can be encouraged to suggest titles for inclusion. Preparing a justification for purchase of an item seen or read in another library can help develop students' writing skills. Students might also enjoy reading reviews of new materials in *Booklist* or *School Library Journal* and completing an order form for titles that appeal to them. If students are assigned to the media center for work-study or as aides, the media specialist should seek their opinions in the selection process and make review of materials part of each person's assignment. All involved in selection should be aware of the selection policy criteria.

Online purchase over the Internet is becoming commonplace. One can order from online bookstores such as amazon.com and barnesandnoble.com or from jobbers with selection lists such as Follett Book Company's *TitleWave* and have access to the same information they would find in *Books in Print.* The jobber's list often allows selection by subject with the added ability to specify only materials reviewed in *Booklist,* which means they are recommended titles. Testimonials and reviews are featured to help with selection in a way that was not dreamed of in the past. School library media specialists may also rely on bibliographies provided by professional associations, if these are current. They may also use *Booklist* and *School Library Journal* for reviews of both books and media or the *Bulletin for the Center for Children's Books,* which reviews books only.

Providing a core collection is the first step in collection development. More important is selecting the remaining materials, which must be chosen to fit the school's curriculum. Meeting curriculum needs is a major criterion for placing items in the collection. Library media specialists can begin to address this task by carefully reviewing the textbooks and review journals in the curriculum area used by each teacher, by finding out the length of time any unit is taught and to how many students, and by discovering what teaching method is used and what the research assignments are likely to be. Next, a bibliography of materials in the collection can be obtained by searching the online catalog for specific subject headings. If the resulting bibliography does not appear to have relevant titles or titles at the ability or interest level of the students in the course, additional materials must be purchased. As a temporary measure, materials may be requested from other libraries in the area.

Selecting Information from the Internet

The Internet, a worldwide communication network, offers both electronic mail and the World Wide Web (WWW) to locate information. With e-mail, students and teachers can communicate with other educational institutions, professional association lists, national lists such as LM_NET, classrooms, and individuals, querying colleagues for answers to questions. One caution is that responses may have files attached to the message that can carry viruses to school servers. Many school districts build firewalls to protect the traffic. If firewalls are not in place, administrators, teachers, and students need to use care in opening attachments and should not do so if the message is not expected.

Access to the Internet provides entrance to the WWW. Created in 1990, information from the WWW can be searched, read, selected, stored, and edited. The WWW permits hyperlinks to more and more distant databases in an ever-expanding realm. Media specialists create home pages for the media center and then link other locations on the Web to their home pages. This greatly expanded access to information requires a new facet to collection development. It also allows students to find better Web sites to search for their topics than to be overwhelmed by the amount of information they find with a search engine.

Information located on the Internet does not resemble the information that media specialists have traditionally anticipated as a part of the selection process. It is not something that will be purchased, processed, and stored for future use on a shelf. However, information from the Internet, available to students and teachers, becomes a part of the media center collection. How to choose the best from the Internet and how to keep what is not appropriate from coming into the media center is a major discussion among all types of librarians and their communities.

Consideration should be given to selecting the Web sites that students should access and to make these the Web sites available on the system as you would select books or magazines or vertical file materials. Lists of excellent Web sites are available from the American Library Association's divisions. Certainly they provide a great deal of access for students from a world that is already overloaded with information—good and bad, accurate and inaccurate, relevant and irrelevant, useful and useless. Attaching appropriate URL addresses to the media center Web page at the time students are studying a particular topic is similar to placing all the books on a topic on reserve at the beginning of a unit of instruction.

An acceptable use policy, created by the media center advisory committee and agreed to by students and parents can help media specialists with this new and very important assignment. Remembering that clever students can locate information even though filters exist, media specialists are less vulnerable if they and their students and parents have agreed that media center computers are available for research rather than random surfing or playing games. The Internet is certainly an exciting new resource, and restricting access limits this potential reference.

One of the most important tasks of the media specialist is to help students and teachers find the best materials available to support teaching and learning. Search engines allow students to locate much more information than they could imagine, and they have no quality control for relevance or accuracy. At the beginning of a unit of instruction, the school library media specialist can add search engines such as Kids Click and Yahooligans that only search kid-friendly sites. Bookmarking URLs with pertinent information works well in middle and high school.

Helping media center users find accurate information on the Internet will be a challenge. This author is less concerned with a student's locating pornography because pornography is instantly recognizable. While filters recognize pornography, they do not identify and block incorrect facts. Misinformation that may be on the Internet is not so readily recognized; students and teachers may have inaccurate facts or statistics and be unaware. Explaining that information from the Internet needs to be confirmed in other sources is a beginning.

Selecting Equipment

Selection of equipment is a further responsibility of many school library media specialists, and some may feel inadequate to make these choices. It is important to keep in mind the user of any equipment as well as the equipment's quality, compatibility, warranty, maintenance, and repair. The first consideration in choosing equipment, as with all items in the media center, is the user. If the user does not use the equipment frequently, it must be easy to use and difficult to misuse. This concern will be of less importance as more schools acquire systems that network audiovisual transmission through stacks of projection or playing devices that project to a remote classroom and even less as the quality of streaming video improves. Electronic transmission of instruction to multiple classrooms is currently available in some schools. It is only a matter of appropriate wiring and purchase of equipment before such technology will be available in every school.

A major concern is quality of the equipment. Many media specialists consider purchasing less expensive home-use equipment rather than commercial-use machines. This is a false economy because home-use machines are not designed to withstand the rigors of school use.

Warranty for the entire piece or parts of equipment should be considered. If the supplier is reluctant to give any warranty, it is better to look elsewhere.

Computers are a particular problem because they are in constant need of up-grading. New software often requires additional memory. Other concerns are the need to purchase and install cards to use computers in a wireless network.

Finally, maintenance and repair are extremely important. If a much-used piece of equipment must be sent away for an extended period, a replacement piece should be available. In an ideal situation, the repair shop should be in the immediate vicinity rather than 200 miles away.

ACQUIRING MATERIALS AND EQUIPMENT

The third part of the selection process includes methods for acquiring and deleting materials and equipment. Many methods exist for acquiring resources for the library media center. Although sometimes the media center receives gifts, most additions to the collection must be selected, ordered, received, and paid for. A first step in the acquisition process is to select a source for purchasing an item.

In many states, selection of a purchase source is based on a bid process when an item costs a specified amount. For example, all items over $100 must be placed for bid. This means that suppliers bid to provide the material or equipment, and the lowest bidder receives the order. This is often true of the jobber chosen to supply library resources.

A jobber is a supplier who buys from a wide variety of publishers, so the library media specialist sends only one order for most resources. Individual publishers and suppliers may give a better discount, but this means that in-dividual purchase orders must be sent. Chapter 9 includes an explanation of why business managers prefer to order from a single source rather than send multiple orders to individual suppliers. Once materials and supplier have been determined, materials are ordered, using the process in place in the school district.

At present, most large school districts order by electronic transmission. A purchase order is returned, often by fax, to the library media specialist to confirm receipt of the electronic order. This replaces the paper copy, multicar-bon purchase orders of the past. No matter how materials and equipment are ordered, great care must be taken in completing the ordering process.

The library media specialist should be aware that jobbers now offer elec-tronic ordering, often as simple as check-marking a box. The availability of all titles ordered will be confirmed, and the materials shipped and billed imme-diately. Many purchasing officers welcome this easy method of ordering. The library media specialist sets a total price limit beyond which the jobber should not send further shipments. This ceiling on purchases allows the media spe-cialist to maximize quick-order opportunities. When the shipment is received, the original order must be checked against the shipment, any missing items noted, and the jobber notified. This acknowledgment is copied to the business office.

School district business managers do not always understand the idiosyn-crasies of the library media world and will welcome assistance with selection and ordering. They may need help in selecting suppliers of materials, especially when the suppliers are not the more familiar sources of other educational items; in writing specifications for equipment; and in confirming that products ordered have been received. This is one way to make friends with those who handle funds for library media programs.

Creating rapport with the business manager is as important as making friends with the administrators in the building and with the custodial staff. Remaining friends with these persons is easier if care is taken to make their jobs easier. One excellent way to do this is to notify them as soon as items are received. This enables them to make full or partial payment to the supplier. Otherwise, the supplier continues to send bills to the business manager, and no one likes to receive second or third notice of unpaid bills.

DE-SELECTION OF MATERIALS (WEEDING)

Weeding is the discarding of materials that are of little value to students and teachers. This is perhaps as important as selecting additional materials for a collection. This may be a temporary loss of value due to a change in focus, or it may be a permanent loss due to curriculum change. Items may be removed due to age, lack of relevance, or wear and tear. A smaller, more attractive collection of relevant, up-to-date materials is more important to students and teachers than a large collection of mostly useless materials that will be virtually ignored. Many school library media specialists find themselves with inadequate shelf space, and their collections must be reviewed frequently to provide space for new additions.

Many library media specialists neglect de-selection, using the excuse that state standards require a certain number of materials in the collection. This is true, but few states have such high standards that collections cannot meet the quantities required. Useless materials on the shelves do not provide quality and should be removed. If the school administration insists that an unusually large number of materials be kept, a separate list could be maintained for these useless materials. They would still be listed as part of the collection but stored out of sight until they can be discarded.

Several factors justify collection reevaluation and de-selection.

1. Changes in the curriculum revise the focus of the collection.
2. Materials must be repaired or replaced if in poor condition.
3. The media center shelves should appear attractive and inviting to users.
4. Numbers of items counted as holdings should represent useful resources rather than appear to be a larger number of unusable items.
5. Students and teachers should have the best possible collection of materials.

De-selection is a continual process. Each person reviews each item as it circulates. It is as much the responsibility of students and teachers as of the library media center staff to evaluate materials regularly. Students can judge whether the material was helpful to them and, if not, why not. Interested teachers who are subject area specialists can be most helpful in evaluating their areas in the collection. The media center staff should conduct a thorough evaluation of the entire collection at least once every three years.

When preparing for an automated circulation system and an online public access catalog, the library media specialist does a thorough job of de-selection. Withdrawing items from many systems is time-consuming and costly; therefore, it is preferable to discard questionable items before retrospective conversion rather than later. It can also be embarrassing when joining a network to have other media specialists note the poor quality of your collection when they seek information.

The school library media specialist is responsible for reviewing the collection for compliance with the selection policy. As with the selection process, de-selection must be regulated by the selection policy, not by personal bias.

In general, four categories of materials are taken from the shelves: (1) materials to be stored until needed, (2) materials to be sent to another school media center for younger or older students, (3) materials in need of repair or replacement, and (4) materials to be discarded.

Materials to be stored are of good quality and accurate but treat topics temporarily not being taught. They are unlikely to become dated and are attractive and at the appropriate level for students in the building.

Materials judged to be below or above the reading levels of students in the building, or those that treat subject areas shifted to another grade level, may be sent to another building. Retaining titles that might be useful in the future is usually not a good plan. It would be easier for the receiving school to return the materials if the situation is reversed.

Materials in need of repair or replacement should be carefully evaluated. Books may be sent to a bindery if the paper is of good quality and the information is important. In-house repair of materials must be reviewed to see that the costs of labor and materials do not exceed the cost of the item.

Finally, materials must be evaluated for retention or withdrawal. Old, worn out materials must be discarded. Out-of-date materials should be removed unless they have great historical value. Duplicate titles may be reassessed if demand for the item has slackened. Biographies of persons unknown to the present generation should not be retained.

Outdated materials may be almost anything in science and technology with a copyright date more than five years old. Psychology, history, business, and education become dated in 10 years. In fiction, certain authors and topics may lose their appeal to an age group. An author read by high school students 15 years ago may be devoured by elementary students today.

In the case of a core collection, a title may be matched to a selection tool. Materials listed in a selection tool should be carefully considered. Perhaps the item should be brought to the attention of students and teachers, or perhaps it should be removed, although it appears in a recommended list.

Reference books, especially, must be reviewed. Encyclopedias need to be replaced every five years, and the old copies should *not* be sent to classrooms. Inaccurate information has no place in a school library media center or in the classroom. Because encyclopedias are so expensive, retaining copies appears to be an asset; it is, however, a great liability. Figure 8.1 lists considerations for retention or discard of materials.

Dewey Decimal Class No.	
000	New editions of encyclopedias are needed every five years.
100	Information in this category is judged by use of material.
200	Religion books are also retained, depending on use. The media center collection should contain basic information about as many sects and religions as possible, and all issues should be as well represented as possible.
300	Controversial issues must be well represented from all points of view. Almanacs and yearbooks are superseded by each new volume. These are seldom of much use after five years, although some library media specialists retain back issues to use in teaching about the almanac. During instruction, facts can be compared to show changes in the information. However, older volumes should not be on the open shelves. Books dealing with historical aspects of politics and economics are determined by use. Timely or topical materials are discarded after five years. These should be replaced with new editions when available. Books on government should be replaced after 10 years. New material on government should supersede older materials.
	Materials in education and commerce should be retained if they are used. Nonhistorical materials in education and commerce should be replaced within 10 years.
	Basic materials in folklore should be retained. Deselection depends on use. At the elementary level, fairy tales represent a popular area of the collection.
400	Basic materials on languages should be retained, based on use.
500	Pure science books, except botany and natural history, are out of date within five years. Collections must be kept current.
600	Historical materials on inventions and basic information about anatomy. Applied science and mechanics become dated in five years unless they have historical information.
	Radio and television materials are dated in less than five years. Information about gardening, farms, and farm and other domestic animals does not become dated as quickly as other sections of the 600s.
	Home economics books are evaluated based on use; however, most cookbooks are retained until they wear out. Business information becomes dated in 10 years, and chemical and food product materials should be removed in five to 10 years, depending on contents. Manufacturing and building information should be removed after 10 years, except books on crafts.
700	Basic art and music materials should be retained. These items are preserved according to their use.
800	Basic literature materials must be retained. Evaluation is based on use.
900	General history materials are evaluated depending on use and curriculum requirements.
	Accuracy, relevancy, and variety of interpretations are of primary concern.
	Materials about countries and geography books must be replaced as soon as new editions are available. These materials are likely to provide misinformation.
	Biography materials, unless the subject has a permanent place in history, should be discarded as soon as use diminishes. Older biographies of mediocre value should be replaced as more literary efforts are available.

Figure 8.1 Considerations for Retention or Discard of Materials

Newspapers and magazine files should be kept up to five years if storage allows. At present, newspapers and magazines are available in full text from several vendors on CD-ROM and online. This technology provides easy storage and quick retrieval. As mentioned earlier, the library media specialist discusses the addition of this type of reference with the principal in order to secure funds to purchase and subscribe to the original product and to future updates. This type of resource access is expected to increase in the future. Media specialists who do not have this technology for their students should begin plans for implementation immediately.

Pamphlet materials are always a concern, and more so because so much information is available on the Web. In the past, this collection, if maintained, was the most up to date in the media center. If it seems feasible to continue with this file, media specialists should stamp a date on each item placed in the vertical file, because most items are not dated. Topics should be reviewed every three years and all folders reviewed before items are circulated to students or teachers. One school library media specialist uses students to evaluate the vertical file and practice their letter-writing skills ordering up-to-date materials.

Equipment can be evaluated with two criteria: use and repair record. Equipment that is no longer used because of lack of appropriate software should be removed from the storage area. Equipment should also be removed when repair costs exceed replacement costs. Keeping a repair record for each piece of equipment is essential. A simple method is to make notations of the date of purchase and type of equipment. Each time the equipment fails to function, a record is made of the malfunction. If a repair is required, the nature and cost of the repair are noted.

A final caution concerns the destination of withdrawn items. If the reason for withdrawal is a change in grade level or curriculum, the library media specialist may wish to relocate these items to another library. If they are old, in poor condition, or contain out-of-date information, they should be destroyed. The less fortunate media specialists will not find them useful even if their collections were destroyed by hurricanes or fires or they are managing a library in a developing nation. Useless to one is useless to all.

OPTIONS FOR CATALOGING

The fourth segment of collection management is organizing the collection to provide for ease of access. Many choices for cataloging and processing materials are available, and the best choice for a given situation should be based on full information. Options for cataloging materials range from original cataloging and inputting electronic records to receiving cataloging for a CD-ROM database, a bibliographic utility, or the jobber who fills the order.

The school library media specialist should always keep in mind that the purpose of organizing the collection is to provide access to the contents for users. Often cataloging and classification courses are taught in library science programs with a major emphasis on such details as the number of spaces after a punctuation mark; thus, the process becomes more important than the product. Although the organization of a collection should be consistent with the national standards for cataloging rules and subject headings, particularly if the media center is part of a consortium, these must be adjusted to the situation. If your media center has not moved into the automated world, you may wish to refer to the previous editions of this book for alternatives.

The most efficient method is to purchase materials with electronic records shipped with the order and bar codes in place on the item. These records can then be downloaded into the OPAC. Books and other materials may come already bar-coded for immediate placement in circulation.

Another source for cataloging and processing services is school districts or intermediate units with centralized processing centers. Materials are ordered centrally, shipped to the processing center where records are entered into the district's database, and then sent to individual buildings.

Cataloging information may be acquired through a bibliographic network, but this is often much more expensive. Previously, joining a national utility meant interlibrary loan capability among all types of libraries. It is no longer as necessary because location information is presently available over the Internet. Costs will be discussed more fully in chapter 13.

In states where statewide networks are in place, updates to the machine-readable database are a regular part of media center management. New materials are recorded for transmission to those responsible for the update, and the media center records are in place.

HOUSING THE COLLECTION

Traditionally, the library media collection has been housed on shelves under the jurisdiction of the library media specialist. That is, materials have been in a room called the media center, locked at the end of the school day, and opened the next morning. When so-called open schools were built, these centers were not closed off. Access was available from all areas of the schools without barriers. As the media specialist increases the integration of the media center, classroom collections for reading move regularly from media center to classroom. As classrooms and homes are connected electronically to the media center resources, this information center becomes truly without walls.

Although media specialists need to formulate a plan for keeping track of hard copy materials so that they can be located quickly when requested, semipermanent loan to classrooms expands their use. With expanding access to online resources, the concern that students need information available on the shelves of the media center is less critical. Although the online capability of access to information may lessen the media specialist's tasks for circulating hard copies, it increases the work to make sure that users can find appropriate and useful information in these oceans of information available electronically.

Exercises

1. Determine whether your state has a law related to confidentiality of records. Compare this with the Pennsylvania and California laws described in this chapter. Ask one or more school library media specialists how they maintain confidentiality of records. Outline a talk you would present to your principal, teachers, and parents concerning your response to the requirements for confidentiality of records in your school.
2. Investigate the strengths and weaknesses of the filtering systems offered to school and public libraries.
3. Prepare a presentation for your teachers concerning ways to overcome plagiarism in student papers.
4. Interview media specialists to see whether they have had any censorship questions and, if so, how they responded.
5. Review *Library Literature* for an update on integrated library systems. Interview one or more school library media specialists who have an ILS. Get their opinions of strengths and weaknesses. Analyze these and compare with information you have located in the literature.

NOTES

1. This information is published annually in the American Library Association's *Handbook of Organization.*

2. *ALA Policy Manual* and Office for Intellectual Freedom of the American Library Association, *Intellectual Freedom Manual,* 4th ed. (Chicago: American Library Association, 1992), 126.

3. ALA *Handbook of Organization.*

4. Unpublished interpretation of ALA Policies 52.5 and 54.15.

5. "Integrated Library System Software for Smaller Libraries," *Library Technology Reports* (May–June 2003): 11.

6. Ibid.

Chapter 9

On the Job:
Managing the Budget

School library media centers expand or disintegrate depending on the amount of money allocated in the school district budget for purchase of needed resources, new materials, and equipment. District administrators plan the district budget and present it to the school board for approval. The type of budget prepared is usually dictated by the state education department and may be directly related to some trend outside education but adopted by educators. The trend in the 1990s was to school-based management, and many districts have continued this into the new century. Rather than allocating resources to schools based on a per-pupil formula, funds are given to the principal, who decides how they are dispersed. Sometimes the money for the entire building is allocated on a per-pupil formula, and the personnel in the building—sometimes the principal and sometimes a building committee—decide how to allocate it within their building.

Whatever the model the school district uses, school library media specialists must conform to that model whenever they have input in the budget process. Whenever school library media specialists respond to requests for budget input, they should show they have conducted a needs assessment and that the budget covers proposed activities for a year, with the supporting rationale for each activity.

Conflicts arise out of the realities of the school district's financial situation, usually defined by local taxation, and the practical need to provide a wide variety of materials for students and teachers. These conflicts can occur at the district level, when the library budget is distributed from a central library budget, or in each school, if district funds are distributed to individual buildings. Because budget items for the library media program are part of the total school district budget, funding requests compete with other units such as academic requirements, art, athletics, and music programs. Budgets distributed

145

in the local school will find the media specialist's requests competing with the classroom teachers' requests as well as with requests from other programs.

Annual budgets for school districts are prepared early in one fiscal year for the next year's expenditures. Superintendents may request assistance from others who are asked for input, but they are responsible for the final decision on items and amounts. Principals and the superintendent's central office staff are usually included by demand rather than by request. An example of others involved would be negotiators for the teachers' bargaining unit. All of these oversee preparation of the budget to make sure no budget decreases will necessitate personnel reductions and to confirm the inclusion of salary increases and other benefits.

Once the budget is prepared, the superintendent presents it to the local school board for approval. In some states, the state board of education grants final approval. In other states, voters are asked to pass a referendum for funding, and budgets can be voted down by the community. The amount of control exercised by local or state boards of education or by the voters in a referendum is in direct proportion to the amount of funds they control. In states where the major portion of education funding comes from state rather than local revenues, state officials maintain closer control over the local budget process than in states where most school funding is locally generated. With the emphasis on education exemplified at the close of World War II by the GI Bill, and followed by President Johnson's Great Society allocations, school district personnel found it easy to create new programs and expand many areas of the curriculum. Changes in the economy in the 1970s and 1980s brought this era to a close. Lack of support for schools was a critical problem in the late twentieth century, and the economic situation in the new century appears even less promising.

Public schools can be defined as service institutions, but measuring the quality of their services can be difficult. Recently, public schools have not been perceived as performing well. According to Peter F. Drucker, one reason that service institutions do not perform well is that they receive budget allocations rather than earning the income to exist.[1] In the past, funding for schools came from the automatic allocations of property tax revenues. State law designated a minimum level of funding, and the state subsidized communities whose tax bases were insufficient to provide minimum funding.

Seldom was there any performance evaluation. Educators did not appear to be concerned about the quality of performance, because they were not held accountable. With reduced funding, the picture has changed. Public school educators are now faced with a public demanding test scores at or above the national average, merit review for teachers, cost accountability for expenditures, and confirmation that the educational program is meeting the objectives set by school personnel. The trend toward reductions in funding for education directly affects funding for the school library media center.

States may mandate a minimum amount to be spent for school library media materials. This amount is usually based on a per-pupil allocation calculated by average daily attendance in the individual schools. If the amount is not specified, the local education agency or school district may grant a specific amount to be spent per pupil. As stated earlier, in other districts principals may receive a sum for the total program in their building, and they decide how much will be allocated to each teacher or classroom program. In other situations, the library budget is allocated through the supervisor of the library media program.

In situations where a sum is specified by the state or the school superintendent, it is much more difficult for individual building-level media specialists to influence the amount they receive. When the budget is given to the district media coordinator for reallocation, the needs of each school may be assessed; school library media specialists present their needs in relation to the possible allocation of funds. A similar case must be presented to the school principal if the library media specialist must justify the budget from a central allocation to the individual schools. Whatever the division of the budget, school library media specialists should understand the method of budget making and the placement of funds in each category.

Although each state may have a different format for placing budget items, most states use line-item descriptions. An example of budget line items is shown in Figure 9.1. This means that each item of the budget is placed on a line next to the account number and description of that item. Usually the budget begins with the revenues accruing to the school district, such as from property taxes. Added to this will be any funds from the state or national government, proceeds from bond sales, sale of property, interest from investments or trust funds, and rentals from facilities.

The next pages of the budget contain the expenditures. Most school budgets reflect the past year's budget with actual expenditures, the current year's budget with actual expenditures, and a column to project the next year's budget. For example, in a budget being prepared for 2010, the first two columns would show the budget for 2008 and the actual expenditures against that budget. The middle two columns would show the budgeted amount for 2009 and the expenditures against that amount as of the date of budget preparation. The final column would show the anticipated budget for 2010.

Budget processes as well as numbering vary from state to state. School library media specialists should locate the persons who can help with questions. Where school districts lack a school library media supervisor, the persons most likely to ask would be a secretary or accountant in the school or the business manager in the central office.

THE FISCAL YEAR

First ask the resource person about the fiscal year. School districts usually match the state government pattern. That is, if the fiscal year is January 1 to December 31, all materials must be ordered, received, and paid for no later than December 31, or the expenditures will be charged against the next year. If the fiscal year is July 1 to June 30, the accounting books will close June 30, and all expenditures not cleared by that date will be charged to the next year's budget.

Business managers often require that all purchase orders be issued in enough time to receive the merchandise, confirm shipment of the appropriate items, and issue payment before the end of the fiscal year. In some cases, no purchase orders are issued within four months of the end of the fiscal year, so that orders will be completed in ample time before closing the books. Library

```
1000    Instruction
        1100    Regular Programs
                100     Personnel Services—Salaries
                110     Official/Administrative
                        111     Regular Salaries
                        112     Temporary Salaries
                        113     Overtime Salaries
                        114     Sabbatical Leave
                120     Professional—Educational
                130     Professional—Other
                140     Technical
                150     Office/Clerical
                200     Personnel Services—Employee Benefits
                210     Group Insurance
                        211     Medical Insurance
                        212     Dental Insurance
                220     Social Security Contributions
                230     Retirement Contributions
                640     Books and Periodicals
                750     Equipment, Original and Additional
                760     Replacement
        1200    Special Programs
        1300    Vocational Education Programs
        1400    Other Instructional Programs—Elementary/Secondary
        1600    Adult Education Programs
        1700    Community/Junior College Education Programs
2000    Support Services
        2100    Supervision of Pupil Personnel Services
        2200    Instructional Staff
        2300    Administration
        2400    Pupil Health
        2500    Business
        2600    Operations and Maintenance of Plant Services
        2700    Student Transportation Services
        2800    Central
        2900    Other Support Services
3000    Operation of Noninstructional Services
        3100    Food Services
        3200    Student Activities
        3300    Community Services
```

Teacher salaries are under 1100.100, and teacher benefits are under 1100.200. The supply account number is 600, with books and periodicals under 640. Therefore, the purchase of books and periodicals from the regular instruction account would be charged to 1100.640.

Figure 9.1 Numerical Sequence for Sample Budget

media specialists seldom have large budgets, and any loss of funds can be crucial. Items that require longer times for shipment should be ordered as early as possible. Moreover, library media specialists should be aware of what happens if a shipment is not received before the books are closed. It may be charged against the next year's budget, in effect costing double. This is because funds were lost from one year and became an unanticipated purchase added to next year, decreasing that budget by the purchase amount. Many of these errors can be avoided if the fiscal officer is aware of the interests of the media specialist.

The need to handle fiscal matters promptly is one of the reasons fiscal officers sometimes wish to limit the media center to one or two book orders each year. Limiting orders seriously affects the media specialist's ability to provide materials for students and teachers when needs arise. Working closely with business managers and clerical staff can help overcome this problem.

The library media specialist should be as supportive of the fiscal officer as possible. Most media specialists present necessary buying information to the purchasing agent by submitting order cards, special order forms, school or district requisitions, or purchase orders. All forms must be completed accurately, from correct spelling and address for the supplier to correct spelling of author, title, publisher for books, and ISBN or ISSN for periodicals. Accurate item numbers for supplies, accurate model numbers for equipment, and accurate quantities desired, unit item costs, and item totals are essential. Any erroneous information on an order may cause an incorrect shipment or incorrect billing, which will result in additional correspondence from the business office for the return or exchange of items. This costs staff time in the accounting office and may lead the business manager to restrict the media specialist's freedom to issue a requisition or purchase order.

As more and more routine ordering is performed electronically, orders may be submitted online. Whatever the method, the school library media specialist should be sure that item numbers, addresses of suppliers, quantities desired, and other information are carefully submitted so that errors are minimized. Orders must also be checked to see that the item supplied meets the written specifications.

WRITING SPECIFICATIONS

Specifications are written to ensure the delivery of materials and equipment to meet the stated need. If you are going to order laptops capable of capturing sight and sound, you might assess whether it would be more convenient and in the end less expensive to purchase them with this capability installed rather than purchasing microphones and cameras as accessories. This is a simplistic example, and, for major purchases, the specifications may be a half page or longer. An instruction book on writing specifications was published many years ago by the Educational Products Information Exchange Institute; however, it has application in the present. Educational Product Report 28, *Writing Equipment Specifications: A How-to Handbook* (updated in 1976) explains the central problem of purchasing instructional hardware: developing purchase specifications. "The fact that the user must write a specification and then go through an extended complicated purchase procedure is just one more frustration of being an educational administrator."[2] However, preparation of good specifications can ultimately "provide better educational systems, at lower cost, for a school or school district," and such a school will give status and credibility to the astute library media specialist.[3]

Purchase specifications must

1. Communicate the desires of the buyer clearly to the potential supplier.
2. Provide more than information about the product or system.
3. Set forth the conditions that govern the purchase.
4. Set forth the purpose for which the equipment will be used.
5. Set forth the results the user desires.
6. Contain definitive requirements as to the expected performance of the delivered merchandise.
7. State how the equipment is to be installed, where it is to be installed, and the standard of workmanship expected.
8. State to whom the equipment is to be delivered.[4]

In ordering technical equipment to meet performance standards, media specialists may wish to consult with others before writing specifications. Collecting suggestions from knowledgeable media specialists on the best product to meet the need can help make sure that specifications cover all contingencies.

Business managers, building principals, and others involved in purchases will usually welcome assistance in writing specifications for unfamiliar materials or equipment. It is essential to obtain assistance in checking the returned bids to see whether the product offered meets specifications. When it does not, the reasons for rejection must be outlined, or the supplier may demand acceptance of the low bid, and an inferior product will be delivered just because it meets the written specifications. When the shipment is received, it must be carefully checked to see that the specified item was shipped and that it meets the specifications described in the bid. If not, it should be returned and another bid issued for the order. When an item is returned, its deficiencies must be described in writing, because the school district will be rejecting a contract for delivery after the bid has been accepted. This is even more problematic than rejecting the initial bid, because the product as it was described appeared to meet the bid specifications.

Demanding quality products for the media center is one step in being cost-accountable to the taxpayers or the sponsors of the schools. The section that follows describes cost accountability in the media center.

COST ACCOUNTABILITY AND THE MEDIA SPECIALIST

Placing a dollar amount on components of a media program is not an easy task. Costing of services is a process of estimating labor as well as materials used. Often the cost of time—whether volunteer, staff, or professional—is overlooked. After all, the library media specialist is on the job anyway. Computing the cost of any service in terms of the time necessary to conduct the service divided into the salary of the person conducting the service will give one cost figure. To this must be added the cost of materials, supplies, or equipment used in the project. A method for building these cost figure estimates, basing them on careful analysis, is shown later in relation to gathering information for a bibliography.

Human costs include professional and clerical staff in the media center. If the annual salary of the media specialist is $40,000, and this person works 180 days per year and seven hours each day, both daily wage and hourly wage are easily calculated. To calculate the daily wage, divide the days worked per year into the yearly salary. This indicates that the director earns approximately $222 per day. Calculate the hourly wage by dividing the hours worked per day into the daily rate. This person's hourly wage is approximately $31 per hour. If the media specialist spends 30 minutes to catalog a book, the cost is $15.50. This would not be cost accountable, because complete processing from a book jobber would be much less. The time saved could be used collaborating with teachers. The cost increases as the media specialist moves up the salary scale.

To calculate the cost of equipment use, list the pieces of equipment and their purchase prices. Divide this by the number of expected years of service and number of days of possible use and then the days by hours of expected use, to arrive at a use-per-hour figure. For example, if a piece of equipment cost $2,700 and its life expectancy is three years of 180 days each year or 540 days of use, and it is anticipated to be used five hours a day, the anticipated use would be 2,700 hours. The cost of use is $1.00 per hour, not counting any replacement parts if the machine does not operate as anticipated. This figure will not reflect any repairs over the life of the equipment. However, unless a piece of equipment is in constant use, the downtime for nonuse should help cover anticipated additional expenditures for repairs.

Material costs are calculated based on their replacement cost, which rises with inflation. This figure may be found in publications, but the average price actually paid can be calculated by adding the total of all purchase orders and then dividing by the number of books received. Using the average cost of a book multiplied by the number of books that were lost, missing, or stolen from the media center can show the replacement cost for a single year.

The approximate cost of a book can be used in another way: to show the total replacement value of the media center and the amount of materials and equipment the manager oversees. If a media center has 20,000 items and an item costs an average of $24 to replace, the director oversees $480,000 in materials. Adding the cost of replacing equipment greatly increases this amount. Book, media, or equipment estimates can also be used to show students and their parents how valuable the media center is to them. That is, if books average $24 and 200 are circulated each week for nine weeks, students and teachers have borrowed 24 times 200 equals 4,800 times 9 equals $43,200 worth of books.

Media specialists in single-person centers are usually concerned about clerical tasks. When a $31-per-hour person spends an hour shelving books, the cost to the district is very high compared with the $10 per hour for clerical staff to do that job. If it takes one hour to gather items for a bibliography for a teaching unit and one hour to produce the bibliography, the cost to the school district is $62 for the single-person center. It would be $20 if a clerk produced the bibliography. Selecting appropriate items to meet the content of the unit and match the reading and interest levels of the students is a professional task. Producing the bibliography is clerical. Costs for this task can be further reduced with an online public access catalog.

For some media specialists, clerical tasks are somewhat rewarding in that they have a beginning and an end. Conversely, media management is ongoing, with one challenge briefly met as another challenge arrives to take its place in the queue of unfinished work. Most media specialists relish the prospect of uninterrupted planning time in the media center, being able to attack tasks with few clerical interruptions. This situation is worth striving for and can be attained by demonstrating to those responsible for budgeting the loss to the district that occurs when the media specialist spends time on clerical tasks.

The greater loss, and one even more difficult to show, occurs when a professional is not available to collaborate with teachers. A media professional who is preoccupied with clerical tasks cannot help students find, analyze, and evaluate materials or assist teachers in locating teaching aids. Certainly a stronger case can be built for clerical assistance in the media center than has been made in the past.

Many school administrators may not see developing budget requests as a function of the school library media specialist. As a result, many media specialists have little opportunity to plan a budget or request funds. Nevertheless, school library media specialists must assume a more proactive role and plan for their programs, establishing a dollar amount for each facet. This process should take into account the present, the immediate future, and long-range plans. Unless media specialists begin to plan for the future, carefully detailing the anticipated costs of necessary services, administrators will remain unaware of the costs of providing for the information needs of teachers and students. Needs and objectives must be established and proposed expenditures clarified. Success is more likely if the requests are presented in a structured format not unlike the formal process of project proposal writing.

WRITING PROPOSALS TO EXPAND PROGRAMS

Many school library media specialists would like to expand their services. One way to do this is to develop a carefully thought out and documented proposal. The information you collect helps explain your need to the persons you are asking. This may be parents, the principal, or the school board. Proposals might stay in the school district, with the administration and school board accepting the proposals and funding the projects with local funds. At other times, the school district budget may be inadequate, and the school library media specialist, with school board approval, may seek outside funding. Whether a project remains in the district or is sent to an outside agency, a proposal must be developed.

The remainder of this section discusses writing proposals for the school district or agencies that fund proposals directly related to school library media center programs. However, sometimes school library media specialists are invited to join other, perhaps larger, agencies to develop a broader proposal. For some agencies, collaboration is either encouraged or required. Because many agencies ask for matching funds, it can be helpful to have more than your school or even the district involved in the proposal. The expertise, experience, or other resources of a co-writer's group can also add value to your proposal.

A project proposal should include the following elements: statement of needs and of goals and objectives, a plan of action or activities and procedures, an evaluation plan, comments about facilities and other resources available, and a carefully planned budget. Additional items, such as employment opportunity regulations, may be required if the proposal goes beyond the school district. You will also need to send vitae of staff and consultants for your project.

Developing the Statement of Needs

Few individuals are willing to allocate money without a needs statement. As children we learn to justify additional allowance requests from our parents. As adults, personal budget decisions to make major purchases are based on a needs assessment. School library media specialists cannot expect additional funding from their school budgets without presenting a strong case of need. Needs are defined in a variety of ways. One is to read research studies that address the problem in your school. You can ask for funds to implement the program that addressed the problem.

Another effective way is to compare the resources available in your school with a similar school in the district or a nearby district where the student body is similar but achievement levels are higher. The difference in resources available could be suggested as a reason for the difference in achievement levels and would give you the opportunity to test the result of adding materials and equipment for student use.

The process will be much more effective if the input comes from the group rather than the media specialist as a single individual suggesting the needs. The composition of the group is very important. Funding agencies want to know if those to be served by the project helped identify needs and if those identified needs were used to help set the priorities. Proposal writers should cite the persons involved in the needs assessment process. In this case, administrators, teachers, and parents are most likely to be those who helped establish the needs because they know when students have problems with reading.

Although a media specialist can say that the collection is inadequate, the statement is more powerful if teachers review the collection in their areas and find it inadequate or if students write lists of missing or inadequate materials for assignments they have researched. It is important that the assessment of needs involves those directly or indirectly affected by the proposed project. It would be foolhardy to ask for an expanded collection of art books if the art teacher did not plan to use the books or make assignments that require students to use them. To confirm the participation of others in establishing needs, the proposal writer should list all meetings held and who attended, tests that were administered and the results, and any other relevant details.

Participation may also be confirmed by letters of support, which are appended to the body of the proposal. Once the need has been established, a goal should be stated and objectives for the project developed.

Preparing Goals and Objectives

A goal is a broad, general statement and is not measurable. Because a goal is such a broad statement, it is not always required for a project proposal. When a goal is required, it should be realistic. Consider reading materials as an example of a goal. Trying to overcome reading problems in an elementary school in a single year might be an unrealistic goal. If children are reading below grade level, if reading at all, a few books and magazines added to the library media collection will not alleviate the problem, and the goal cannot be met.

Objectives, conversely, must be measurable. They are designed to help solve the needs that have been determined, and they should state the precise level of achievement anticipated and the length of time expected to achieve them. Objectives must be an outgrowth of the stated needs. They should describe where the school library program should be in this time frame in relation to where the program is currently and who or what is involved in the project. The better the objectives are written, the easier it will be to prepare the evaluation later. An attempt to increase reading scores will need to include the number of students, how much increase will occur, and in what time frame. This becomes the objective.

Goals and objectives themselves may be evaluated. Context evaluation is the assessment of goals and objectives to see whether they are written in terms of the intended constituency of the project. This evaluation reviews the number of students who will benefit from the project, for they should be part of the stated objectives. For the reading project, you might choose to work only with third grade students for one year, and you would suggest that each student would raise reading scores by two years.

Objectives are often confused with activities. Rather than state the expected outcome, novice proposal writers often list the methods to achieve an outcome. These methods are activities rather than stated objectives, and they are a part of the plan of action.

Establishing the Plan of Action

The section of the proposal that states the plan of action, or proposed activities, describes the methods to be employed to meet the stated objective and alleviate the needs. A general statement of the overall design of the project includes the population to be served, how the population will be selected, and how the project will be managed. But the activities themselves must be directed to the objectives, and that relationship must be clear. Procedures to attain the objectives must follow from the objectives. If the relationship between objective and activity is ambiguous, those reading the proposal may reject it. Funding agencies and school administrators prefer projects with a step-by-step plan of realistic activities to meet the objectives and alleviate the need. The activity for third-graders might be to give them books to read that they will want to read and allow them unlimited access to these books.

When a project planner is unsure that proposed activities will meet objectives in the anticipated time frame, alternative plans of action may be presented. A rationale for each alternative may include a brief statement about why the first plan of action was proposed and how, when, or why it will be decided to use the alternative plan. If providing a large collection of reading materials does not seem to be encouraging their reading, providing more reading opportunities during the school day and asking parents to help children read more at night at home could be an alternative plan of action or even a second activity. Whenever possible, proposal writers should include relevant research supporting their choice from the array of possible activities.

As the project activities are stated, a time line for each of the activities may be presented. The time line shows the sequence of separate activities that have gone before, what is in progress, and what will be done. This helps the reviewers understand how the activities relate—that is, if and when the initiation of one activity depends on the completion of another, when activities overlap, and the progress necessary for project completion.

Planning for Evaluation

After the activities have been designed, proposal writers must then determine the best methods to evaluate the activities to see whether they are, indeed, meeting stated objectives. To do this, two kinds of evaluation are helpful: formative and summative. Formative evaluation processes occur throughout the life of the project. At each step, an evaluation may be made to see if the activities are accomplishing the planned improvements. If the project does not appear to be successful, an alternate plan of action may be put into place. Progress using the new activity will then be evaluated to see if it demonstrates more success than the previous plan. Formative evaluation further determines whether project progress is within the anticipated time period.

At the close of any project, a final, or summative, evaluation is conducted. At this time, each activity is evaluated to determine the degrees of progress made to meet the stated objectives. Proposal writers must detail the means by which they or their agency will verify for the funding source that the project has accomplished the objectives as stated and the degree to which the objectives have been met. Information to be collected must be described, methods to analyze the information must be outlined, and the degree of success that should be expected must be stated. With this example proposal, the obvious summative evaluation would be a reading test to see whether test scores have increased.

This is often not an easy task, and many proposal writers seek help from persons in tests and measurements offices in colleges and universities and in local or state agencies to help define the evaluation procedures to be used after the project begins. Many funding agencies prefer the summative evaluation be conducted by an outside evaluator to eliminate or modify the possibility of bias and add validity to the evaluation statements. When seeking project funding from outside agencies, choosing an outside evaluator—especially one highly regarded by the funding agency—may increase the likelihood of the project's approval. Someone not directly related to the project may be better able to measure the degree of success. Certainly the evaluation is one of the most important aspects of project planning and should be given full attention.

Deciding the Dissemination

Although outside funding agencies may not ask about any presentation of the project and its outcome to the general public, the school library media specialist should be prepared to share the results of any project with the appropriate audience. Just as government agencies and foundation staffs need to know the degree of success of their investment, they anticipate credit for the contribution they made to the project. For locally funded projects, the school library media specialist reports project success to the superintendent and principal. They should be given material they can use for publicizing a successful project. It is no virtue to hide project success.

Funding agencies need good publicity to continue awarding money for projects; likewise, the school library media center is more likely to receive additional funds when successful projects are reported in the news media. Therefore, the media specialist must consider carefully how to present information to appropriate audiences beyond the project. It may be letters sent home to parents or full coverage in the news media, both newspapers and television. The school district may have a public relations director to handle this, or the library media specialist may need to send out press releases to reporters.

Information presented for publication must be well written, accurate, and complete. If photographs of students are submitted, permission for publication must be obtained from parents.

Finally, successful school library projects should be reported to the school library community through activities in professional journals and presentations at conferences and workshops. The media specialist must share the outcomes of projects with other professionals so that successful activities can be replicated in other school library media centers. A list of publications of special interest to school library media specialists is provided in Appendix G.

School library media specialists may be reluctant to make presentations. If you are the person in charge of the project, in developing the proposal with all its parts, the needs assessment, preparation of objectives, activities, evaluation, dissemination, you are the best person to share how this happened and the results of the project. Even if the project didn't meet its objectives, you will have some idea of how things could have been done differently. You need to share your expertise with your colleagues, and your professional associations may be the best place to do this. As you write the proposal, you will need to list all the ways information will be disseminated about the proposal.

Describing Local Resources

Project proposals should also describe the facilities where the project will be conducted. If the school or school district has excellent facilities in place to support project activities, there is a greater chance for success. Conversely, if an elaborate program is described, but the school does not have adequate space for it, there is a greater likelihood for failure. Describing facilities and additional resources available, human and material, will help the funding agency realize that the school library media specialist has a better chance of conducting a successful project. If special equipment is needed for the project, the equipment must become part of the project proposal, or the method of securing the equipment must be shown in the project narrative and budget as in-kind equipment.

Proposal writers should list all resources that add credibility to what, or who, is being proposed. If a school library media specialist lacks long experience in the library media world, assistance may be available from a district coordinator. The community may be supporting the school library media specialist in some unique or special way, and this should be explained. Additional funding may be available for the project from other sources—the community, individuals, or the state department of education. This support should also be cited.

Personnel who work on the project must be listed. If they are available as in-kind contributions to the project, this means their salaries will be paid by the school district and will not be part of the cost charged to the project budget. All personnel to be added must be listed. Job titles, job descriptions, qualifications expected, and length of time assigned to the project must all be described. Resumes should be attached for all persons who are identified as part of the project staff. This includes project director, coordinator, consultants, clerical and technical staff, teachers, and evaluators. These resumes must be brief, and the activities and positions described in their backgrounds should be only those showing skills related directly to the project.

Before submitting a person's name as part of any project staff, proposal writers must secure permission from that individual. Most people are annoyed if their name is submitted without permission. Often, an implication exists that these proposed project consultants or staff have approved the proposal in principle, even if they did not actually participate in writing it. Also, there is the danger of including someone's name in a proposal when that person is writing a proposal in response to the same request for proposals.

When competing for limited funds, the proposal writer should try to find out whether project staff under consideration is known to the funding agency. The agency may be more willing to fund a project if they recognize the capabilities of those directly involved. Also, the funding agency may insist on approval of the categories of persons to be hired, such as researchers, technicians, media practitioners, or clerical staff. Finally, many funding agencies are reluctant to approve the hiring of new persons for a project if there is no indication of how this staff will be continued after the project is completed. School district administrators may find themselves obligated for any unemployment benefits for furloughed staff unless they can be placed in other positions.

Building the Budget

The final part of project planning, the budget, includes the anticipated costs of the project, item by item. Government agencies provide a form to be completed. If no form is provided, some suggestions of items to be included are found Appendix H. These items can be used to verify that the information usually required is included in the project budget.

Two budget items that may cause unexpected problems are fringe benefits and overhead. Fringe benefits are part of salary statistics. The percentage figure used to calculate fringe benefits for proposed project personnel will be the same used for all school district salaried staff. Fringe benefits for a district employee are determined by the monthly salary, percentage of time and length of time of the project. That is, if a school library specialist with a $2,000 monthly salary is to be employed half-time for six months, the project would show $1,000 times 6, or $6,000 for the project. If the school district has a fringe benefit package of 27 percent, $1,620 must be added to the project costs.

Overhead percentage may be set by school districts, universities, and private agencies. Overhead is an assessment of the use of staff, equipment, and facilities that will not be specifically included in the proposal budget. Examples of overhead are the preparation of purchase orders, checks for payment, bookkeeping, use of office furniture and equipment, heat and lighting, and computer use. The overhead costs are then added to the total costs for the project. This is sometimes discouraging to a proposal writer when the overhead costs add another charge to the project. It sometimes means cutting other parts of the project that seemed essential in order to submit a proposal that has a reasonable budget.

Some agencies such as state departments of education may limit or prohibit assessment of overhead percentages or limit the amount that can be added. This needs to be determined before you begin the project proposal so that it is not an unexpected cost to the planning. If your district has a contract with the agency to which you are submitting the proposal, you will need to put a copy of that contract with your proposal.

If space or equipment is to be rented, those costs must be calculated. Consultant or contracted services also must be listed. Consultants may be paid a per diem amount rather than a salary, in which case fringe benefits need not be calculated. School library media specialists should keep in mind that telephone charges, mailing costs, duplicating fees, online database searches, and office supplies should be added to the budget if the school budget cannot absorb these additional charges. Finally, if the staff or consultants require travel funds, these must be included.

Additional Considerations

When planning the project, proposal writers should check to see if evaluation points have been assigned to each part of the proposal. The number of points assigned is the highest score that proposal readers can give each part of the proposal. Careful attention must be placed on all parts of a proposal, but special attention should be given to the sections that have been assigned the most points.

Throughout project planning and proposal preparation, school district administrators must indicate their support. It is heartbreaking to complete a project proposal and have the principal or superintendent refuse to send it to the funding agency. It is even more difficult when an agency awards funding and the school board refuses to permit the school district to accept the funds. Not all administrators or school boards welcome funding from an outside source, especially if they perceive that strings are attached. This is especially true when personnel must be added, because, as stated earlier, these persons may expect to become permanent employees at the close of the project. A successful project may encourage other administrators to demand similar materials, staff, or services from already overextended district funds. Convincing administrators of the value of the project and the potential benefit to the school building and school district is important. This is better accomplished when the school library media specialist provides an honest, realistic assessment of the regulations and requirements for the school district at the close of the funding, the probable level of enthusiasm for similar projects in other schools, and the funds required to continue even a small portion of the project.

After preparing the proposal, the writer should reread it to make sure it is written without jargon, to be sure the plan of action is logical and will achieve the objectives, to eliminate extraneous words and unnecessary materials, and to correct any spelling or grammatical errors. Finally, the proposal should be neatly typed in an easy-to-read format or in conformity with the format outlined in the request for proposal. Format instructions might include spacing requirements, number of pages for each section of the proposal, length of abstract, and other details.

Be sure that all necessary documents are included, but do not send materials that are not requested. It would be unfortunate to lose evaluation points because a required item, such as a copy of the district's selection policy, was not sent. Further, some agencies require confirmation that equal employment opportunity requirements are met and other legal regulations are in place.

Most funding agencies are interested in what will happen to the project at the close of the outside funding. If parts of the project will be continued with school district funding, the project may have a better chance for outside funding. If administrators are involved in planning throughout, they can help determine how to continue the project.

Those who are required to sign the proposal must be available to do so. If the proposal requires school board approval, copies must be distributed to members prior to the board meeting, and someone from the proposal preparation team must be ready to answer questions at the meeting. It may not be possible to call a special meeting of the board, so the school library media specialist must pay attention to the closing dates of all requests for proposal, to allow time to secure board approval and all appropriate signatures.

Proposals must be submitted on time. If a deadline exists, this date must be met. Proposals that arrive after the deadline are usually returned unopened.

Writing proposals is a way of life in many situations. In others, it may be a way to get additional funds, expand a program to meet a specific need, add equipment, add materials, or try a different way to provide materials to help teach students.

Most persons who have had one proposal funded are very willing to write another. They have been given an opportunity to improve their school library media center, test a new method, offer a new service, or provide more materials for students and teachers.[5]

To write a proposal is to enter a competition, and the process is similar to any other competitive endeavor; sometimes you win, sometimes you lose. Sometimes it may seem better to lose. One gains all the applause for the effort to establish needs, develop objectives and plans of action, and write and submit the proposal. It is an opportunity to meet new colleagues and reestablish communication with old acquaintances. Sometimes you win, and then you have to work to see that the project succeeds.[6]

Exercises

1. Develop a budget policy statement for a school library media center.
2. Choose a service currently offered in a school library media center and determine the cost of providing this service for one week.
3. Determine a service that patrons seem to use less, and, after establishing its cost accountability, justify adding a new service to replace this one.
4. Locate an active request for proposal for funding for a school and brainstorm ideas that could be written into a project proposal. Then write the proposal for a school library media specialist who would appreciate having the assistance.

NOTES

1. Peter F. Drucker, *Management: Tasks, Responsibilities, Practices* (New York: Harper & Row, 1973), 141.
2. Educational Products Information Exchange Institute, Educational Product Report 72, *Writing Equipment Specifications: A How-to Handbook*, rev. ed. of EPIE Report 28 (New York: Educational Products Information Exchange Institute, 1976).
3. Ibid.
4. Ibid.
5. Blanche Woolls, *Grant Proposal Writing: A Handbook for School Library Media Specialists* (Westport, CT: Greenwood, 1986), 96.
6. Ibid., x.

Chapter 10

On the Job: Managing Services

Four components of school library media programs—personnel, materials, equipment, and facility—are highly visible. School personnel can readily observe the library media center staff at work. The materials collection, because it is heavily used by students and teachers, is a recognizable part of the school's assets. Because teachers, students, and administrators use the media center often for reading, research, and meetings, it is considered an essential room in the building. It is also more comfortable and more attractive than the regular classrooms. Management and coordination of these individual components culminate in the program of services offered, and, services, though less immediately visible, are the media center's reason for existing.

Teachers and students may take the components of the media center for granted or they may not expect many services. If there is a media specialist because the state mandates the position or the regional accrediting agency dictates it, this manager is on-site; therefore, there is a room and a collection. Users then take the services for granted and may not recognize when one service no longer exists or is replaced with another. When equipment wears out and is not replaced, or reduced budgets do not permit renewal of magazine subscriptions or online resources, users may be surprised, but they probably did not recognize the need for their replacement to continue the service.

Teachers and students may expect few services because they have not been introduced to the wide variety of experiences they may choose in the media center. Deciding which services to offer and in what depth are the management decisions of the media specialist, and these decisions are based on the staff and facilities available. Services are limited only by the creativity of the media specialist who must work with a given number of staff, within a given space, with a given collection of materials and equipment, within a given budget, and within the limit of materials available from other locations. These are the factors that form the base of possible activities. However, once these factors have been analyzed, the most important consideration is delivering what is needed to integrate media services into the curriculum.

Services are planned with full knowledge of the curriculum, teaching methods, assignments given by teachers, planned activities in classrooms that require media center support, and activities in the media center itself. To plan services for teachers, the media specialist must understand how they teach and what assignments they will make; to plan services for students, the media specialist must understand how students learn. The major task of the school library media manager is to turn units of curriculum into opportunities to blend classroom activities with use of the media center and its collection. The ultimate goal is to blend classroom and subject areas across the curriculum and across the school. To make this happen, school library media specialists become leaders in the instructional team.

UNDERSTANDING CURRICULUM

The 1998 American Association of School Librarian standards, *Information Power: Building Partnerships for Learning,* listed 10 learning and teaching principles for media programs. Principle 3 states, "The library media program models and promotes collaborative planning and curriculum development."[1] This is reconfirmed in *Standards for the 21st-Century Learner,* with "School librarians collaborate with others to provide instruction, learning strategies, and practice in using the essential learning skills needed in the 21st century."[2] Media specialists collaborate with teachers to meet the intellectual needs of students. They collaborate with teachers regularly to provide resources for course, unit, and lesson integration. To model and promote collaborative planning and curriculum development, library media specialists are aware of the curriculum in their schools.

Media specialists who have elementary teaching certification or a subject specialty at the secondary level in addition to media certification already know a good deal about curriculum. These persons are highly knowledgeable about the relationship of the curriculum to the classroom. Most media specialist preparation programs provide some experience in the development of curriculum units in course work and in the practicum setting, so that each media specialist will have practical knowledge to plan for guided inquiry—which

> offers an integrated unit of inquiry, planned and guided by an instructional team of a school librarian and teachers, allowing students to gain deeper understandings of subject curriculum content and information literacy concepts. Guided inquiry combines often overlooked resources with materials in the school library.[3]

In order for this planning to happen, media specialists gather materials and information about the curriculum in the local school.

One way to begin this process of understanding the curriculum is to create a professional reference collection of all textbooks used in the building. This also will be useful to teachers who need to know what has been covered in previous courses and what will be covered in the future. Media staff reviews textbooks used by teachers (as discussed in chapter 4) to help plan for the semester's probable units of work. Throughout the year, the media specialist expands on the projects reviewed during the first week in the building, determining what each teacher teaches and integrating the method of teaching, the materials needed beyond those provided in the classroom, and the probable use to be made of media center materials and materials secured from other libraries.

A second professional reference collection includes copies of curriculum guides developed at the building and district levels and at the state department of public instruction. If possible, curriculum guides from all grade levels should be available to help teachers understand their students in the context of their previous and future classroom experiences. The media specialist can continue developing this professional service by participating in textbook selection and curriculum planning.

Volunteering to serve on textbook committees provides an inside view into new topics to be covered. This gives advance warning so that the media center collection can be assessed to meet new needs. When a topic is added, new materials must be located, purchased, and added to the media center holdings; new Web sites must be found; and the collaboration process for developing units of instruction begins in advance of the arrival of the textbooks.

Media specialists also serve on curriculum committees. By serving on these grade level or subject area committees, media specialists are better able to integrate the media center into unit plans of all teachers. Managing time to participate in these meetings may appear to be difficult or even impossible. However, this is the primary role of the media specialist in the education of students, and it must be given high priority. The need for backup assistance so the media specialist can attend meetings and still keep the media center open can be used to justify additional help in the media center. The media specialist should ask for the services of a substitute teacher when curriculum planning meetings are scheduled for more than one period in the day. Justifying this need emphasizes the importance of working with teachers and curriculum and keeping the media center available with a professional replacement when the media specialist has responsibilities elsewhere.

In the process of developing curriculum, library media specialists are able to take a leadership role because they teach all the students, work with all the teachers, and understand the curriculum throughout the school. As *Information Power* suggests, "The library media specialist models and promotes creative, effective, and collaborative teaching."[4] By taking the lead, the media specialist suggests curriculum units that go across grade levels and across subject areas, making the instructional program an integrated whole rather than separate, segregated components that students have difficulty relating to what they have learned before, what they are learning in other classrooms, and how this affects their everyday life.

Once curriculum units have been defined, media specialists work to help in the instructional design of units and to suggest materials that will assist the teacher in teaching these units. The advent of the word processor greatly facilitates the creation and maintaining of bibliographies. Recorded unit activities on a database management program can also be updated as changes are made. A unit evaluation form can be integrated into this single database, helping teachers and media specialists assess and understand outcomes of one unit's presentation.

The process of understanding the curriculum, encouraging collaboration between teachers, and leading in the integration of learning across grade and subject levels is not easy. Curriculum changes, some teachers change, and new teaching methods come into the school. Yet, not all teachers want to change or to adopt new teaching methods. Some may even rebel against changing any part of the curriculum.

Keeping a record of collaboration between teachers and library media specialists can be facilitated through the use of a computer program. One such program has been designed by Nancy Miller. Her *Impact*[5] makes it possible not only to record collaboration but also to create the reports to share with principals showing the time spent with teachers and planning. The record maintained of curriculum units prepared can help expand into instruction across the curriculum.

The move to integrate instruction across the curriculum that made some progress in the 1990s needs to continue. The role of the library media specialist is one of leadership in helping to accomplish this. The in-depth knowledge of what is being taught and what will be taught in each classroom provides many opportunities to suggest combining learning experiences. Educational leaders are suggesting teaching across the curriculum and across the school. The media specialist, with knowledge of curriculum units being taught throughout the year is in a unique position to help this happen.

This integration is being threatened by the focus on student testing. When teachers are evaluated for merit increases based on test results, many will fear the consequences of teaching other than to the test. Rote memorization will replace critical thinking unless media specialists can help them understand the value of assignments to help students prepare for lifelong learning.

When curriculum is discussed, the media specialist should be an aggressive advocate of expanding student learning into real-world experiences. Again, this is a trend in education today—to place the learning of students into the context of how they will function in the future. The media specialist helps teachers focus on activities that will help students develop critical thinking skills and prepare them for tasks that they will be doing after they leave school and join the work force.

The media specialist keeps teachers aware of trends in all areas of education so that they can determine which changes they wish to implement. Because professional journals come into the media center, the media specialist can suggest articles that teachers will find of benefit. Ideas gleaned from a review of each table of contents can target information literacy–related activities to match the discussion in the subject area. For the principal, the media specialist helps interpret national and state government regulations. Preparing frequent collections of articles on particular subjects will help administrators make informed decisions.

ANALYZING TEACHING METHODS

Despite efforts of education leaders who suggest the need to use a variety of resources and teaching methods to accommodate students' different learning styles, many teachers still use textbook and lecture as their primary—if not only—teaching method. One colleague of the author insists that this tradition is a product of the faculty in schools of education, who teach almost exclusively by textbook and lecture. This textbook model does not demonstrate to the future teacher how or why to make use of instructional design strategies to incorporate variety of methods to teach and a variety of library media materials into lesson plans to reach every student. Moving beyond the textbook encourages many things and can expand to teaching across the curriculum. It allows media specialists to plan experiences that will help teachers both expand curriculum experiences across the school and to encourage their use of more individualized and group activities that will meet the needs of students.

Teachers who anticipate student learning through a variety of methods make heavy use of materials beyond the textbook. Planning projects with teachers to ensure that students can explore a topic of interest and report this learning in a meaningful way requires much more time than preparing a lecture and developing a test on the content. Projects must be coordinated with the media staff to confirm the availability of materials. If a topic is too narrow, expanding it to a wider area, yet permitting the student to conduct the research originally suggested, takes a great deal of planning among teacher, media specialist, and student. Many teachers are better able to manage classroomwide assignments than independent study or group projects. Media specialists can do much to encourage alternative teaching methods and materials for covering the curriculum. *Standards for the 21st-Century Learner* suggests expanding assignments to be done by groups. It states: "Participate and collaborate as members of a social and intellectual network of learners,"[6] and "Share knowledge and participate ethically and productively as members of our democratic society."[7]

The use of media beyond the textbook can be a positive experience for students and teachers. The author recalls one first-grade teacher who used textbook and workbook exclusively. This teacher taught in an elementary school that was designated a model school, with a wide variety of media available in the media center. To minimize efforts to locate equipment, each classroom was issued audiovisual equipment for permanent use in that classroom. One afternoon, the teacher decided to try an audiotape designed for alphabet skill practice. As she said later, "The children perked up, and I perked up, and I realized that media can provide a change of pace that is beneficial for all."

Kristen Fontichiaro has many suggestions in *Active Learning through Drama, Podcasting, and Puppetry* to help perk up students. In her introduction, she suggests

> Imagine your media center alive with energy as students actively engage with books and research. Imagine that, while the quality of their work deepens, the number of behavior management issues decreases. These are just some of the benefits of integrating drama lessons into the media center curriculum.[8]

Research studies are ambivalent about how successful certain media are for accomplishing certain tasks. Certainly when media are used incorrectly, it should be no surprise if there is little improvement in learning. However, media provide a different approach to the learning task, and the media specialist must be aware of the collection in order to offer this change of pace. For some students, media are the best way to learn because they do not rely on reading skills. If teachers are to use media, they must be accessible. Accessibility is a management role that goes hand in hand with the personnel role of helping teachers to change. Teachers can be encouraged to change their teaching methods only if the alternative is perceived to be no more, and preferably less, work than their previous method. Remind them that working together means at least two and maybe more teachers to design the strategies.

Using instructional design to develop projects requires extensive planning, but the rewards are well worth it. Working closely with teachers, media specialists help plan units of work, decide on appropriate teaching methods, activities related to the unit, help teach the unit, decide methods of testing, and finally, help score the products, and assign the grades. This can be very time consuming and the media specialist should not be discouraged if few instructional design projects are accomplished in a single semester. However, it is better to accomplish one a semester than none.

If examples are needed to show projects and how they are evaluated, *Assessing Learning: Librarians and Teachers as Partners*[9] provides a sample lesson for elementary and one for high school. A wide variety of assessment models are also shown in this volume.

The willingness of the media specialist to participate in teaching a lesson and reviewing the final products may encourage teachers to plan units of work with media specialists. To have someone help make teaching both easier and more effective and assist with the assessment of student progress should be irresistible. Teachers quickly realize that one plus one equals two, and students now have the skills of two teachers focused on their project rather than one. This simple equation should help other teachers recognize how teaching across the curriculum and across grade levels might take a little extra planning time, but the return on the investment in the learning of students seems a small price to pay.

At the beginning, attempts at instructional design must be done one on one with carefully selected teachers so that the attempt is successful. Because all teachers, particularly at the same grade level or in the same subject area, have basic expectations of assistance with classroom assignments, most will want to work on similar projects. It is a short step to helping one or more teachers join to teach a combined unit until one major project could go across the school.

However, it might be difficult to coordinate the collaboration of teachers who may not, at first, feel comfortable in joint teaching experiences. It requires the best efforts of the media specialist to lead the teamwork to make this happen.

ASSISTANCE WITH CLASSROOM ASSIGNMENTS

A common use of the media center for classroom assignments is the book report. At the elementary level, the assignment may be as unexciting as "Read a book with at least 100 pages." From the management standpoint, this is simple. It does not take long for the media specialist to spot books with more than 100 pages. The assignment lacks creativity, and this is not lost on students. Only the most motivated will be inspired by this approach. Offering teachers the opportunity to make creative assignments using media materials is a major responsibility of all media specialists.

The library media specialist need not rely solely on personal imagination. References to clever, successful ideas can be found in books that should be in your professional library. You should also subscribe to periodicals with lesson plans and suggestions such as *School Library Media Activities Monthly* and *Library Media Connection.*[10]

A second response to classroom assignments is to encourage the use of appropriate references for research papers. This means that the media specialist must teach students and encourage teachers to accept forms of bibliographic reference that may not be found in every style manual. Teaching students to use a style manual for their citations and then assisting teachers with grading the bibliographies are both part of the library media specialist's curriculum responsibilities.

Helping a teacher with a different and more creative assignment may seem like relying too heavily on gimmicks. But suggesting new ways to do old things can change attitudes of teachers and students and can encourage other, more exciting projects, which will engage students in their own learning.

TEACHING THE NEW KINDS OF LITERACY

The ever-increasing quantities of new information being generated daily dictates the role of the library media specialist as responsible for teaching many kinds of literacy to students. The 1998 *Information Power* suggested

> With its focus on information literacy and its promotion of a vital and exciting culture of learning, the school library media program sets the stage for students' entry into the larger learning community and for others' continued participation in that community.[11]

Teachers are reminded that assignments should promote information literacy so that all students become information literate. Helping teachers help students learn how to access, evaluate, and use information is more than showing students how to find information through the Internet, on a CD-ROM, or through the online public access catalog. It begins with a student who recognizes the need for information.

This author remembers an in-service session in the mid-1960s where the guest speaker suggested that schools in the next century would no longer exist. Rather, a child would see a caterpillar in the backyard. Carefully picking it up, the child would move to a central building, where an information specialist would be available to help find out where the caterpillar came from, what it eats, and how long it will live, among other questions. The questions would come because of a need for information, and information specialists would assure that the information located was accurate and complete. Teaching the sources of information would only be necessary *after* the student had developed the research question. These are all part of teaching the research process.

Many models[12] exist for teaching the research process, but Carol Kuhlthau's six principles of guided inquiry have been thoroughly tested.

- Children learn by being actively engaged in and reflecting on an experience.
- Children learn by building on what they already know.

- Children develop higher-order thinking through guidance at critical points in the learning process.

- Children have different ways and modes of learning.

- Children learn through social interaction with others.

- Children learn through instruction and experience in accord with their cognitive development.[13]

A second component of information literacy is that students can evaluate the information they find. Just as media specialists establish the authority of authors and publishers before selecting materials to add to the collection, the student learns to establish the authority of all information presented. Is the information written, collected, photographed, and stored on a CD-ROM or found on a search of the World Wide Web accurate and relevant? Students must learn to expect to find all sides of controversial issues and be able to distinguish fact and the opinion of the author and to find the sources to correct inaccurate information or to expand into another point of view if accurate information is missing.

Students who locate information are taught and retaught how to write a research paper. This process begins in the early grades and continues through high school. At the most basic level, students construct an outline of information after they determine the organization of the report. Drafts of the report are shared with other class members so that the editing process is two-way. That is, when one student's draft is being evaluated, the student is reviewing a colleague's paper. Current performance evaluation models include the student's oral and written products, again with the student's self-evaluation as well as evaluations of other students' products.

Teaching information literacy is more easily accomplished with the use of Kuhlthau's information search process. The steps include (1) the teacher's initiation of the unit of study; (2) the students' selection of a topic; (3) exploration to find a focus; (4) formulation of a focus for the research; (5) collection of information; (6) presentation; and (7) assessment with self-reflection. When the media specialist joins teachers in planning classroom assignments, it is easy to move into the inquiry process.[14]

Assistance with classroom assignments also involves evaluation of student performance. While the current focus is on testing, media specialists can encourage teachers to continue to focus on individual students and their preparation for the workplace and lifelong learning. The media specialist can be actively involved in several ways:

1. Locating the various methods of assessing student progress reported in the literature

2. Assuring that assessments of student progress include an analysis of their ability to locate and synthesize information from a variety of resources

3. Working with students and teachers to make judgments about what was learned and, if the presentation was disappointing, what needs to happen for learning to occur.

Planning inquiry-based units of instruction through evaluating student performance brings the media specialist into the classroom environment.

THE MEDIA SPECIALIST IN THE CLASSROOM

The role of the media specialist in the classroom is one of teacher rather than manager, but the management aspects of this role must be considered. When the media specialist is in the classroom, another individual must be placed in charge of the media center. Also, when the media specialist takes materials to the classroom to demonstrate or teach, these resources will be missing from the media center. When the media specialist is demonstrating online database searching using the media center's wireless laptops in the classroom, this may mean that other students will not have computers to search during that time. While this type of situation presents a strong argument for having a wireless network throughout the school, it may be some time before funding to do this will be available in all schools. Media specialists must be able to leave their media centers to go to classrooms to instruct, but the potential obstacles will require clever solutions.

The placement of the media specialist, media, and equipment in a location away from the media center must be planned in advance. Students who wish to use the media center throughout the day will expect to find it open and all reference materials readily available.

One solution is for schools to provide every classroom with online connections, a mounted projector in the ceiling, and a projection screen. This does not solve the problem of windows, which make it difficult to see what is being projected. However, this solves the problem of scheduling many materials and equipment away from the media center. Another solution is to use the media center as a classroom.

THE MEDIA CENTER AS CLASSROOM

Teaching in the media center is much easier when the media center contains a classroom in the facility. The media specialist schedules the use of this space, but priorities are established by the media center's advisory committee. The media specialist is given first preference, and teachers who wish to begin a lesson in the media center rather than the classroom or move to the media center in the middle of the period are considered a second priority. Non–media-related activities, such as testing students by guidance counselors, should have a lower priority.

When a media center classroom is available, media materials and equipment may be easily moved into this room for teaching and practice. Immediate access to reference books, media, and computers and other equipment makes lesson planning much easier than if the lesson and its examples must be moved into a classroom elsewhere in the building. This room should have a mounted projector and screen, and, if it is not an inside room, the windows must have covering.

When no separate room is available, a space in the media center should be set aside for this type of instruction and use, and attempts should be made to close off the area so that activities there do not disturb other media center users. This is a real challenge when the room is small. At the elementary level, storytelling should be conducted in an area away from other students so that neither group disturbs the other.

Another management dilemma occurs when resources are being projected in the media center, and it is not possible to turn off the lights or limit sound to that area. This becomes a scheduling and even a room-arrangement problem if more than one group wishes to use the media center while an online product, telecast, video, or slide show is being operated. It is an architectural design problem, too, if the media center is designed with high, uncovered windows—beautiful but not functional.

Once the curriculum, teaching methods, assignments, and classroom activities have been determined, the units to be taught in the media center are reviewed. Media specialists as teachers have a library skills curriculum to integrate into classroom units so students learn how to use reference books, read a table of contents, consult an index of nonfiction books, view videos or DVDs, locate and select references for a research paper, search databases, avoid plagiarism, and, perhaps, discover "truth." As access opens students to library collections around the world, databases including full text, interactive video, and e-mail communication, among others, teaching students to discriminate will become an ever-increasing task for the media specialist. Access to the world also allows students to communicate with other students perhaps practicing their knowledge of another language. They can communicate with authors, politicians, journalists, and others. Establishing these links are all part of the activities provided in the media center.

MEDIA CENTER ACTIVITIES

Some activities that a school library media specialist provides may be determined at the state level. That is, specific curriculum components may be required by state department of education regulations. In other instances, the district library media coordinator may direct programs to cover a districtwide library skills curriculum to ensure that all students can access information, take adequate notes, and create accurate bibliographies while they increase their literacy skills. With the movement to restructure schools, a schoolwide committee may decide what is taught. At all times, the media specialist must integrate library skills instruction with students' classroom assignments so that the skills are not taught in isolation.

The remaining services to be offered should reflect not only the requirements of a good media program, but also the needs and desires of school personnel, teachers, students, administrators, and parents. One major objective of the media specialist is to try to discover these needs and desires.

One method to determine needs is to expand or modify the listing of services suggested in chapter 4 that the media specialist sends to teachers and students early in the school year. The list could contain present and proposed services. Expectations of additional services could be solicited with an open-ended question and space to write. Asking for such input will give the library media specialist an indication of the reference and research sophistication of the potential users of the library. If their lists are short and most request rather traditional services, it may be that these teachers and students have little or no idea of what should or could be available to them. Their expectations may also be based on their experiences with traditional, limited services in other school library media centers. If they request services that are currently offered, the media specialist must plan an awareness campaign.

A second method to determine library users' needs is to ask respondents to assign rankings of 1 (low preference) to 5 (high preference) to a list of services. This system, with no limits, allows teachers and students to assign a high priority to all items, because no penalty is attached to recognizing the importance of all. That is, teachers can choose to place a high priority, 5, to all services rather than ranking or weighting their preferences. An example follows:

low **high**	
0 1 2 3 4 5	Provides weekly story hour for primary children
0 1 2 3 4 5	Presents book/material talks to encourage reading

The numbers assigned to each service could then be summed, and those with the highest scores given highest priority. If no method of forcing choices between services is attached, it is possible that each service would be rated equally, which would not help the media specialist with setting priorities. The possibility of respondents believing they could receive all services may raise false expectations.

A third way to find out what kind of services library users expect is to offer a list of services that have been, are being, or could be offered. In doing this, the library media specialist might ask which services teachers and students perceive they are receiving. Media specialists may be dismayed to find that teachers are unaware of services available to them, or they may not understand what is being described in the list of services. If a wide discrepancy exists, the media specialist should meet with faculty and try to sort out the confusion. One great value in asking users to select new or expanded services is that it provides new directions for planning.

The sample list of media center services shown in Figure 10.1 can serve as a guide to the development of more specific services for a media center. They may help the media specialist choose wording and add suggested services. This shopping list can become a subtle communication device to increase interest in expanding services into new areas. Teachers may be given 100 points and asked to use them to select from among the choices. A service given 50 points would indicate that the respondent considered that single service as very important. Thus, with this method, the most important services score the highest number of points. A final list shows teacher perceptions of needed services in priority order. That list will help the library media specialist decide which services to offer first and which might be postponed until more staff, materials, equipment, or space is available.

___ Students are helped to improve reading through lists developed to match their interests and to interest them.

___ Media center staff assists students to develop information literacy skills.

___ Media center staff assists students to develop digital literacy skills.

___ Media center staff assists students to develop technology literacy skills.

___ Media center staff provides links to appropriate Web sites to support unit assignments.

___ Photo-duplication service is provided.

___ Online database searching is available for students, teachers, administrators.

___ Interlibrary loan service is provided for students, teachers, administrators.

___ Internet access is available for students, teachers, administrators.

___ A wireless cart with 25 laptops is available for classroom use.

___ Students are told about materials available in academic, public, and special libraries in the area.

___ Materials in heavy demand are reserved for individual students and teachers.

___ Individual students may come to the media center.

___ Classrooms may visit the media center.

___ Instruction in the use of resources in the media center is tied directly to the curriculum unit being taught.

___ Online database searching is taught to all students.

___ Access to the online public access catalog and online databases is available in classrooms.

___ The media specialist regularly provides information about new resources for teachers.

Figure 10.1 Sample List of Library Media Center Service

However the original list of services is selected, responses should be studied to determine the feasibility of the requests. A second list should then be compiled and resubmitted for further priority ranking. This can be accomplished in a variety of ways. Perhaps the simplest is to ask teachers and students to indicate "yes" if they would like the service and "no" if not.

If this survey is less successful than one might wish, it may be that some teachers and administrators do not use the media center because they are unaware of the possible resources available to them. They do not know how to select materials, operate equipment, search online databases, or collaborate in the development of units of instruction, which will include guided-inquiry principles. They may have attended schools where they were not taught these skills, or they may have had unpleasant experiences trying to find information. One important service that media specialists may offer teachers is a good in-service program to acquaint them with the resources of the media center and their potential uses and to introduce them to new resources and new technologies as they arrive or demonstrate how to collaborate effectively with other teachers.

CONDUCTING IN-SERVICE TRAINING SESSIONS

The school library media specialist is a catalyst in planning and leading in-service training sessions. Some of this responsibility may be undertaken by the establishment of new professional learning communities. School administrators are under exceptional pressure from the requirements of No Child Left Behind legislation, individual state standards, district mandate, and community interests to change, improve, and produce high student achievement test results. The challenges of educating students to high standards are complicated by the needs of various at-risk student populations, such as students with disabilities, socioeconomically disadvantaged, English language learners, and ethnic groups. Increasingly, educators speak of professional learning communities as a strategy for school improvement.

When in place, professional learning communities focus staff development activities on change processes to improve student learning. Professional learning communities have five important attributes:

- Supportive and shared leadership
- Shared values and vision
- Supportive conditions
- Shared personal practice
- Collective creativitiy[15]

Library media specialists can be major players in carrying out these attributes. They understand the values and vision of the school; and they know all the teachers and how they teach, all the students and how they learn, and all the curriculum. The library media specialist can make sure that programs are supporting these goals. Library media specialists are a part of the collaborative teaching teams because they know the resources available when teachers are making unit plans. Because they don't belong to a particular department or grade level, they can integrate lesson plans across grade levels and across curriculum areas. When library media specialists have an open schedule for the media center, they are available to help students and teachers at the exact time they need help.

A professional learning community allows library media specialists to consolidate the collective creativity of teachers, providing an active role within subgroups in the school. Library media specialists are teachers with no vested interest in any curriculum area or grade level. They can organize teachers into collaborative efforts to present lessons that span the curriculum. This effort can be a part of the professional learning community.

The professional learning community is based on continuous adult learning, and time is scheduled for teachers to collaborate with other teachers and support staff. Democratic participation leads to consensus about the school culture and environment, and, most importantly, how individuals will work together to attain the results they want. Educators talk with one another about their practice, share their knowledge, observe each other, and applaud one another's success.

Setting aside time for professional learning communities to meet allows new relationships between teachers and library media specialists. Having assigned time to meet was not possible in the past. Library media specialists strive to attend these planning, collaboration, and staff development meetings so that the scheduling of the media center is in place and resources can be available when needed. An effective school librarian will see many opportunities to integrate information literacy lessons "just in time" for major projects and units of instruction teachers are planning.

When there is no professional learning community, the school library media specialist assumes responsibility for good in-service programs. Good in-service programs grow out of problems perceived as significant to teachers or administrators. A needs assessment is necessary to determine these problem areas, although the needs assessment may be an informal query. Few teachers and even fewer administrators are eager to admit they lack information-seeking skills; they are reluctant to ask for assistance in finding or using resources or equipment, and they may be fearful of technologies they have not used. They may be reluctant to want to use technologies because they don't have the skills they know their students have. It is up to the media specialist to train them.

Certainly, if the library media specialist hopes to have an effective in-service program, teachers should be involved in planning it. Their input will ensure that the media specialist starts where the group is and takes it as far as possible in the time allocated.

The library media specialist sets goals and objectives for any training session, and then keeps these in focus. Some teachers may try to turn the group in another direction. Keeping an audience on task, particularly a group of peers with whom one works on a daily basis, is accomplished more easily when objectives are shared and accepted by the participants.

One of the most important services the media specialist can offer staff and students is training sessions that will keep them aware of and capable of participating in educational innovations and, most especially, using the new technologies as they evolve. This is a complicated issue simply because the technologies change so rapidly.

Keeping faculty aware of educational innovation is an ongoing process, not a yearly presentation. This awareness has several levels. The first is the quick presentation at regular teachers' meetings. This type of update will occur frequently because new resources, new trends, and new technologies are evolving constantly. These presentations must always be interesting and short—a preview designed to draw those interested into the media center for more.

A next level is being asked to help plan in-service days for teaching staff where the media specialist is expected to recommend presenters and consultants. This list is made up of faculty at schools of education in nearby colleges. Checking with administrators and teachers in your school and in other schools in the district who attend professional association meetings may add to this list. If they have heard someone who has a message for the staff, the person and the topic are recorded. If more funding is available, knowing who is outstanding on the state or national circuit is important. Not all experts are good presenters. If the media specialist cannot hear the speaker before scheduling a date at the school, it is essential to ask those who have heard the speaker for their opinion.

More likely, the media specialist will be planning in-service for the building-level personnel only, during regularly scheduled in-service days or a teachers' meeting. The media specialist who is trying to teach the use of any resource or technology should allow participants time for ample practice. Nothing is as futile as explaining the use of a digital camera to a large audience, many of whom cannot even see the camera. If the purpose is to teach simple photography, each participant should have an opportunity to take several shots and download the images during the in-service sessions. If teachers are going to learn how to access a new database or use a new Web site, they must first be taught how to access the database, how to locate information, and how to download any chosen resources. Hands-on experience is essential.

To conduct effective in-service sessions, the media specialist must have necessary resources and materials on hand. Enough digital cameras or computers with online access must be available for each participant. The size of the audience should be limited to provide sufficient resources to conduct the training session. The time when two people could share a computer is in the past. Now each person needs to directly experience the technology being introduced.

Expertise is essential for the trainer. If the library media specialist is uncertain about to how the training should be presented, an outside consultant should be brought in. In some situations, an outside consultant may be preferable even though the library media specialist is competent to conduct the training. This is especially true if the media specialist is trying to sell the faculty on a new technology or a new service. An outside presenter can help strengthen the case without appearing to be self-serving.

The successful in-service trainer takes the group as far as possible in the time allotted. To do this, each participant must be made to feel a vital part of the experience. Careful attention should be paid to individuals in the audience to confirm that they are following the process and understanding the instructions, keeping up with the pace of the presentation, and succeeding at the assigned tasks. One person lagging behind should be helped individually, allowing the trainer to continue. Depending on the difficulty of the proposed session, additional staff may be needed to make sure the presentation moves forward as rapidly as possible.

Evaluation of the in-service session will help determine the audience's approval of the information received, the success of the experience, and the need for the next level of this training or a change to another topic. As with any evaluation process, the changes that are needed before presenting another session will be apparent. The skills of the outside consultant are assessed to determine whether this person should be asked to present again.

Whatever is planned, the program must be considered as it affects the instructional program and use of the library media center. Through an effective in-service training program, the library media specialist has an opportunity to reach reluctant teachers and to expand the services of the media center into all classrooms.

Certainly no library media specialist should promise to provide a service that is beyond the present staff, facility, collection, or budget. However, no change can be made in the condition of the media center if no new services are suggested. Small pilot programs may be implemented to see whether they result in better service to teachers and students. Successful pilot programs can be proposed for continued funding in the next year's budget. Costing out the pilot, using methods discussed in chapter 9, will help the media specialist assign a real dollar cost to a service rather than an estimate.

This author is concerned about some less-critical services offered to students and teachers to the neglect of essential services. It is far more important to work with teachers and curriculum than to catalog and process books. It is far more important to work with students on their research projects than to send them fine notices, and the time expended in both cases may be equal. Helping to complete projects at the end of the school year and doing preliminary planning for the next year are far more important than taking an inventory. Weighing services to meet needs against management tasks should show services in the winning column.

The most creative media specialist can plan the most helpful services. Even with sufficient staff, quantities of materials, and a pleasant facility, enticing users into the media center remains a major management task. This is discussed in the next chapter.

Exercises

1. Create a list of three or more services you would like to offer your teachers and students. For each service, determine the actual cost in personnel, resources, and equipment.
2. Choose a new technology and design an in-service program to teach students and teachers how to use this technology. Remember to include the supplies, equipment, and other items you will need to present the program.

3. Create a 15-minute presentation to explain information literacy to a group of teachers or parents and the community.
4. If you have access to a school, ask the library media specialist if a teacher makes an assignment that needs to be modified and plan those modifications.

NOTES

1. American Association of School Librarians and Association for Educational Communications and Technology, *Information Power: Building Partnerships for Learning* (Chicago: American Library Association, 1998), 58.

2. American Association of School Librarians. *Standards for the 21st-Century Learner.* (Chicago: American Library Association, 2007), 3.

3. Carol C. Kuhlthau, Leslie K. Maniotes, and Ann K. Caspari, *Guided Inquiry: Learning in the 21st Century* (Westport, CT: Libraries Unlimited, 2007), 1.

4. AASL and AECT, *Information Power*, 58.

5. Nancy Miller, *Impact* (San Jose, CA: Hi Willow Research and Publishing, 2003).

6. AASL, *Standards for the 21st-Century Learner*, 6.

7. Ibid., 3.

8. Kristen Fontichiaro, *Active Learning through Drama, Podcasting, and Puppetry* (Westport, CT: Libraries Unlimited, 2007), xi.

9. Violet H. Harada and Joan M. Yoshina, *Assessing Learning: Librarians and Teachers as Partners* (Westport, CT: Libraries Unlimited, 2007).

10. *School Library Media Activities Monthly* is a publication available from LMS Associates, 17 East Henrietta Street, Baltimore, MD 21230; *Library Media Connection* is published by Linworth Publishing, 480 E. Wilson Bridge Road, Suite L, Worthington, OH 43085.

11. AASL and AECT, *Information Power*, 72.

12. California School Library Association, *From Library Skills to Information Literacy: A Handbook for the 21st Century*, 2nd ed. (San Jose, CA: Hi Willow Research and Publishing, 1997); Michael B. Eisenberg and Robert E. Berkowitz, *Information Problem-Solving: The Big Six Skills Approach to Library and Information Skills Instruction* (Norwood, NJ: Ablex, 1990); Barbara K. Stripling and Judy M. Pitts, *Brainstorms and Blueprints* (Englewood, CO: Libraries Unlimited, 1988); Carol C. Kuhlthau, *Seeking Meaning: A Process Approach to Delivery and Information Service* (Norwood, NJ: Ablex, 1993; and Alice H. Yucht, *Flip It! An Information Skills Strategy for Student Researchers* (Worthington, OH: Linworth, 1997), among others.

13. Kuhlthau, *Seeking Meaning*, 25.

14. Ibid., 17–18.

15. Richard DuFour, Robert Eaker, and Rebecca DuFour, *On Common Ground: The Power of Professional Learning Communities* (Bloomington, IN: National Education Service, 2005).

11

On the Job: School Library Media Centers and the Reading Program

One of the common beliefs in *Standards for the 21st-Century Learner* is that "Reading is a window to the world,"[1] naming reading as a fundamental skill. If students are to learn, to grow, and to enjoy school, they must be able to read and understand text. Knowing how to read goes beyond success in school and becomes a lifelong skill that helps them comprehend and interpret information and develop new understandings. This is not a new belief.

A major priority of school library media programs has traditionally been the reading program. Henry Cecil and Willard Heaps, in their 1940 *School Library Service in the United States*, credit Governor De Witt Clinton and William L. March of New York and Horace Mann of Massachusetts with traveling to Europe to bring back the best ideas for educating children to put into practice in the United States.

> These educational leaders and others of the day realized that the development of intelligent citizens depended not only upon teaching reading but also on providing reading opportunities. It was for the purpose of providing such opportunities that the school district libraries came into being.[2]

Unfortunately, the educational thinkers of the late nineteenth century did not specify the development of libraries in schools as the ultimate method to teach reading. Certainly library services in elementary schools did not begin or progress with the enthusiasm that these leaders might have envisioned. Two explanations account for this. The first is the activity of the public library. The expansion of public library services to children through the creation of children's rooms and the beginnings of training for children's librarians in the Carnegie Library of Pittsburgh in the early 1900s seemed to meet the need for reading opportunities. Children's librarians provided room collections of 30 or more library books for elementary classrooms and some programming for children. Public librarians were assigned to high school library rooms, and entire library collections were provided. These services thus released school officials from that responsibility in schools. This continued until public librarians realized they could no longer afford the high cost of their service to schools.

The second reason for the slow beginnings of school library services in schools relates to the method of teaching. Reading was taught from reading textbooks written by so-called reading experts. These textbooks did not always appeal to children, particularly children from varied cultural and family backgrounds. The occupations and racial background of parents, life-style, family composition, and the language spoken at home excluded large numbers of children from any relationship to their reading texts. Nevertheless, the basal reader dominated reading instruction through much of the twentieth century.

Individualized reading proponents in the 1960s tried to move children from textbooks into school library books. Each child's spelling and writing exercises were individually created from their choice of book. This was very difficult to implement because it required a great deal of planning for the teachers and also because few school libraries existed in elementary schools. The movement to provide school libraries was more directly related to the need to increase understanding and competency in students, particularly in science and foreign languages, not necessarily to help children learn to read better or faster.

The emphasis on creating and expanding school library programs in the mid-1960s provided the resources for library media specialists to begin extensive reading motivation in the media center. The Right to Read and Head Start programs focused attention on the need for children to learn to read, and media specialists began to offer reading guidance to children. However, this did not seem to progress beyond suggesting books that children might enjoy or giving book talks.

Stepped-up emphasis on getting children to read resulted in the whole language movement, somewhat a revisit to individualized reading from the 1960s, because both used library books rather than readers. California proposed halting the use of reading textbooks and turning to children's books to teach reading, confirming the perception that the whole language movement had great promise to increase reading skills in children. Other states followed. This has seemingly not been any more successful than other methods for teaching children to read. It took only a short time until teachers, with the encouragement of their principals, began to "basalize" children's books, creating work sheets and tests for this new challenge. Textbook publishers eagerly provided classroom collections with multiple paperback copies of popular children's titles. Students were forced to plow through works that were intended by their authors for the enjoyment of reading.

At the present time, many teachers are mandated to use basal reading programs. State test scores are taken yearly to find out the annual progress students are making toward meeting the No Child Left Behind (NCLB) legislation requirements. State departments of education have based their frameworks on the findings[3] reported by the National Reading Panel of the National Institute of Child Health and Human Development. While the findings of this panel have been much debated, the library media specialist should understand the basic components of the report to support teachers.

Reading First, a part of the No Child Left Behind Act, focuses on improving reading instruction. Five key components of effective reading instruction have been identified to guide instructional decisions, and each are to be included in daily reading instruction:

- Phonemic awareness
- Phonics
- Fluency
- Vocabulary
- Text comprehension

Phonemic awareness describes the reader's ability to think analytically about the sounds in words. For example, students who are phonemically aware can blend individual sounds to make words, /k/ + /i/ + /k/ = kick. They can segment the sounds in words, such as the three separate sounds in the word cat = /k/ /a/ /t/. They can isolate initial sounds and identify alliteration in speech. They can also isolate terminal sounds and identify rhymes. They can manipulate sounds within words—for example, changing the medial sound /u/ to /a/ in the word run to get ran. If asked to remove the last sound in the word bark, they will be able to identify the word bar. Phonemic awareness is auditory and oral, meaning it does not include decoding skills or recognizing sound-symbol representations. Phonemic awareness is fundamental, though, to mapping speech to text. If a child cannot hear and identify the initial sounds in baby and buddy as the same, this is a predictor of the inability to connect sounds with their written symbols. Additionally, children who are unable to blend sounds may have great difficulty with blending their symbolic representations during phonics instruction.

Phonics is the systematic relationship between letters of written language and the individual sounds. Phonics instruction must be direct and explicit. For those who have had no introduction to methods of teaching reading, the English language presents some distinct challenges. One reading program developed in the late 1960s in England tried to overcome the challenge of the English alphabet where one letter represents one sound, two or more letters can represent one sound, and many words have letters that are silent. Readers were developed with an "initial teaching alphabet" using additional "letters" to carry the appropriate sound. Students were expected to be able to transfer to regular reading texts after their beginning instruction. Phonics instruction, according to the National Reading Panel, should be taught systematically to kindergarten and first grade children.

Fluency, according to Ellery, "represents a level of expertise in combining appropriate phrasing and intonation while reading words automatically."[4] Teachers regularly record the accuracy and speed of oral reading to assess a student's reading level and fluency, but this also occurs during silent reading. Some might equate fluency only with speed and accuracy, but to be truly fluent, the reader must understand the content and be able to interpret it. Fluency is the link between phonetic decoding and comprehension. One suggestion for helping students increase their fluency is to do choral reading and readers' theater. The library media specialist can help with materials to do this.

Students must be able to understand the meaning of words they read in the text. This is the vocabulary part of the key literary topics. They must be able to recognize and understand words and use these understandings to construct meaning in a text. Furthermore, vocabulary is not only a key factor in reading comprehension, it is also essential for effective listening, speaking, and writing.

Students who understand what they are reading learn and grow into life-long readers. Comprehension skills require students to be active and purpose-ful participants in the processing of text. They must understand why they are reading, use strategies and self-monitor for understanding during reading, and process the text after they have read. Teachers can help before students begin by trying to determine the students' past knowledge about the subject and discussing any unfamiliar words the reader might encounter. While they are reading, students should be making connections between the text and what they know. Text-to-self connections occur when something they read re-minds them of something in their own life experience. Text-to-text connections occur when they relate something they are reading now to something they've read in the past. They also can make a text-to-world connection, where they connect the text to something they heard or saw, perhaps on radio or televi-sion. Additionally, comprehension includes visualization, meaning students create pictures in their minds of the text. Students should be able to create questions about what they have read, make inferences and predictions based on evidence from the text, and explain how a text is personally meaningful. Post reading activities might include writing activities that summarize, review, analyze, or evaluate the text. Writing a personal response, dramatic activities, and extended research are creative ways of asking students to show their com-prehension of what they read.[5] Many post reading activities give teachers and media specialists opportunities to collaborate.

The above discussion addresses the challenge of teaching reading in the elementary grades. An even greater challenge exists with students who have not learned to read in the lower grades and now need intensive intervention in high school. If you are working with high school students, you may need to help the teachers even more, because they will have had less experience with teaching reading than their elementary counterparts. Bromley has a list of nine things high school teachers should remember about words and word learning in vocabulary in their content areas.

1. English is a huge and unique collection of words.
2. The rules of English are simple and consistent compared to other languages.
3. Language and proficiency grows from oral competence to written competence.
4. Words are learned because of associations that connect the new with the known.
5. Seventy percent of the most frequently used words have multiple meanings.
6. Meanings of 60 percent of multisyllabic words can be inferred by analyzing word parts.

7. Direct instruction in vocabulary influences comprehension more than any other factor.

8. Teaching fewer words well is more effective than teaching several words in a cursory way.

9. Effective teachers display an attitude of excitement and interest in words and language.[6]

This list doesn't promote any specific activity for the school library media specialist except to share it with teachers. Ten strategies to promote literacy are proposed by Thomas and Wexler. Their evidence-based strategies to use in the classroom, include the following:

1. Ask for help.
2. Support word recognition needs.
3. Select appropriate materials.
4. Develop reading fluency.
5. Foster vocabulary acquisition.
6. Build comprehension.
7. Monitor student progress.
8. Differentiate instruction.
9. Group students effectively.
10. Embrace more flexible ideas about reading materials.[7]

With regard to this list, the school library media specialist can help especially with selecting appropriate materials and promoting flexible ideas about reading materials. Helping the teacher select appropriate materials to encourage reading and working to build more flexible ideas about materials to encourage reading are a part of the role. A broad collection of materials is needed to fulfill this role.

Another writer suggests that "when we inundate older struggling readers with superficial and lifeless reading and writing tasks that bear no resemblance to the reading and writing they encounter in the real world, we ensure their status as outsiders in the real literate community."[8] We need to surround students with a library media collection that will be interesting to them and that will have a wide variety of books using a vocabulary that they can read, not necessarily easily, but with the possibility of achieving meaning as they read.

Middle and high school teachers might be encouraged to read briefly to students at the beginning of the class period. It is a good method to help students settle in their seats. Library media specialists can offer teachers suggestions of quick reads from current news, biographies of persons important to the subject being taught, or anything relative to the course. This can give students something else to consider beyond the immediate assignment. It also shows that all the teachers believe reading is important.

Perhaps the greatest damage to high school students is that poor readers fail in their classes, and they are at greatest risk of dropping out of high school. Having materials that they can read and use to complete their assignments is critical. They need ready access to good books.

Ready Access to a Good Book Helps
Improve Reading Skills

When Stephen Krashen revised his landmark publication, *The Power of Reading,* in 2004, he retained:

> There is abundant evidence that literacy development can occur without formal instruction. Moreover, this evidence strongly suggests that reading is potent enough to do nearly the entire job alone.[9]

Krashen reports the results of "read and test" studies, where students read text with vocabulary that is unfamiliar to them. They were not told they would be given a vocabulary or spelling test. Rather, they were tested to see whether they learned any of the meanings of unfamiliar words. Acquisition of vocabulary and spelling occurred without skill-building or correction, which shows that literacy development can occur without instruction.[10] Krashen summarizes

> In-school free reading studies and "out of school" self-reported free voluntary reading studies show that more reading results in better reading comprehension, writing style, vocabulary, spelling, and grammatical development.[11]

To apply these research findings in elementary schools, school library media specialists must allow as much free voluntary reading time as possible. A case can be made for using the entire time students are assigned to the media center to read and read and read. This research supports the value of having free voluntary reading in schools where students are assigned to the media center during the teacher's planning period.

Rather than attempting to teach some isolated library skill, the librarian can teach reading by allowing students to read.

> Average reading scale scores for 9- and 13-year-old students were higher in 1996 than in 1971. Scores for both 13- and 17-year-old students showed a positive linear trend, indicating a gradual rise in scores for the period 1971–1996. Scores for both 9- and 17-year-old students showed a negative quadratic trend, indicating that scores had increased, but then either declined or flattened out. Reading scores for most but not all student subgroups were higher in 1996 than in 1971, particularly in the 13- and 9-year-old age groups. Black students recorded increases in all three age levels. However, scores for many subgroups showed a pattern of increase in the 1980s, followed by a decline or a flattening out in the 1990s. Reading scores for 17-year-old black students have been increased even as dropout rates have been falling.[12]

In January 1998, the National Center for Education Statistics reported "Long-Term Trends in Student Reading Performance." Their conclusions were as follows:

> Acceptable levels of literacy are achieved by most pupils, in most systems, despite a diversity of reading methods and traditions. In general, however, achievement is greatest when the educational systems are well

endowed financially, when teachers are well educated, when students have ready access to good books, when they enjoy reading and do it often, and when their first language is the same as that of the language of the school.[13]

While the financial endowments of school systems and the educational qualifications of teachers fall outside the responsibility of most library media specialists, we are responsible for a students having ready access to good books. Research confirms the need for a wide variety of materials to entice interest in reading for students.

The connection between the amount of reading done and reading proficiency has been well known and accepted for a number of years. Less well known but of equal importance has been the finding that more access to reading materials *leads* to more reading, and subsequently higher reading achievement, and can itself explain a great deal of variation in reading scores.[14]
Elley found that the size of the school library was the number one factor distinguishing the reading scores of nine-year-olds between the high and low scoring nations, with an impressive effect size of .82. Frequent silent reading time was the next most important variable, with an effect size of .78.[15]

McQuillan closes his book with

There is now considerable evidence that the amount and quality of students' access to reading materials is substantively related to the amount of reading they engage in, which in turn is the most important determinant of reading achievement. Many students attend schools where the level of print access is abysmal, creating a true crisis in reading performance. . . . I do *not* wish to argue that simply providing books is all that is needed for schools to success. . . . But just as we would not ask a doctor to heal without medicine, so we should not ask teachers and schools to teach without the materials to do so.[16]

Commercial Reading Incentive and Software Programs

School library media specialists are often asked by their administrators to participate in and coordinate reading initiatives. In an effort to increase reading, schools may implement a commercial computerized reading incentive program. Scholastic's *Reading Counts* and Advantage Learning System's *Accelerated Reader* are the two industry leaders of this type of computerized reading program that have proliferated in the past 10 years. With these programs, students read from specific books, generally obtained from the core fiction collection of the school library. After reading the book, the students then take a computer test over what they just read. Points are awarded based on the correct number of answers and the length and difficulty of the book. Although both the incentive industry and educators agree that these tests do not measure true comprehension or higher-order thinking skills, it is also established that they do measure basic recall and the amount of text that has been processed.

Disagreement about the effectiveness of these programs is often debated with two major recurring themes: (1) teachers may use points to assign reading grades; and (2) reading is not connected to its misuse of the points and program intrinsic rewards, but instead an external reward is used to coerce reading as a means to get prizes. The literature has articles in favor of and against the use of such external reward systems. Unfortunately, some of the research has been conducted by the developers themselves rather than independent researchers, and it is not surprising that their research reports that the programs are effective.

Commercial incentive programs can become a real problem or a boon to library media specialists. On the positive side, libraries will generally require a larger and newer book collection to support the increased demand and use of books. Administrators and parents that support these programs will generally provide funds to implement them. As long as the money is *in addition to* the amount needed to implement a balanced collection development policy, this is a way to grow a library media center's collection. Initially, at least, the students will also tend to read a significantly larger number of books and visit the library more often in their quest for points. Teachers are likely to rely more heavily on the library media specialist to support the reading program, and to realize the importance of increased access opportunities for their students. Difficulties can occur if the collection development policy is ignored when teachers (or parents) insist that only books available from and tested by these programs be added to the collection. Additionally, a school that makes a small initial investment in one of these programs may have a very limited number of quizzes. This can cause students to limit their selections to a small number of options and discourage reading choice based on interest. Once a school is firmly entrenched with an incentive program, library media specialists may find that students will resist checking out books (even the brand new fiction) unless a quiz is available because they can't earn credit for reading them.

It is debatable whether extrinsic rewards provide the literacy development that reading alone can do. School library media specialists can help teachers understand that the score from a computer test taken by their students does not necessarily indicate an understanding of the content of what has been read. Using the computerized reading program as a way of measuring reading practice and time on task may simplify record-keeping and verify that students have actually read books, which is something that self-reported reading logs do not. Krashen reports

> Despite the popularity of [a reading management program], we must conclude that there is no real evidence supporting it, no real evidence that the additional tests and rewards add anything to the power of simply supplying access to high-quality and interesting reading material and providing time for children to read.[17]

School library media specialists may implement creative reading initiatives that are successful by keeping reading voluntary, linking it to intrinsic rewards, and maintaining a relationship with teachers to support a strong reading instruction program instead of supplanting it.

Sharing Reading Research

No one doubts that the world is welcoming the advent of telecommunications to provide instantaneous access to information, but this merely intensifies the emphasis on reading. To understand most information on a computer screen, one must be able to read and interpret the language of the information. Students must know how to read, and they will learn when they are in schools with strong reading programs. Research shows that reading programs are stronger when they are supported with an excellent collection of materials in the school library media center. This and other research on reading helps teachers learn best practices. School library media specialists should be aware of the latest reading research and share it with teachers.

Fisher and Ivey[18] suggested that the traditional practice of assigning all students to read the same book at the same time results in a singularly unenthusiastic approach to the enjoyment of literature. Even high-achieving students take shortcuts just to finish assignments. In some cases, this is a part of state content standards, but school library media specialists can help teachers move away from requiring students to read the same book by providing a list of quality options within a theme that will allow students choice and keep them engaged.

Because the media center has current and ongoing subscriptions to professional journals in the professional collection, school library media specialists should search the reading research for results they can share with teachers. Teachers are often pressured to implement the next educational fad, just as they have been with NCLB. Keeping teachers informed will help them structure programs using the media center. Examples include the Partners in Reading, Partners in Life program, in which eighth grade language arts students read books with senior citizen volunteers,[19] and Moss and Hendershot's "Exploring Sixth Graders' Selection of Nonfiction Trade Books."[20] Sharing research creates the opportunity for you the library media specialist to share in the implementation of a reading program, and everyone wins. When library media specialists work with teachers to improve reading proficiency, they are helping learners use their skills, resources, and tools to inquire, think critically, and gain knowledge as prescribed in *Standards for 21st-Century Learners.*

Exercises

1. Visit an elementary classroom teacher and talk about how he or she has been working with students to improve their reading. Try to determine how the media specialist might work with this teacher and that plan.
2. Choose a middle or high school teacher and create a bibliography of resources for quick reads for the beginning of classes either every day or weekly.
3. Propose a program that would encourage readers in a school. This could be a very short program or it might be one that continues for a semester.

NOTES

1. American Association of School Librarians. *Standards for the 21st-Century Learner.* (Chicago: American Library Association, 2007), 2.

2. Henry L. Cecil and Willard A. Heaps, *School Library Service in the United States: An Interpretative Survey* (New York: H. W. Wilson, 1940), 41. Reprinted in Melvin M. Bowie, *Historic Documents of School Libraries* (Englewood, CO: Hi Willow Research and Publishing, 1986).

3. National Institute of Child Health and Human Development, *Teaching Children to Read: An Evidence-Based Assessment of the Scientific Research on Reading and Its Implications for Reading Instruction: Report of the National Reading Panel* (Washington, DC: National Institute of Child Health and Human Development, National Institutes of Health, 2000).

4. Warwick B. Ellery, *Creating Strategic Readers: Techniques for Developing Competency in Phonemic Awareness, Phonics Fluency, Vocabulary, and Comprehension* (Newark, DE: International Reading Association, 2005), 77.

5. Elaine M. Bukowiecki, "Teaching Children How to READ," *Kappa Delta Pi Record 43* (Winter 2007): 63.

6. Karen Bromley, "Nine Things Every Teacher Should Know about Words and Vocabulary Instructions," *Journal of Adolescent & Adult Literacy* 50 (April 2007): 528–37.

7. Cathy Newman Thomas and Jade Wexler, "Ways to Teach and Support Struggling Adolescent Readers," *Kappa Delta Pi Record* 44 (Fall 2007): 22–27.

8. Douglas Fisher and Gay Ivey, "Evaluating the Interventions for Struggling Adolescent Readers," *Journal of Adolescent & Adult Literacy* 50 (November 2006): 182.

9. Stephen Krashen, *The Power of Reading*, 2nd ed. (Englewood, CO: Libraries Unlimited, 2004): 20.

10. Ibid., 13.

11. Ibid., 17.

12. National Center for Education Statistics, *NAEP Facts*, U.S. Department of Education, Office of Education Research and Improvement, *NAEP Facts* Vol. 3, No. 1, (January 1998).

13. Ibid.

14. Warwick B. Elley, "Lifting Literacy Levels in Developing Countries: Some Implications from an IEA Study, in *Promoting Reading in Developing Countries: Views on Making Reading Materials Accessible to Increase Literacy Levels*, ed. V. Greaney (Newark, DE: International Reading Association, 1996), xxi–xxii.

15. Elley, "Lifting Literacy Levels," xxi-xxii.

16. McQuillan, *The Literacy Crisis*, 86.

17. Krashen, *The Power of Reading*, 121.

18. Douglas Fisher and Gay Ivey, "Farewell to 'A Farewell to Arms': Deemphasizing the Whole-Class Novel," *Phi Delta Kappan* 88 (March 2007): 494–7.

19. Anne DiPardo and Pat Schnack, "Partners in Reading, Partners in Life," *Educational Leadership* 60 (March 2003): 56–58.

20. Barbara Moss and Judith Hendershot, "Exploring Sixth Graders' Selection of Nonfiction Trade Books," *The Reading Teacher* 56 (September 2002): 6–17.

Chapter 12

On the Job: Advocacy and the Media Center

The importance of the school library media program seems apparent to media specialists. However, this is not an automatic reaction for all teachers, administrators, and parents. For school library media programs to be given the appropriate high priority in funding and staffing plans, an advocacy program must be developed, implemented, and kept on the alert. Being aware when attention is needed to the keep the media program at the center of the school is a major assignment for library media specialists. If no such efforts are made, the media program becomes one of the first areas to be targeted for reduction or elimination when budget cuts are mandated. Advocacy begins with an analysis of the program and determining the best way to market its components.

Many media specialists lament inappropriate use of materials and facility by their colleagues, who sometimes send students from the study hall to the media center with no assignment or who do not give students assignments that encourage them to use the media center. Moreover, support of colleagues is often lacking when the need for funding cuts arises. When the school media program lacks affirmative perception in the eyes of teachers, students, parents, and administrators, the media program becomes an easy mark. While marketing a poor program is false advertising, the media specialist with a good program must make sure that the community recognizes the impact of the media program and services on teacher success and student learning. Only when users are aware of the quality and importance of the services will they fight to preserve them.

Appropriately marketing the media center builds a proper image and encourages appropriate use of the media center. When library media specialists understand, plan, and implement successful marketing projects, they draw affirmative attention to the media center program. This chapter outlines some measures for marketing a school library media program. Others suggestions are in the literature.

Several books[1] address the topic of public relations in libraries and specifically for school librarians. This section begins with a broader view of the topic, looking to the marketing world for models to build a public relations program.

According to Philip Kotler, marketing is the "purposeful coalescence of people, materials and facilities seeking to accomplish some purpose."[2] If this definition is translated into the coalescence of teachers and media specialists seeking to prepare students for adult society, marketing the media center should involve the selling of services and use of the collection. The media center staff plans how to sell these services to teachers. Teachers, in turn, join with the staff to sell available resources and information to students to increase their ability to learn. The media center staff markets its image to gain budget support for increasing services, and the circle continues.

The success of the marketing campaign can be confirmed when it is the campaign of teachers and students to halt any proposals for cutting media center services. When teachers and students are able, willing, and eager to articulate the importance and value of the media center in teaching and learning, the media center will, indeed, be the center of the school.

Before discussing the process of a successful marketing plan, it is necessary to present some aspects of the media center that produce bad impressions. Teachers and administrators, not understanding the administrative process in the media center, may misinterpret an activity. The school library media specialist must exercise care to ensure that activities in the media center that are observed by persons other than media staff are acceptable to most. Activities that produce negative reactions should take place elsewhere or not at all.

Among the ill-favored actions of media specialists are levying fines, closing the library to take inventory, returning misbehaving students to the teacher, and reacting negatively to student and teacher requests for service. Conversely, positive image builders include collaborating with teachers, participating in a helpful manner in all curricular changes, searching for needed information in a variety of sources outside the school, and making special efforts for teachers and students. Paying attention to the ambiance of the media center means changing bulletin boards and showcases frequently, displaying student work, and keeping the center busy with happy users. Media specialists use a variety of activities to draw users to the library.

Because administrators and teachers often view the media center based on past experiences, they may need to be reminded of its true role in teaching and learning. The school library media specialist needs to understand marketing techniques that go beyond suggestions made in a meeting or anticipating a response to an idea discussed over lunch. It may seem that too few hours are available in the school day even to consider such an uncertain return on the investment of time; in fact, marketing is an essential investment for the media center manager.

From a management standpoint, marketing is the "managerial process involving analysis, planning, implementation, and control."[3] In the broadest sense, it is the bringing together of producer and consumer. To carry on the marketing function, the individual must attract sufficient resources; convert resources into products, services, and ideas; and distribute outputs to various consuming publics.

The marketer, by giving something, acquires something in return. The successful marketer researches the anticipated needs of the persons to whom this exchange is directed, designs a product they cannot ignore, generates an absolute need for the product in the potential recipient, and communicates at an appropriate time and in an appropriate place.

School library media specialists are in the unique position of being able to provide large numbers of materials for clientele at no immediate or apparent cost to them. The media center is full of products that can easily become "gifts" the teacher or student cannot refuse if those gifts are marketed at the appropriate time and place.

Marketing has three facets the library media specialist must consider: public awareness, dissemination of information (which may be a part of public awareness), and development of services to meet needs based on marketing research. The first, a public awareness program for the media center, is centered on the person in charge.

A basic problem for marketing remains with personnel, a problem not unique to education or media centers. Media center staff—both personally and through the programs and information services they offer—must project a strong, helpful image to all the students and adults in the building, from kindergarten through high school, and including custodians, clerical staff, cafeteria workers, bus drivers, teachers, administrators, and parents. Media specialists represent all persons in the library and media world to the clients they serve, particularly if those clients make little or no use of any other information agency.

Dissemination of information as part of public awareness to draw attention to the media center and its services includes providing information that may not be perceived as essential but that will be useful. Patrons might not seem to be eagerly awaiting a list of recently purchased materials. Only the more aggressive media center clients ask, "What's new?" Nevertheless, sending a list of new materials and additional access to new databases to classrooms will draw students and teachers into the center to pursue topics that interest them.

The process of developing services based on marketing research is another facet of the marketing process and was discussed in chapter 10. Obviously, the services offered by the media center should be a combination of services that users deem necessary (determined through market research) and services the media specialist identifies as necessary and appropriate for curriculum integration and support.

A wide gulf exists between offering services and clientele use of those services. Getting users to the media center to use the services is another component of the marketing process. If teachers receive a warm welcome when they appear to collect media, produce a sign, search a database, or look up the price of materials they wish to purchase, they will carry away with them a positive image of media personnel and services. If students are treated as serious scholars rather than nuisances, they will come. If selection and distribution of materials from the media center are simple processes efficiently managed, and if information is provided willingly, correctly, and quickly, the recipient will be willing to enter the center. Placing as few limits as possible on the use of information in the media center or for circulation from the media center keeps the media customer a happy customer. The next question is what offerings will keep the client returning.

WHAT TO MARKET

"Marketing in the firm begins and ends with the customers."[4] To the media specialist, the customers are the media center clientele. To determine what to market, an organization chooses which of its desirable assets it wishes to place for "trade." The primary commodity of any media program is its services. The secondary commodity is the collection itself. Plans should be developed to market the following:

1. Those services determined as priorities by the majority of users. These are the services that must be provided because they are most often requested.
2. Other services that are offered because the need exists. Some of these may be the same as those listed above. Once services are selected to be offered, it is important that all teachers and students be made aware of their existence.
3. Those services that should be provided but may not be requested because teachers or students are not aware of them. Advertising these services will provide a pool of potential users.
4. New services that should be provided and will be used if an area of interest is developed in teachers and students.
5. New materials and databases added to the collection.
6. New equipment available for use in the library or classroom.
7. Special collections available for teachers and students.

Once media personnel have chosen which services to market, they must decide what methods will be most effective to carry out the marketing process.

HOW TO MARKET

The marketing environment comprises consumers and producers and is part of the societal environment. The marketing environment for school library media centers varies from state to state and between regions and local districts within states. Included in the marketing environment is competition from other information agencies, such as bookstores and college, public, home, and classroom libraries. Also included in this environment are the suppliers and producers of products and services that are secured by media professionals to place in centers. Producers of materials for media centers include commercial vendors as well as staff and services of the production center in the media center itself. Finally, it is hoped that happy media center users will become consumer advocates.

Media specialists become *producers* who must anticipate the consumer marketplace and then offer something of value to the media center clientele as *consumers*. A planned market offering of products, services, promotion, distribution, and, in some cases, pricing (e.g., copying costs) is developed. Certainly, school library media specialists want to anticipate the market. Just as commercial vendors send sales representatives out to do just that, the media specialist must leave the media center and meet the clientele in the classroom and the corridors. If media specialists are to anticipate markets for their products and services using the business model, they must leave the library media center to learn about clientele needs.

In the marketing world, the consumers return something of value to the producers. If the product is offered for a cash value, the return is a dollar amount. For media specialists as producers, the value received is a much less tangible reward, such as a satisfied customer's smile, a thank you, or "Boy, was this a good book!" The teacher's return to plan another unit is another reward.

The *market offerings* of product or service for the media program are the media (products) and the methods of using them (services). *Promotion* becomes a marketing plan, which will be discussed in depth later in this chapter. *Distribution* is the system that provides the product, service, or information requested by the consumer. Distribution in the media center is translated into access to and ease of use of information. In most areas of the media program, *pricing* is not a consideration because services are and should be free. All types of librarians have been debating fee versus free services, usually connected to a need to be reimbursed for some recurring cost that may or may not be used by all students, such as photocopying or making prints of resources found during database searching. However, funding for photocopying or paper and printer ink might be better provided by a project of a school club. The library media specialist might be able to limit the number of copies made by a single student. When the ceiling is reached, a student might be asked to help support the system.

Market planning is the "act of specifying in detail what will be done, by whom, to whom, with what and when, to achieve the organization's objectives."[5] Market planning resembles the process described in the section on proposal writing in chapter 9. It begins with setting goals and objectives for the planning process for the district or school media program, developing a proposal for funding, or writing educational objectives for a new facility. The four steps in this process and some additional suggestions follow.

The first step is to analyze the situation—that is, conduct a *market analysis*. A market analysis may resemble the needs assessment conducted for program planning. Media specialists should not spend time trying to convince teachers or students to use services they consider of little value. Library media specialists have products to sell that are essential if teachers are to have the best teaching materials and students are to be given the best opportunities to learn. At times, these products may be perceived to be less helpful because of the difficulty of securing them, the lack of quality of the products, or simply the audience's lack of awareness of their existence. To use an example of a library media specialist who determines the need for better management of the current events literature, the market analysis might include addressing the following considerations. Should print periodical subscriptions continue at their present level or should these funds be reallocated to online databases? Students are unable or unwilling to locate current information for class reports in print resources and are concerned about the length of time between requesting a periodical from the stacks and receiving it. Also, they want to use a simple search engine to retrieve a topic.

The second step is to develop a strategy for what to do and how to do it. This also resembles a step in responding to a request for proposal, that of planning activities. What can be done to meet the need within the constraints of the media center and its services and yet help students find relevant information? For the current events literature example, the media specialist, collaborating with the teacher, bookmarks Web sites with appropriate information on the topic and plans to present effective search strategies for online databases. The clerk records the provision of research information in periodical literature for two weeks in comparison to the use of the Internet.

A test is completed using two measures. The first is to ask students preparing a research paper for one class to record their success or failure in finding information in the periodical collection and also to note the amount of time between requesting and receiving a magazine from the stacks. The second measure is for the library media specialist to record use of computers available for this research. The library clerk is asked to turn through three years of *Time* magazine and note the number of articles that have been cut from the issues. Finally, a review of the bibliographies in the research paper indicates the sources of information.

The probable result of this brief marketing strategy will show that providing back issues of periodicals for research is less useful and that the solution is to provide fewer periodicals in print and others from full-text databases with collaborative teacher and media specialist teaching about using appropriate online resources rather than a short-cut search engine. This moves to the second outcome, the need for more computers and more training in the use of online resources.

Because online access to full-text articles may require sharing limited equipment, media specialists offer in-service sessions with teachers and students to demonstrate any new equipment and new database searching processes so that searching will be efficient. Students can be involved in developing the rules for sharing computers in the media center. Although many schools are moving into wireless technology and others are providing laptops for students, this is still an expensive alternative.

Step three evaluates the effectiveness of all activities. A good evaluation technique is to keep brief records of any comments made about the quality of materials located. From the pre-project record of the number of uses of print periodicals, it will be easy to determine whether this number goes down and online database use goes up by that amount or more. If students begin using excellent Web sites as much as or more than print, the marketing is successful.

The fourth step is final evaluation. A brief questionnaire is distributed to teachers and students, asking them their opinions about online copies of periodicals, with some questions about if, how, or why they accept or reject these rather than print. The evaluation of papers by the teacher and media specialist with particular attention paid to the bibliographies will also point out the use of online rather than print current information.

A final application of use statistics could establish the need for the availability of more computers in the media center. Documentation that students are not able to find the information they need in the resources on hand in a timely fashion leads to a request for additional computer stations with access to the Internet. It could also indicate a need for an increased budget for a different budget item—for example, printing costs (printer ink cartridges and paper).

In the above example, a marketing strategy is planned and the "sale" is an easy one. It is not difficult to sell students and teachers on the use of online information. The objective is to achieve acceptance of a new format for materials in the media center. When a strategy is less successful and the product is still important, the library media specialist should analyze the marketing process and try a new strategy.

A marketing program is ongoing, and statistics should be available for media center staff to respond instantly to inquiries from parents, community members, teachers, and administrators. For example, major corporations and university athletic departments publish fact books for the news media. General information on the media program should include statistics about the media center—its size, amount of seating, numbers of volumes, media and databases, budget, amount of use by class and individuals, and type of use (e.g., storytelling, viewing, research, online searching). Output measures such as circulation figures should be included, as well as interesting input measures such as the number of new resources purchased each year and the average cost of each, from books through databases and hardware. The fact book might also contain a description and photos of the facility. Finally, information should be included concerning collaborative unit development using the computer-generated graphics described in chapter 10.

Marketing experts also suggest that an image be selected for the media center—an image that can change from time to time. Students might be asked to help choose a theme for the year and to suggest ways to follow through with an ongoing plan to keep the media center in the center of attention at the school.

To maintain a full marketing program, the media specialist should ask the following questions. First, what is the time frame for market planning? Weekly, monthly, or annually? If survival is an issue, more frequent market planning should be done. Otherwise, a regularized system can be maintained during monthly staff planning sessions. If this does not happen, then the market plan should be discussed during the first staff meeting of the school year with a follow-up at the beginning of the second semester.

Who should do this planning? In a single-person media center, the planning is done with the advisory committee. Additional assistance is needed for marketing, especially in a single-person center. If the media center has more than one on staff, they must all be involved in planning, because they will all be involved in implementation.

As stated earlier, a marketing plan follows the format of proposal writing. Objectives are developed, the current situation is described, and the expected progress is outlined. Alternative strategies are written for achieving the objectives, with reasons given for each strategy. Specific actions are then listed and any needed budget proposed. Staff members are assigned to specific implementation tasks. Finally, evaluation of each step is indicated, with a time line showing how often to review.

PROMOTION

An important point to remember in marketing planning is that promotion is a form of communication. Kotler lists several promotion tools, which have been modified for the school library media program setting.[6] The first tool, *space and time advertising,* could take the form of an article for the school newspaper. If the school publishes a literary newsletter or magazine with articles by students, the media center could sponsor a well-written book review or other media review. A media column with critiques of films in local theaters could be patterned after the entertainment column in the local newspaper.

Loudspeaker advertising of the media center could be offered through school intercoms. Sometimes the only public relations message that school library media specialists provide is a notice about returning books at the close of the semester (penalty noted: grade cards withheld); this is clearly not a positive marketing mechanism. A better plan would be to announce the winner of the latest reference question quiz. The message should publicize happenings in the media center that will attract students and teachers to the center.

The equivalent of *mailings,* another method of marketing, could be achieved by putting information in teachers' boxes or distributing notices during students' homeroom period. All such messages must be carefully planned with thought given to the type of ads used to sell products. Examples that come to mind are the enclosures highlighting new products or sale items that often accompany billing from credit cards, department stores, or oil companies. If the message is clever, brief, and attractive, it will be read. If not, it will be discarded immediately.

The *sales presentation* could be equated to the presentation of new materials at the teachers' meeting. The presentation should be relaxed, with some "reward" at the close of the meeting, when teachers are given sample products described during the presentation. Demonstrations provided at these meetings may promote the use of a new piece of equipment. Certainly, any demonstration should provide new information and offer something the audience will be eager to use. A brief demonstration should leave teachers eager to use the product.

Contests are another successful ploy when they pique the interest of the intended audience. Contests should be planned with specific goals and objectives to expand the market, not just to bring attention to an existing service. One does not need to offer a prize to the teacher who used the most videotapes in a year when videotape use is high. However, providing a prize for the best research paper using media center materials should expand students' use of the center.

Free samples are another marketing tool. Students love bookmarks. Posters from professional meetings can be shared with teachers or students. A production workshop in which teachers or students create something they can take away from the media center is an excellent strategy.

Displays of posters, signs, and show cards produced in the media center can bring teachers and students in to create their own for classrooms and clubs. Posters, signs, and show cards are also excellent tools to advertise the media center. If production of attractive posters is not possible in the school, the district or regional production center should be used. Library media specialists should try to locate sources for developing in-house posters, because the local aspect of this type of advertising adds a positive dimension. Microcomputer software and desktop publishing provide excellent poster and sign graphics that are sought after by teachers and students.

Another marketing device is the *point-of-sale display,* often used in grocery stores to feature a certain product. A poster and a stack of books near the charge-out desk encourage students to borrow something to read.

Sales literature could take the form of bibliographies generated to show users what is available on a single topic. Other forms of sales literature are flyers to describe a workshop or a guest speaker and an exhibition book about a special exhibit that a student or teacher might place in the media center.

In developing another marketing device, the *brochure,* one should consider the development of the copy. Most advertising personnel choose a particular theme. If several themes are possible, media center staff or students might help select the best via an in-house contest. The possibilities of the product to be sold should always be kept in mind as the sales literature is being developed.

Another marketing tool is the *formal presentation* made by the library media specialist to groups both inside and outside the school. An enthusiastic, carefully orchestrated talk with interesting visuals can draw far more positive attention to the media center than many of the methods discussed earlier. Such a presentation, followed by a lively question-and-answer period, can do much to change any negative images of media professionals and media programs.

The author has been asked to present media centers to service organizations. These groups meet weekly, and the person in charge of programs is always looking for a new speaker. Offering to show a slide set or video of students at work in the media center could provide the introduction to a pleasant after-lunch speech. Often these organizations will make a small donation to purchase something for the media center. Also, the school's parent and teacher association and a local school foundation may respond after you present a program to them.

PREPARING PRESENTATIONS

Many books have been written to help the novice prepare and deliver a speech. Persons who have managed to make as few formal presentations as possible in their high school and college years are probably not as comfortable in front of a group as they perceive their colleagues to be. Yet it is essential that the media program be articulated to a wide variety of audiences if the program is to be understood and given the high priority that it deserves. A few simple suggestions may help the reluctant speaker accept this responsibility.

First, the length of the presentation should be predetermined and observed. No audience wants to sit longer than they expect to sit, as demonstrated by

e who begin to yawn or wriggle in their seats. Nor does a host wish to
the program come to a close too quickly.

ie media specialist should prepare an outline of the presentation to con-
the sequence of points to be made. The outline should then be followed. A
,entation that wanders will confuse the audience, and the point will be lost.

The shy speaker should plan visuals to help illustrate points and to reduce
the speaking time required. It is useful to distribute copies of important visuals so the audience listens rather than trying to make hasty notes.

For those who are totally unsure of themselves, Joyce Kasman Valenza has
prepared *Power Tools*,[7] which, in addition to ideas, provides actual slide presentations. These are included with a CD-ROM so that you can adapt her work
to fit your situation. The slides for presenting the results of Keith Curry Lance
studies are available in *Powering Achievement*.[8] The Web site www.davidvl.org
contains up-to-date presentation ideas.

Successful speakers tell their audience what they are going to say, say it,
and, finally, summarize what they have said. If the speaker is enthusiastic
about the topic, that enthusiasm will be transmitted to the audience. Bringing
along written testimonies, or having children present their projects in person
will add substantially to the audience's enjoyment of the presentation.

Marketing the media center is a continuous activity. It begins with a welcoming facility with a pleasant ambiance through the provision of appropriate resources. However, one of the media specialist's easiest marketing techniques is
to greet everyone who comes in the door with a smile and an eagerness to help.

Exercises

1. Match a media center activity or service with each of the promotional
   tools listed below:

   Space and time advertising
   Loudspeaker advertising
   Mailings
   Sales presentation
   Contests
   Free samples
   Displays
   Point-of-sale display
   Sales literature

2. Design a brochure to advertise the addition of new materials or equipment to the media center.
3. List the contents of a "media book" you would develop for your media
   center.
4. Outline a presentation for teachers or parents describing a needed
   addition to the media center. "Sell" this to the group to get their support
   for administrative approval of additional funds.
5. Describe a presentation you would make for a service organization,
   including what visuals you would share with them.

NOTES

1. Among these books are Sue Alman, *Crash Course in Marketing* (Westport, CT: Libraries Unlimited, 2007); Feona Hamilton, *Infopromotion: Publicity and Marketing Ideas for the Information Profession* (Hants, England: Gower, 1990); Ken Haycock, *Program Advocacy* (Englewood, CO: Libraries Unlimited, 1990); Cosette N. Kies, *Marketing and Public Relations for Libraries* (Metuchen, NJ: Scarecrow Press, 1987); Rita Kohn and Krysta Tepper, *You Can Do It: A PR Skills Manual for Librarians* (Metuchen, NJ: Scarecrow Press, 1981); Mildred Knight Laughlin and Kathy Howard Latrobe, *Public Relations for School Library Media Centers* (Englewood, CO: Libraries Unlimited, 1990); Benedict A. Leerburger, *Promoting and Marketing the Library*, rev. ed. (Boston: G. K. Hall, 1989); Louise Condak Liebold, *Fireworks, Brass Bands, and Elephants: Promotional Events with Flair for Libraries and Other Nonprofit Organizations* (Phoenix, AZ: Oryx Press, 1986); Anne F. Roberts and Susan Griswold Blandy, *Public Relations for Librarians* (Englewood, CO: Libraries Unlimited, 1989); Mark Schaeffer, *Library Displays Handbook* (New York: H. W. Wilson, 1991); Steve Sherman, *ABC's of Library Promotion*, 3d ed. (Metuchen, NJ: Scarecrow Press, 1992); Ann Montgomery Tuggle and Dawn Hansen Heller, *Grand Schemes and Nitty-Gritty Details: Library PR that Works* (Littleton, CO: Libraries Unlimited, 1987); Suzanne Walters, *Marketing: A How-to-Do-It Manual for Librarians* (New York: Neal-Schuman, 1992); Elizabeth J. Wood, *Strategic Marketing for Libraries: A Handbook* (New York: Greenwood, 1988).

2. Philip Kotler, *Marketing for Nonprofit Organizations* (Englewood Cliffs, NJ: Prentice Hall, 1975), 5.

3. Ibid., 6.

4. William J. Stanton, *Fundamentals of Marketing* (New York: McGraw-Hill, 1978), 35.

5. Kotler, *Marketing for Nonprofit Organizations*, 238.

6. Ibid.

7. Joyce Kasman Valenza, *Power Tools: 100+ Essential Forms and Presentations for Your School Library Information Program* (Chicago: American Library Association, 1998).

8. Keith Curry Lance and David Loertscher, *Powering Achievement: School Library Media Programs Make a Difference the Evidence*, 2nd ed. (San Jose, CA: Hi Willow Research and Publishing, 2002).

13

On the Job: Managing Program Evaluation and Assessment

Library educator David V. Loertscher often asks his audiences, "If you had 10 cents for each time you had helped a teacher with a curricular unit, what could you buy: a new suede jacket or an ice cream cone? If you were arrested for contributing to the education of a student, would there be enough evidence to convict you?" Both are actually thoughtful questions, and progress toward the dual goals of helping teachers and contributing in the education of students must be documented if these successes are to benefit the media program.

Documentation is the result of careful evaluations of many aspects of the program, and it involves counting things. However, your program is not evaluated only in terms of what you have and the number of times you offer programs; you also must assess student learning, which is different from evaluation.

Evaluation has many definitions. According to one dictionary, to evaluate means "to ascertain or fix the value or worth of: to examine and judge, appraise."[1] Determining the worth of a project, product, service, person, or program to fix a value to it can be threatening. The judging process is frightening, because it may reveal that what was thought to be helpful is, in fact, not helpful at all. From early years, children are tested and retested for scholastic achievement, experiences that are often anxiety provoking. This tension is not easily outgrown, and adults are seldom secure in what they perceive to be a test atmosphere. The same is true when the outcome of the evaluation is to fix a value to a program or a service. It becomes more complex when one tries to assess learning.

A less threatening approach is to analyze a program through *measurement* rather than evaluation, particularly when evaluation is viewed as assigning a rank order score from high to low, good to bad, or A to F. Top programs receive As, and a less effective program earns a B. Just as in assigning grades to scores in the classroom, cutoff levels on the scale of scores appear to be arbitrary. Students

201

regret missing an A by one point or enjoy having their grade raised from a C to a B when the teacher lowers the scale by one or two points. For example, a media program with 19,999 books fails, yet 20,000 books are considered successful. Therefore, evaluation of the media center is presented, whenever possible, in the context of quality rather than a numerical quantity.

Evaluation of the school library media program and its components is undertaken for one or more reasons. The school library media specialist may choose to test a single program facet. School district administrators may wish to compare all programs or any part of their media program at the local level, or they may wish to receive approval by a regional accrediting agency. In other instances, the school library media program may be part of a network that requires an analysis of a media service. If school library media programs are to continue to exist and to be managed by a certified media specialist, statistics showing student learning gains are critical. In each of these cases, a different approach may be necessary to provide the proper responses to evaluation.

Two perspectives of program evaluation exist: (1) to find out what is right, and (2) to find out what is wrong. Both perspectives are useful. Certainly, school library media specialists need to learn what is wrong so that the repairs, changes, or alternatives can be put into place. Finding out what is right is satisfying, because it confirms that proper decisions have been made, adequate procedures are in place, and the program is running smoothly in those areas. Evaluation is not a threat when it confirms accomplishment or provides constructive plans for improvement.

One major problem with any numerical test is that most elements of the school library media program are not easily quantified. Many quantity measures are not real measures of a program. For instance, circulation statistics reveal only what materials have moved out of the media center. They do not tell the amount of use or, for that matter, whether there was any use at all.

A second major problem with quantitative evaluation is that few yardsticks exist against which to measure. One yardstick is national standards or guidelines. Because library media standards are typically developed solely by school library media specialists or with minimal input from others, they are sometimes questioned by school administrators and others in the education community, especially when they are based on intuition rather than research results. To measure against content area standards, media specialists must read them carefully to find library media relationships.

Standards for media centers exist in many states, but these tend to outline minimum requirements that are within easy reach of school library media programs. When they are mandated by the state, the quantities cited are meager. State standards that require large numbers of materials, a substantial amount of special equipment, many professional and clerical workers on staff, and large facilities are often challenged by school board members who say they cannot raise adequate funds for implementation. Then local officials demand that state funding be supplied to meet state-imposed standards, and this is never politically popular.

Local standards may be established by administrators to ensure that all programs have minimum materials, staff, and services. When local standards are developed, they should be designed to judge the progress of the school library media program to meet district-wide objectives. This type of evaluation helps with planning all programs, with policy making, and with the revision, continuance, substitution, or cancellation of program components or media center services.

Evaluation can also serve as an awareness device for teachers and administrators. It is particularly useful for those who have misunderstood the purpose of the media program. Most school personnel base their expectations on models they observed when they were in elementary and high school, in teacher training programs and in student teaching or practicum experience. These library media specialists who served as role models in previous teaching and learning situations may have been mediocre to excellent.

After graduation, teachers and administrators added to their perceptions when they accepted positions in schools and observed the media program and its relationship to their classes. Although some of these experiences may have provided excellent models, many did not. An effective evaluation designed with teacher and administrator input can raise their awareness and expectations.

Simply saying that the school library media program is essential to the learning environment of the school is not enough. Media programs can be scrutinized by program appraisal methods that test their value. Program appraisal helps analyze which services are meeting the needs of the school. Do services meet the objectives established by the media center advisory committee? Measuring progress toward these objectives is the first step in evaluating the media center. For example, if a program objective is to provide online database searching for research papers, the evaluation could be simple. "Yes, online database searching has been added to the library media center services." A better value statement tells how many searches were made for how many students, the number of students trained to do their own searching, the average length of time for each search, and the number of relevant citations found. If the media center has not been able to provide this information, analysis should be done to show whether the problem is lack of funding, equipment, staff time, or staff training.

The importance placed on the role of the media specialist and the concept of the media program must be assessed in relation to the school district and the community. If students and teachers have access to a wide variety of information sources such as public and academic libraries, they may need a totally different type of collection and service program in the school. If the library media center is the only source for students, a different concept may prevail. Relationships among nearby information agencies and the use of these outside sources should be part of the evaluation process.

When school staff and students are involved, they must understand the evaluation process so that an accurate study can be conducted. All must view the process as a self-evaluation that requires responding with accurate and well-considered answers. Again, it is impossible to improve a program if the media staff does not recognize the flaws. The counterpoint is that successes should be confirmed rather than assumed.

Methods for testing must be designed with care to determine exactly who will be queried, which items measured, and what procedures used to acquire the needed information. Careful consideration must be given to the choice of statistical methods used to tabulate and analyze the responses. Furthermore, individual components of any media program should not be measured in isolation.

The statistics gathered in the many studies by Lance and colleagues have shown the importance of the school library media center and its staff in the achievement of student learning.[2] These studies will continue to be replicated in other states, and such statewide analyses are significant from a wider perspective. However, the curriculum is the essential element in the planning and evaluation of the individual school's media program, because the major test is the degree to which the media program complements, supplements, supports, and integrates into curriculum offerings. Collections are tailored to meet the needs of teachers and students, and these needs change as the curriculum changes, as grade levels are shifted among buildings, and as teachers are replaced. Students and teachers may need more audiovisual materials or high-interest/low-vocabulary materials rather than a larger collection of higher-level materials. The types of learners in the school affect the collection, just as the teaching method dictates some aspects of collection development.

Four components of the media program can be measured without much difficulty: staff, collections, facilities, and services. They can be measured by quantitative or qualitative methods patterned after existing models or planned by the total media staff with assistance from other building-level or central administrative staff. Documents are available that show measuring techniques. A search of the recent literature will point to these.

QUANTITATIVE MEASURES

As mentioned earlier, school library media standards and guidelines often provide quantitative measures, but they may be too high (as in the case of the 1975 standards) or too low (as in the case of most state standards). The 1988 *Information Power* used statistics gathered by the Office of Educational Research and Improvement of the U.S. Department of Education.[3] Survey data collected by the Center for Education Statistics in 1985 and 1986 were available on computer tape. Schools were stratified by elementary, middle/junior high, and high schools with fewer than 500 students; elementary, middle/junior high, and high schools with more than 500 students; high schools with between 500 and 1,000 students; and high schools with more than 1,000 students. They were further divided into 75th, 90th, and 95th percentiles for services offered. Statistics for each strata were available for the library media specialists to count personnel and collections in their particular situations and compare them with these guidelines. A similar survey was taken in 1994, but the "services offered" component was not included. Therefore, similar data will not be included in future guidelines documents.

A major flaw of quantitative measures is that administrators place too much emphasis on counting things with little regard for their quality. To meet a requirement size for the media center, areas such as equipment storage closets or even a storage area in the basement may be designated part of the media center with little regard for proximity or access. The necessity of providing a certain number of books or videos per pupil may result in neglect of the weeding process. Collections may meet an arbitrary numerical count but be out of date, in poor condition, or of no value to the current curriculum. Obsolete or broken equipment may be left in closets gathering dust because its disposal would place the media center below the required numerical code. Administrators may also buy inferior products to achieve a standard number of holdings rather than purchase high-quality merchandise.

Quantitative measure of services can be performed, but this may result in a one-dimensional perspective. School library media specialists may distribute a checklist asking teachers to indicate which services they are receiving. A wide variety of services may be offered, but such a survey will yield inaccurate results if most students and teachers are unaware that these services exist, or if many services are offered that are not requested by teachers or students. It will not matter whether a service is available if no one makes use of that service for any reason. Although quantitative measures are often less helpful, some output measures are useful in describing the media program. Counting output will certainly confirm media center use. Output includes the number of teachers and students who come into the media center each day, an estimate of the number of materials that circulate, the percentage of the student body using the media center at least once a month, and other similar statistics. The better measure is the relationship of quantity to quality.

QUALITATIVE MEASURES

Because quantity measures are specific and have little cause-and-effect value, they do not test a program adequately. Quality measures are much more significant but much more difficult to determine. One measure of quality, shown in Table 13.1, is to compare *what is* to *what should be.*

Administrators, teachers, students, and media staff can measure what is against what should be and calculate the discrepancy as an actual dollar amount. Although this sounds as if it is a quantity count, it is not. The *what is* becomes a qualitative count of professional and staff time allocation to tasks, equipment, materials, or the qualitative standard before it can be counted. *What should be* outlines what is needed to provide quality. These qualitative factors are applied to facilities, staff, collection, and services. Thus, an obsolete projector would not be eligible for the tabulation of holdings in audiovisual equipment.

Two volumes on evaluating school library media programs include Everhart's, which provides forms as well as standards of measure from state guidelines and reports statistics gathered by the U.S. Department of Education through

TABLE 13.1 Qualitative Measures

What Is	What Should Be
A place to send students for teacher's 50-minute break.	A place with open access for research and reading based on collaborative programming.
Share list of available resources to use in a unit of instruction.	Collaborate with teachers in planning, conducting, teaching, and evaluating a unit of instruction.

its National Center for Educational Statistics;[4] and Yesner and Jay's which suggests ways to recognize negative elements and identify missing elements in the operation of school library media programs.[5]

APPRAISING THE FACILITY

Analyzing the facility is discussed in chapter 6 under planning and remodeling the media center. Students and teachers may be asked to make suggestions for improving the ambiance of the media center. In so doing, they may take responsibility for helping raise funds to make simple adjustments.

STAFF OR PERFORMANCE APPRAISAL

Performance appraisal is easy in the world of sports, where the height of the basketball player and the weight of the football player are easily determined facts. Success is calculated by baskets scored, rebounds made, yards gained, or number of tackles or passes completed. The ultimate test for the team is not the score for the individual players but that season's number of wins and losses and invitations to end-of-season tournaments.

Such statistics are not readily available for media center staff, and the calculation of wins and losses is arbitrary most of the time. Asking teachers or students to determine wins and losses is difficult, because the qualities that appeal to one student or teacher may not appeal to another. Frances Henne's basic rule for media staff, quoted in chapter 7, bears repeating:

> For some students, and in certain schools this may be many students, the only library skill that they should have to acquire is an awareness, imprinted indelibly and happily upon them, that the library is a friendly place where the librarians are eager to help.[6]

The score for "friendly place" and "librarians eager to help" may be determined in part by the numbers of students who seek the advice and counsel of the media specialist, not only for curriculum needs but also for matters that go beyond the scope of the classroom. Compatibility of personalities is difficult to score. Interpersonal relationships, though identified, are not easy to describe in terms of quantity or quality. Communication patterns among media center staff and users of the media center can best be determined if someone spends time observing such patterns, and this method is seldom possible to implement. Another measurement is to ask students and teachers to describe what they like best about the media center. If a student likes the media specialist best, this would indicate rapport between the student and the media specialist. Conversely, if the response to a question about what students like least about the media center elicits the same response (the media specialist), one would evaluate this as lack of rapport. In-between measures on the scale are much more difficult to determine or analyze.

In some states, evaluation of all teaching staff is mandated, and a state-approved form is provided. Most library media specialists lament the fact that the items do not seem to apply to their unique assignments, and their evaluation by this mechanism, though not accurate, is incomplete. A better method is to match performance to previously determined job expectations. George B. Redfern suggests the following basic components of performance evaluation:

1. Clarification of performance criteria or definition of the scope of the job
2. Establishment of performance objectives or job targets
3. Formulation of performance activities or a plan of action for implementing objectives
4. Agreement on monitoring techniques for measuring the effectiveness of activities
5. Development of a means of assessing the monitored data
6. Arrangement for one or more conferences with follow-up to utilize the feedback gained from the process[7]

The application of these components is discussed in chapter 7 in the section on evaluating personnel. However, the activities expected of the media specialist should be the baseline for appraisal of that person's success or failure. Expectations should be written as job descriptions and discussed with each individual.

Clerical staff should also be measured on pre-established performance criteria. These criteria are related to their job descriptions, and evaluation may be based on a district-wide process. If not, the director must maintain documentation of the staff member's work falling below the established standard if changes in behavior are to be expected.

Another measure of performance is the ability of the media center personnel to provide information for the media center's clientele. If materials are well organized, if patrons are given correct and pertinent information in an efficient manner and with a minimum of difficulty, the staff is performing well. If patrons are reluctant to ask for assistance or if they are consistently provided with misinformation, performance of the staff is considerably below adequate achievement levels.

Staff may be evaluated on how many services they offer as well as on how well they deliver their services. Mary Virginia Gaver verified the assumption that size of staff can affect the number and quality of services offered.[8] It was later confirmed in a study by Keith Curry Lance and colleagues, when they replicated a national study that showed the number of staff in the school library media center affected the achievement of students.[9] This was shown to be true in a statewide replication study in Colorado. As mentioned earlier, these two studies have been conducted in many other states, and more are in process.

If the number of staff is large enough to permit a media center to offer a wide variety of services and it does not, one would investigate why not. Similarly, it is not practical to attempt to offer a wide variety of services with limited staff. Media specialists would not be exercising good judgment by offering many services but offering no service well.

The principal may define quality as the ability of the media center staff to get along with teachers, to control the behavior of students in the media center, and to limit the number of books lost during the school year. Although these items may be helpful in the evaluation of the media specialist, it is unfortunate if theses are the only criteria for performance appraisal.

COLLECTION MEASUREMENT

Although analysis of the media collection should be done yearly, this is impractical in most situations. Rather, part of the collection may be analyzed each year. Certainly, each item in the collection should be reviewed at least every five years. Several measures are useful for evaluating the collection. Some are simple, and others are more time consuming.

In the past, collection mapping would allow a review of the collection matched to particular curriculum areas. When materials were needed by teachers and students to carry out assignments, those that were missing were ordered. With the availability of information on various Web sites, the collection is evaluated to make sure that these curriculum areas do have print and audiovisual materials as needed for students to confirm what they find on the Internet. Materials are also needed for students who prefer to read a book about a topic of interest being studied rather than locating shorter bits of information online.

Records should also be maintained for materials, if any, that are borrowed from outside the school district. Items used more than once a year should be purchased, if available, for the media center, except in the case of very expensive items that may be borrowed from a regional or state center or rented from a rental library. Collecting statistics on materials borrowed will help in budget requests for future years.

The relevance and timeliness of the collection can be easily measured. Different areas of the Dewey Decimal Classification System have different copyright date requirements. The books and other materials in classification 310, almanacs and yearbooks, should be superseded by each new edition, because they have little value after five years. Conversely, a history of the Civil War that is accurate and well written, relevant to the curriculum, and suitable to the reading ability of most students might be used for many years. A simple chart that tabulates shelflist holdings can help determine the quantity and timeliness of the collection, with specific areas outlined (see Table 13.2).

As shown in Table 13.2, more than 50 percent of the reference books in this collection are more than 20 years old, and 75 percent are more than 10 years old. If the five counted as copyright after 2004 are sets of encyclopedias, students would have general up-to-date information. However, one would be skeptical about the quality of reference information in this school and its relevance to the curriculum.

Relevance can be measured only by asking teachers and students whether the materials they used were relevant to their needs. This does not mean an item should be discarded because it did not meet a specific need for one assignment. However, an item lacking relevance for the topic it covered under all circumstances should be discarded. This was made evident to the author when she counted materials in school districts and found 20-year-old books on aeronautics (classification 629.9).

TABLE 13.2 Collection Age Inventory

Dewey	Copyright Date									
Decimal Class	Before 1985		1986–1994		1995–2004		After 2004		Total	
	Number of Items	Percentage of Collection	Number of Items	Percentage of Collection	Number of Items	Percentage of Collection	Number of Items	Percentage of Collection	Number of Items	Percentage of Collection
0	40	50	10	25	5	12.5	5	12.5	60	100
100										
200										
300										
310										
320										
340–350										
360										
etc.										

Many school media specialists with computerized circulation systems can program the system to tabulate the circulation by each Dewey class number. Then the media specialist can analyze use or lack of use of materials in each area. Individual books can be tracked to see how often they circulate. Although neither of these procedures can determine how the materials were actually used, knowing the topics being researched may be helpful.

Actual use can be identified in many ways. Teachers and students can be interviewed concerning their use of materials when they return them. Students can also be asked to keep a log of materials they select to note how they use them. They might also be willing to record materials secured from other sources. The usefulness of all materials should be assessed.

At the completion of a unit of work, a citation count, long a favorite in academic research, can be applied to students' research papers. Citations can then be checked against the media center's holdings to see whether materials are available in the collection or students chose items from other libraries. If a bibliography is generated for the unit or if a collection is pulled to be placed on reserve or for use in one classroom, teachers and students can be asked to indicate use and to evaluate the quality of items on the bibliography or in the classroom collection.

Collections can be checked to see how many materials have not circulated in the past three years. If these materials are relevant and useful, why have they not been located and used by students or teachers? If they do not appear relevant or useful, they should be reviewed to determine whether they would be more appropriate at a different grade level or in a different building. Some materials cease being relevant when curriculum changes, in which case they can be stored until later. If they are not being used, are unlikely candidates for use in the near future, or are unused because they are out of date or in poor condition, they should be discarded and all records removed. No collection, no matter how large, can be judged high quality when it is cluttered with out-of-date, worn, unused, or irrelevant materials.

ADMINISTRATOR'S PROGRAM APPRAISAL

Principals and superintendent should understand the complete program of the library media center and its relationship to teaching and learning. These administrators should have a simple means of evaluating this contribution to student learning, effective teaching, and the relationship to the school's curriculum. Because administrators seldom have any instruction concerning the role of the library media specialist, you may need to locate up-to-date suggestions in the literature.

When it is time to make program cuts in any school setting, the principal must believe in the necessity of the school library media program. This is not something that is accomplished in one day but rather something that goes on constantly. If program appraisal is essential for any reason whatsoever, it is to convince principals and superintendents of the worth of the library media center in terms of student achievement. Ongoing evaluation with regular reports of results is the key. It may seem that evaluation is more difficult and more time consuming than a school library media specialist can afford, with the other facets of the program that demand attention. However, when program evaluation is the road to survival, its importance is better understood.

CONTRIBUTING TO THE EDUCATION OF STUDENTS: ASSESSING STUDENT LEARNING

Assessing the contribution to the education of students is the key to the survival of the position of school library media specialist. Brian Kenney, editor of *School Library Journal* has pointed out that

> Neither better relations with our colleagues nor more preaching about the importance of information literacy will save our jobs. Data—that measurement of a library program's impact on student learning—isn't something we traditionally collect, or even know how to collect, but if we are to survive, it's the information we desperately need.[10]

Lance and colleagues have shown how to conduct impact studies at the state level, but few studies are undertaken at the school level—where the focus is on individual students. Harada and Yoshina explain that assessment is different from evaluation, because assessment is "an ongoing activity that provides critical *formative* information about what the student is learning and how that learning is taking place.[11] Learners who are involved in their own assessment are learning in the process. These authors discuss assessing authentic learning and information literacy and how they are related to the content standards.

> The critical point is that school library media specialists must seize the opportunity to show how our teaching reinforces and enhances class-room learning. By noting both the content as well as information literacy standards in our instructional plans, we make visible the synergistic relationship between student engagement in both the classroom and the library media center. The bottom line is that teachers need to see how the classroom-library partnership targets their own goals and priorities.[12]

They explain and share assessment tools such as checklists, rubrics, rating scales, assessment conferences, logs, personal correspondence, graphic organizers, and student portfolios. They also provide elementary and high school examples. As soon as possible, school library media specialists should begin working with teachers to assess student learning; results should be reported so the impact on student learning can be demonstrated.

AFTER THE FIRST YEAR

Evaluation is a process of deciding what to tell, whom to tell, and why to tell. Sometimes one set of statistics can be used for two purposes. When large numbers of students use the media center for assignments, these numbers can be used in a positive report showing media center success, and such reports are made regularly to administrators and teachers. When students cannot find materials because the collection is out of date, the same statistics become part of a failure report that is also shared with teachers, administrations, and parents. By the middle of the media specialist's second semester on the job, the year's goals and objectives should be under scrutiny for their success to date. The degree of accomplishment may be high, and this should appear in the annual report to the principal. If accomplishments have been much lower than expected, a careful analysis of the reasons should be made, so that needs for the next year may be stated. This analysis becomes the blueprint for the second year and into the future.

Exercises

1. Meet with one or more school library media specialists to find out what program evaluation they have conducted in the past year and to whom they reported their findings. If no evaluation has been conducted recently, volunteer to help design and implement an evaluation project to test one component of the library media program. Prepare a written report of the data analysis that will be suitable for a presentation at a school board meeting.
2. Conduct a simple study of the numbers of staff in school library media centers and the budgets for purchasing new materials and equipment in your immediate region. Report your comparison to these centers.
3. Discuss with a school principal the appraisal process being applied to the school's media center, staff, and services.
4. Locate one or two articles to share with your principal on the role of the principal in working with the school library media specialist. Describe how you would share these articles with your principal when you first begin your job.

NOTES

1. *American Heritage Dictionary of the English Language* (Boston: American Heritage and Houghton Mifflin, 1969), 453.

2. James C. Baughman, *School Libraries and MCAS Scores: Preliminary Edition* (Boston: Graduate School of Library and Information Science, 2000); Keith C. Lance, Marcia J. Rodney, and Christine Hamilton-Pennell, *How School Librarians Help Kids Achieve Standards: The Second Colorado Study* (San Jose, CA: Hi Willow Research and Publishing, 2000); Keith C. Lance, Marcia J. Rodney, and Christine Hamilton-Pennell, *Impact of School Library Media Centers on Academic Achievement* (Castle Rock, CO: Hi Willow Research and Publishing, 1993); Keith C. Lance, Marcia J. Rodney, and Christine Hamilton-Pennell, *Information Empowered: The School Librarian as an Agent of Academic Achievement in Alaska Schools* (Juneau: Alaska State Library, 2000); Keith C. Lance, Marcia J. Rodney, and Christine Hamilton-Pennell, *Measuring up to Standards: The Impact of School Library Programs & Information Literacy in Pennsylvania Schools* (Greensburg: Pennsylvania Citizens for Better Libraries, 2000); Keith C. Lance, Marcia J. Rodney, and Christine Hamilton-Pennell, *Good Schools Have School Librarians: Oregon School Librarians Collaborate to Improve Academic Achievement* (Salem: Oregon Educational

Media Association, 2001); Keith C. Lance, Marcia J. Rodney, and Christine Hamilton-Pennell, *How School Libraries Improve Outcomes for Children: The New Mexico Study* (Santa Fe: New Mexico State Library, 2002); Marcia J. Rodney, Keith Curry Lance, and Christine Hamilton-Pennell, *Make the Connection: Quality School Library Media Programs Impact Academic Achievement in Iowa* (Bettendorf, IA: Mississippi Bend Area Education Agency, 2002); Ester Smith, *Texas School Libraries: Standards, Resources, Services and Students' Performance* (Austin, TX: EGS Research & Consulting, 2001).

3. American Association of School Librarians and Association for Educational Communications and Technology, *Information Power: Guidelines for School Library Media Programs* (Chicago: American Library Association, 1988).

4. Nancy Everhart, *Evaluating the School Library Media Center: Analysis Techniques and Research Practices* (Englewood, CO: Libraries Unlimited, 1998).

5. Bernice L. Yesner and Hilda L. Jay, *Operating and Evaluating School Library Media Programs: A Handbook for Administrators and Librarians* (New York, Neal-Schuman, 1998).

6. Frances Henne, "Learning to Learn in School Libraries," *School Libraries* 15 (May 1966): 17.

7. George B. Redfern, *How to Evaluate Teaching* (Worthington, OH: School Management Institute, 1972).

8. Mary Virginia Gaver, *Services of Secondary School Media Centers* (Chicago: American Library Association, 1971), 39.

9. Keith Curry Lance, Lynda Welborn, and Christine Hamilton-Pennell, *The Impact of School Library Media Centers on Academic Achievement* (Englewood, CO: Hi Willow Research and Publishing, 1993).

10. Brian Kenney, "Getting It Together," *School Library Journal* 53 (July 2007): 9.

11. Violet H. Harada and Joan M. Yoshina, *Assessing Learning: Librarians and Teachers as Partners* (Westport, CT: Libraries Unlimited, 2005), 1.

12. Ibid., 13.

14

On the Job: Cooperation, Networking, and Social Networking

Cooperative activities among schools and other entities most often existed with public libraries, and their relationship was discussed in chapter 1. Cooperation started as early as both schools and public libraries existed, but it was institutionalized in 1896, when the National Education Association made librarians eligible for membership.[1] Relationships flourished, and the Certain Standards, the first school library standards, stated that,

> To relate the work in the high school library to that of the public library and to make clear the uses to pupils, after school days are over, of an institution which should be a factor in their future mental development, classes should be taken to the public library, where its book resources, rules, methods, departments, catalog and support can be briefly explained by one of the staff. . . . Where visits to the library are an impossibility in school hours because of distance, competent members of the library staff may be invited to talk on the subject.[2]

By the early 1960s, increased attention to research in schools—particularly scientific research—and the lack of good school libraries created a problem for public libraries. The effort to accommodate student use of public libraries appeared to be adversely affecting service to other clients. The passage of the Elementary and Secondary Education Act assisted efforts to meet students' needs in the schools, but even those funds did not provide all the materials needed. As stated in chapter 1, neither schools nor public libraries alone can offer the quantities of materials needed to allow students to conduct the type of research projects that will prepare them for a global society. Only through cooperation between these two agencies can the best use be made of public funding.

When funding for public institutions comes under scrutiny, talk arises of making one agency serve both audiences. This generally happens when funds are being cut from one or the other. Joining forces to show the differences between the types of services to be offered may be the only way to save both types of libraries. Criteria for combined libraries are detailed in chapter 1 and will not be repeated here. However, combining libraries is not cooperating. It is removing one or the other, and children need both public and school libraries if they are going to be lifelong learners.

Cooperation among other types of libraries is predicated upon the proximity of users to libraries and any restrictions on use that may be in place. Cooperation is most often successful when participants need each other and are willing to give more than they receive. Cooperative ventures between or among information agencies exist as long as those who are in charge want the cooperation to be successful. More formal arrangements with contracts that are binding happen during the creation of consortia and networks.

The original need to share resources resulted in a variety of efforts at cooperation and networking, and consortia and networks were created to link academic and large public libraries. These grew in number and expanded in size to include smaller public libraries, special libraries, and school library media centers. As information became more available online and the costs of both software and hardware dropped, school library media specialists were no longer so isolated and could function independently.

At the present time, the most likely shared resources are found in those states that have a statewide database. Having the state legislature fund a statewide database makes the resources of the database available to all agencies as well as all citizens of the state in their homes. School library media specialists, by having access to these databases, then use their local funds for additional resources. With this type of resource, school library media specialists and public librarians provide access to the database for students who do not have online connectivity in their homes.

While providing online access to persons who do not have this in their homes is one reason for the existence of libraries, cooperation among libraries may help build the case for professional assistance with users of online resources. As will be discussed later, users of search engines are often not able to discern good information from poor information. Cooperation among librarians in all types of libraries can help describe the role of the information professional in the lives of library users.

School library media specialists will continue to provide such materials as books, videocassettes and DVDs, word-processing programs, periodicals, tele-facsimile transmission, and connections to the Internet and other online resources available through local purchase or a statewide resource. These greatly increase the information available to teachers and students, and the library media specialist's role is to help them make the best use of the Internet.

THE INTERNET AND THE WORLD WIDE WEB

The Internet is the largest telecommunications network in the world. It began in 1969 under the name ARPANET (Advanced Research Projects Agency) and was part of the U.S. Department of Defense. Research conducted by ARPANET allowed messages to flow from one computer to another. When the military released this system to the academic community, it was quickly adopted as a question-answer system that allowed communication among researchers who were not necessarily aware of each other. Messages requesting information were sent out over the network, and persons with responses simply returned a message.

Once access to the Internet was established, it was easy to navigate. It is almost impossible to imagine any school library media center today without access to the Internet and the World Wide Web (WWW) even with the perceived problems this may cause. Internet access adds to the role of the school library media specialists because they must be leaders in their schools—helping administrators, teachers, and students keep on the cutting edge of the ever-expanding uses of the Internet.

Helping teachers and students use the Internet wisely is one of the most important assignments for school library media specialists. Moving users from the crutch of Google to the broader use of the WWW gives them lifelong learning skills. Opening them to the constantly changing opportunities provided through this resource is both a challenge and a blessing.

Because the Internet is global, it offers exciting opportunities to school library media specialists to help their students and teachers locate person-to-person information in other parts of the world. For example, if a class wants to know something about special foods for a particular holiday in any country, they can e-mail another class in that country and ask the students there to tell them about the customs and the foods. One school library media specialist in Sydney, New South Wales, Australia, sent an e-mail message to the South Pole to confirm the temperature there. This kind of assignment provides writing experiences to both classrooms. Students studying French can e-mail their counterparts, who can respond in French and, perhaps, correct any grammar that is traditional rather than the most modern use. Helpful communication avenues are also available to school library media specialists.

LM-NET, established at Syracuse University, is a national forum for library media specialists who debate issues, request assistance to help solve their local management and professional problems, answer questions, and announce new opportunities. Most state school library associations have lists available for their members to share information. When a teacher asks for a book she read about a girl who grew up in the west in many different homes, keeping a diary of the experience, a message can be posted to see if anyone recognizes the plot and can supply the title and author. Many are used for announcements of conferences, workshops, and other learning experiences—once limited to print publications or mailed brochures—which are now also published on bulletin boards.

Information technology has grown to provide the school community access to a virtual world. The growth of the WWW has changed the ways students can locate and share resources. This presents a challenge for the school library media specialist who needs to see that students are information literate when they move ahead. The speed with which students can access a search engine such as Google or Yahoo challenges their ability to make decisions about the relevancy or authority of what they do find. Research has found that young students aren't very skillful in developing good search strategies or choosing search terms, which means that much of what they may find, download, and print may not really be what they need. Students seldom evaluate what they find, and what they are finding may well be information placed there by another student.

> The emergence of social web sites is changing the nature and fabric of the World Wide Web; we have moved from an internet built by a few thousand authors to one being constructed by millions. . . . users creating and posting content for themselves, blurring the age-old distinction between information producers and information consumers.[3]

The WWW's social networking sites and simple-to-use and very attractive desktop publishing software allows students to create and post their findings. The sophistication of their documents is such that another student might not recognize it was written by a student with little or no actual research.

Bulletin boards and chat groups give students opportunities to participate in discussion groups across the country and around the world. MySpace and Facebook allow the sharing of personal information. MySpace gives a Web page to a user, mostly teenagers, to customize, and they may link to other friends. They can post pictures, and this has created some concern among parents and teachers because of predators who lurk online.

Facebook concentrates on a particular community; to join, the e-mail address must be linked to that community. Such new spaces change rapidly, and the media specialist knows when one resource such as MySpace becomes passé and something new, such as Facebook, takes over. Another concern about social networking sites is cyber-bullying, which is not confined to students bullying other students. Administrators, teachers, and even media specialists may be the object of false rumors, information, or doctored photographs.

Other problems with social networking sites, in addition to online predators and bullying, include viruses from Web sites. Children aren't as likely to be concerned about identity theft, but they can become the targets of stalkers. It is a difficult choice to make, but the benefits of the sites should overcome the disadvantages if parents, teachers, and other adults are aware of the problems and care is taken to minimize the potential harms.

Another challenge is to help students learn to evaluate what they find on the WWW. Because children do not evaluate what they find and do not recognize the relevance or accuracy of information, school library media specialists must work closely with teachers to ensure that students are becoming information literate. The fact that the speed of searching has not increased students' ability to evaluate what they find, more attention should be paid to helping students develop effective search strategies. Providing access to information is no longer enough. Students must become skillful searchers who do evaluate the information they find. If a student leaves elementary school and hasn't been taught how to develop a search strategy, identify search terms, and evaluate what is found more than simply looking at the first page, it becomes even more critical in high school. Once the student graduates, it is too late to create a lifelong information-literate user. To be able to keep up with the challenges of teaching information literacy, the school library media specialist must learn about new technologies.

EMBRACING NEW TECHNOLOGIES

According to Elizabeth L. Black, "The term Library 2.0 first appeared in September 2005 in a post by Michael Casey in his *LibraryCrunch* blog."[4] Rather obviously, it is based on the concept of Web 2.0 which is an expansion of what the WWW has offered to society. This new concept is one which anticipates the collaboration and connections of users through such devices as blogs.

The person who thought it would be great fun to be a librarian, sitting around reading books all day and sharing the love of reading with those in the library is a dinosaur. It becomes more apparent every day that the library media specialist must keep up with Web 2.0 and Library 2.0 and all the new opportunities these and all the new technology advances bring. Among these are blogs, wikis, and podcasting.

The first, the blog is set up by a provider. Those who wish to participate are invited to join. In some instances, the information on the blog may be considered private and a password is needed to join. Blogging software uses a Really Simple Syndication feed (RSS), an XML-based format. One recent use of a blog was with a library conference planning committee whose members were from a wide area of the U.S. Another was set up to allow LIS students in the U.S. to share their progress with communicating with LIS students around the globe.

The wiki was designed to allow programmers to share their knowledge as they worked on projects. This ability for a group to place and edit content regardless of location of any member of the group makes virtual group work simple. The best known wiki is the Wikipedia Encyclopedia. While one might question the true accuracy of this encyclopedia since anyone can alter the content, it is certainly a first search place. The fact that it is updated constantly gives it a timeliness not found in other sources. Studies have compared the accuracy of Wikipedia with print encyclopedias and found it to be comparable. An encyclopedia is a very ambitious use of a wiki and much simpler applications are good starting points. With the help of the library media specialist, teachers can set up wikis within their classrooms for joint projects among students. If they have online access at home, they can revise their reports 24/7.

Another innovation with great potential is podcasting. The word, *podcasting*, is a combination of "broadcasting" and "iPod." This particular technology is growing rapidly and it has particular applications to library media centers. Kristen Fontichiaro[5] suggests the use of podcasting for third grade and higher students to create radio plays. Podcasting is an excellent way to conduct book talks and story time. The technology allows the recording of live events, which can be transmitted later. The value of this technology may need to be demonstrated to teachers who fight students having MP3 players in their classrooms as a distraction.

Podcasting does have some legal considerations. When a speaker is recorded for future podcast, he or she must grant permission for the recording and subsequent use. When students are using music for their podcasts, this music requires permission. Students can find the online sites providing access to music that is safe for use as a podcast.

Many other new technologies are being developed constantly. These are detailed in library publications, discussed on blogs and wikis, and presented at library media conferences. It is not necessary to understand how each innovation works, but it is essential to learn what they can do and help teachers make good decisions about integrating these into the way they teach. Keeping up with new technologies and their application makes the library media specialist an essential component of teaching and learning in each school.

ELECTRONIC PUBLISHING

Changes in methods of publishing are already making an impact on higher education and public libraries. Textbook publishers are allowing faculty members in universities to choose parts of their texts for their classes, downloading those parts rather than trying to sell the complete book. For-profit providers are moving from the more traditional printed formats (books), which are expensive to purchase, organize, shelve and reshelve. Print formats require human intervention at all steps. E-books have not been as popular as they were thought to be, but they are certain to become more popular with handheld devices. Project Gutenberg was built with public domain books, which were manually typed by volunteers; there are more than 19,000 volumes available. Most e-books can be easily searched, making this technology most attractive for reference books.

While most people who were born before the advent of the microcomputer prefer to read a book rather than hold a handheld device, this may not be the choice of new generations as they live in an increasingly electronic world. To ignore the potential that e-books provide would not serve them well.

CONTINUING ACCESS TO INFORMATION IN ALL FORMATS

School library media specialists are responsible for ensuring that students and teachers have access to the best information possible. They must be vigilant to see that the educational needs of youth are kept in the plans for implementation of networks; access to a statewide database; or any joint library effort at the local, state, and national levels. The ability of youth to become a part of the global community will partly depend on their awareness of the opportunities provided through the use of networks and advanced technologies. When parents and teachers recognize that even the youngest child needs access to materials that may be beyond the ability of the local school or public library to provide, school library media specialists play a key role in finding resources from other locations, whether print or electronic. School library media specialists are charged with opening the world of information to their users, and, to do this, they remain on the cutting edge of new technologies.

Exercises

1. If your state does not fund a statewide database, how would you go about collecting the information to help your principal, the parents in your school, and your local and state legislatures understand the savings to individual school districts?
2. Plan an in-service workshop to introduce the use of blogging, wikis, or podcasting to your teachers. Think of applications for them to use.
3. Create a list of the hardware and software you need to initiate podcasting in your library media center.

NOTES

1. Melvil Dewey, "New Library Development of the National Education Association," *Public Libraries* 1 (September 1986): 185.

2. C. C. Certain, *Standard Library Organization and Equipment for Secondary Schools: New York State Library: Library School Bulletin 45* (Albany: University of the State of New York, 1920), 22.

3. "Information Behavior of the Researcher of the Future," CIBER briefing paper, January 11, 2008, http://www.jisc.ac.uk/media/documents/programmes/rep pres/gg_final_keynote_11012008.pdf.

4. Elizabeth L. Black, "Web 2.0 and Library 2.0: What Librarians Need to Know," in *Library 2.0 and Beyond: Innovative Technologies and Tomorrow's Users,* ed. Nancy Courtney (Westport, CT: Libraries Unlimited, 2007), 1.

5. Kristen Fontichiaro, *Active Learning through Drama, Podcasting, and Puppetry* (Westport, CT: Libraries Unlimited, 2007), 155–66.

Chapter 15

Leadership and Professional Associations

"The time has come," the Woollsrus said,
"To talk of many things:
Of shoes—and ships—and sealing-wax—
Of cabbages—and kings."

With apologies to Lewis Carroll, the time has come for all school library media specialists to step out from behind the looking glass and assume a leadership role in both of their professions, educator and librarian. They must then move into a leadership role as advocates for the information professions, becoming active participants in the political process on all levels.

In the 100-year history of professionals in school library media centers, it has seemed difficult at times for many media specialists to become leaders in either role. Difficulty has occurred in the role of educator for these reasons:

1. The first school librarians were more often part-time librarians and part-time teachers in academic classrooms. Or, as librarians, they were often responsible for two or more schools. Either way, it was difficult to establish a power base.

2. School library media specialists were considered specialists rather than regular teachers.

3. The perception of the school library media specialist was that of a quiet, retiring person, not a dynamic, assertive program advocate.

Difficulty occurs in the role of library professional for these reasons:

4. Media specialists have 9- or 10-month contracts and may be unavailable to meet with other professionals for two or three months each year.

223

5. Some media specialists, often because of their undergraduate preparation in schools of education, are identified as educators rather than professional librarians.

6. Many professionals, librarians included, consider members who work with youth rather than adults as somehow less likely to lead.

For these reasons, school library media specialists must continue working to change perceptions of their profession. They can employ a variety of strategies to overcome these difficulties.

School library media specialists who still work part-time between schools must exert a true leadership role to change this. School district administrators will argue that some schools are too small to merit a full-time principal, art teacher, music teacher, or library media specialist. The media specialist who is a leader can convince the superintendent that the ability to work with teachers and students in support of curriculum will make the principal's shared appointment an easier one. With site-based management, the media specialist can serve as leader of the site-based team to determine expenditures. As mentioned previously, media specialists hold no allegiance to a particular part of the curriculum or a specific grade level.

When the school district provides clerical assistance in place of the building-level media specialist, state regulations should be checked to see if this person is liable for the safety of students in the absence of a certified teacher or media specialist. In addition, a case may be made against depriving students and teachers of professional assistance. As sophisticated technologies continue to emerge, teachers and students need professionals to respond to queries, confirm the best choices of items from the wide array that can be located on the Internet or requested from interlibrary loan, handle technical problems with equipment, and suggest sources from the ever-increasing numbers of references available. This will dictate the requirement for a full-time media specialist.

The perception of the media specialist changes as media programs change. The degree of change resides in each individual media specialist in each library media center. While organizations such as the American Association of School Librarians develop publications such as *Information Power* to help define the role, only individuals can create the image for their schools, students, teachers, administrators, and communities. Media specialists who understand and describe for others the importance of their place in the present and future world of education will be able to help teachers become more effective teachers and students become better learners. This must be accomplished within the parameters of local, state, and national education policy, guidelines, and regulation. Most particularly, trends in education, changes in budget, and expanding new technologies will affect the ability of the media specialist to change.

The movement to year-round schooling will change media specialists' current status of working 9- or 10-month contracts. Electronic access to the holdings in a media center collection creates the need for someone to be available on site to respond to queries and to monitor technologies over a longer school day and longer vacation periods. Network administrators are able to do systems work from off-site locations, and media specialists can, via e-mail, respond to student queries while away from the media center. However, this means a different use of off-site time than media specialists have anticipated in the past. It also requires a professional to choose on-site as well as off-site resources and to make sure the system is up when users need access.

Finally, information professionals whose primary assignment is the youth of our nation must accept the fact that their responsibility is one of the most important in the world. The education of youth for a global society is paramount, and this is only accomplished when students become information literate, with enhanced critical thinking skills they can apply to information available to them now and in the future. This is the assignment of the library media specialists and the youth librarians in public libraries, working in concert with teachers and parents. A first step in this process is to join professional associations of both educators and librarians and work within them as capable, creative, confident members and leaders.

EDUCATION ASSOCIATIONS

An exciting number of opportunities exist for media specialists in a variety of education associations. At the national level, educators choose to join either the National Education Association (NEA; www.nea.org) or the American Federation of Teachers (AFT; www.aft.org). Both associations have state and local affiliates, and school library media specialists may teach under contract to a local affiliate of NEA or AFT that acts as the bargaining unit. Although affiliation may not be mandatory in a local school district, it is usually an uncomfortable situation for a media specialist to refuse to join fellow teachers in the negotiating contracts for their units. Resentment directed at the media specialist who does not join may extend to resentment toward the media program.

When the school district has a local bargaining unit, membership in both state and national associations is required and automatic. Also, the teacher and media specialist cannot join only the national association but must join their local and state associations as well. These teachers' associations offer media specialists the opportunity to attend local and state meetings and possibly to become a delegate to the national association.

Media specialists who belong to their education association should work within that association to improve perceptions of the media program. Teachers, especially at the elementary level, often feel the media center is their free period. The author is aware of one situation in which a grievance was filed against the media specialist because this person was not assigned lunchroom duty. Helping teachers understand the importance of having the media center open for students throughout the day is part of the role of the media specialist.

It is also important that at least one media specialist be a member of the contract unit's negotiating team. In this way, library media specialists can represent the needs of the media center as part of the bargaining team. When library media specialists neglect this important opportunity, they risk being moved into a special category, apart from the teaching staff. When this happens, additional time may be assigned to the media specialist role. For example, in one state, it was ruled that, because library media specialists did not have student work to take home to grade, they were expected to report to school 30 minutes earlier and stay 30 minutes later than classroom teachers.

School library media specialists with interests in specific subject areas may join the relevant associations to help keep the library media center visible to other educators. Special subject associations include the National Council of Teachers of English (www.ncte.org), the International Reading Association (www.ira.org), and the National Council of the Social Studies (www.ncss.org).

Related organizations include the Association for Supervision and Curriculum Development (ASCD) and the International Society for Technology in Education (ISTE). Choosing to become active in ASCD (www.ascd.org) brings library media specialists in direct contact with superintendents, principals, and curriculum directors in school districts. The mission statement states that ASCD is a diverse, international community of educators, forging covenants in teaching and learning for the success of all learners. ASCD represents 160,000 educators from more than 135 countries and 66 affiliates. In 2007, ASCD switched its report of membership to percentage of the total. The membership is comprised of 38 percent principals and assistant principals, 18 percent classroom teachers, 16 percent directors or supervisors, 7 percent superintendents and assistant superintendents, 4 percent professors, and 7 percent building-level specialists; 3 percent are not currently employed, and 3 percent designate "other."

ISTE (www.iste.org) provides leadership and service to improve teaching and learning by advancing the effective use of technology in K–12 education and teacher education. It boasts a worldwide membership of leaders and potential leaders in educational technology. Visiting the Web sites of these associations helps prospective members determine which they might wish to join in addition to their school library media associations.

LIBRARY AND MEDIA ASSOCIATIONS

Library media specialists who wish to meet others working in school library media centers may be able to participate in a local association, which is usually an informal group of librarians. In the Pittsburgh area, the Council of School Librarians meets twice a year. The first is a fall Saturday visit to a school, with workshops and speakers followed by lunch. The spring meeting, a dinner session, features a children's book author. These provide an opportunity for school library media specialists to meet and discuss their concerns with others in the area. Membership is inexpensive, and participation time minimal, except perhaps for the officers.

The California School Library Association, located in a very large state in size and population, has two spring meetings each year—one in the north and one in the south. These one-day continuing education events allow school library media specialists to participate as officers and presenters and to get up-to-date information about what is going on in other schools.

Some states have two media-related associations and others only one. Pennsylvania has the Pennsylvania Association for Educational Communications and Technology (www.paect.org) and the Pennsylvania School Librarians Association (www.psla.org). The Florida Association for Media Educators (www.floridamedia.org) is the only association in that state for media professionals.

Annual conferences provide workshops, speakers, exhibits, and communication with other library media specialists. The success of a state association relates directly to the willingness of members to volunteer their services. Few state associations have sufficient income to maintain paid office staff. Participation in the state association provides an excellent opportunity to build leadership skills. At this level it is often easy to become active in committee work and present at the annual meeting.

Included among national groups are the Association for Educational Communications and Technology (AECT; www.aect.org) and the American Library Association (ALA) and its division, American Association of School Librarians (AASL; www.aasl.org). AECT (www.aect.org) provides members with three publications, *Tech Trends: Linking Research and Practice to Improve Learning,* the bimonthly *Educational Technology Research and Development,* and *Journal of Instructional Development.* Members also have the opportunity to attend a yearly conference. AECT is governed by a president, elected annually, a council, and an affiliate council. AECT members may write articles for *Tech Trends* and make presentations at the annual meeting. Exhibits for this association specialize in audiovisual media and equipment. Many state library/media associations are affiliates of AECT.

A second national association is the ALA (www.ala.org), with 60,000 members representing all types of librarians, information professionals, and trustees of public libraries. The AASL is a division of ALA, and members of AASL receive the benefits of ALA membership, including a lobbying effort in Washington, DC. Two meetings are held each year—a midwinter conference and an annual conference. The midwinter conference is for members of the ALA executive board, council, officers, members of boards of directors of divisions and roundtables, and ALA and division and roundtable committees. Many exhibitors provide new items for participants to consider for purchase.

The annual conference, a much larger event, offers not only meetings of boards and committees but also speakers, preconference workshops, exciting meal functions such as the Newbery/Caldecott dinner, and a vast array of exhibits. A number of library-affiliated groups gather at the same time, including membership in the Black Caucus of the ALA, the American Indian Library Association, the Asian/Pacific American Librarians Association, the Chinese-American Library Association, and the membership meeting for Beta Phi Mu, International Library Science Honor Society.

In addition to the national conference of ALA, AASL holds its own national conference every second year. These are planned by AASL members, and all programming is directly related to school library media services. Many members find these an excellent way to become acquainted in a smaller setting, rather than plunging into an ALA conference. This conference also provides an opportunity for practitioners and researchers to present information on their program and research results. Exhibits are directly related to school libraries.

AASL is governed by an executive board made up of the past president, the president, the recording secretary, the president-elect, a member elected by the board of directors from the board, and the executive director and deputy executive director, ex officio. In addition to the executive board, a board of directors is elected by membership and by other sections in the association and the Affiliate Assembly membership.

A wide variety of committees exist for AASL members. These include the AASL Intellectual Freedom Committee, the AASL Legislation Committee, and several awards committees, among others. The AASL Editorial Advisory Committee reviews the publication of the association journal, *Knowledge Quest.* Their research journal is a second publication, *School Library Media Quarterly,* which is available online. Members also receive the monthly *AASL Hotlinks,* which is sent to them online. AASL maintains relations with state associations through its Affiliate Assembly, which is made up of officers or delegates elected from state associations. These state associations may affiliate with AASL only if their president is a member of AASL.

Some school library media specialists suggest that dues for national associations seem very high, and they question what they get out of their membership. An article by Helen Adams in *School Library Media Quarterly* listed the following AASL membership benefits:

- Toll-free number to the AASL office
- Provision of the *Information Power* national guidelines
- Written policy statements on such issues as the role of library media specialists in site-based management
- Advisory telephone services by trained library media professionals
- Access to strategies for defending library media programs
- Access to statistics and research about library media programs
- Access to intellectual freedom assistance
- Access to a national network of fellow library media professionals
- Access to public relations information and activities about school library media programs through a variety of media
- Subscription to two AASL publications (*Knowledge Quest* and the electronic journal *School Library Media Quarterly*)
- Reduced registration rates at national AASL conferences, preconferences, and regional institutes
- Discounts on AASL publications
- Eligibility for AASL awards and scholarships
- Opportunity to serve on more than AASL committees
- Leadership training[1]

For school library media specialists who enjoy meeting their counterparts from other nations, two organizations are available. The International Association of School Librarianship (IASL; iasl-online.org) is open to school library media specialists from all over the world. A graduated dues schedule allows persons from developing nations to join for a reduced fee, and members are encouraged to adopt a member from a less-wealthy nation. Two scholarships are available for someone from this category to attend the annual meeting.

Members can present papers at IASL conferences and hear speakers with national and international viewpoints on education and school librarianship. Many of the social events allow visits to school libraries and homes of school librarians in other countries as well as historical sites. Preconference and postconference tours and educational experiences add to the value of membership in this association.

The governance structure of IASL includes an executive board with a president, three vice presidents, and a financial officer. The board of directors includes the executive board and six directors who represent their regions of the world. The executive secretary serves ex officio on both boards. IASL members receive the research journal, *School Libraries Worldwide*, a newsletter, an up-to-date Web site, and an active e-mail list.

The School Library Section of the International Federation of Library Associations and Federations (IFLA; www.ifla.org) also provides a forum for school library media specialists worldwide. Because IFLA is primarily an association made up of associations (e.g., ALA and Special Libraries Association) and major research libraries (New York Public, Harvard University Library), fewer individuals join as personal members, but rather participate as voting representatives of their professional associations.

Both of these associations allow school library media specialists from the United States to meet and discuss library media programs with professionals from around the globe. Because media programs in the United States are usually more advanced than in other locations, discussing activities provided in a media program here helps a professional in a country with less well-developed programming plan for the future. Understanding the state of a media program in another country may encourage media specialists to adopt an international media program and collect funding for materials for that school. As others are able to access the Internet, e-mail will expand the exchange of information and widen the boundaries of schools in countries around the world.

Because both associations meet in other countries, active membership means the library media specialist will travel to an international location and be able to visit libraries of all types. This places a different perspective on cultures and clarifies any impression of persons from that country as well as from other countries. It is obviously a more costly investment in time and funding, but the outcomes as we move into a global society are incomparable.

The School Library Section's elected chair is responsible for planning school library–related programs at the annual meeting of IFLA. These programs are available at the conference in hard copy (limited numbers) and CD-ROM, are posted to the IFLA Web site, and are often translated to other languages.

Certainly more associations exist than many school library media specialists can hope to join. Nevertheless, choosing as many as possible and participating actively is essential to the effectiveness of the school library media specialist and the profession. Membership in an association exposes library media specialists to the most recent trends in education and librarianship and enables them to join forces with peers to lobby for the continuing expansion of school library media programs at local, state, and national levels. Membership information is available from the Web sites of each professional association.

SCHOOL LIBRARY MEDIA SPECIALISTS AND THE POLITICAL PROCESS

School library media specialists are well aware of the need to become effective in the political process, but this does not mean that individuals are stepping forward to take responsibility in this important arena. The media specialist's role in the school and responsibilities for improving the image of the media center in the minds of students, teachers, administrators, and parents have been discussed in previous chapters. This section presents ways to improve the library media center image in the state and national arena.

That school library media specialists are a public asset is a fact that has not been universally acknowledged. This will happen only when effective methods are used to bring the status of media centers into public view. One method of doing this is for media specialists to learn how to sell a program—to lobby.

For some school library media specialists, the word *lobby* may seem threatening or beneath or above the abilities of a building-level person. Lobbying is the process of making opinions heard and getting ideas to decision makers. It is collecting appropriate information and using it for advocacy. Finally, it can result in influencing legislation. Library media specialists need not begin their lobbying efforts by trying to change federal laws. It is much easier and obviously much more effective to begin at home.

Lobbying begins at the local school building when the library media specialist promotes the needs of the media program to students, parents, teachers, and, most of all, the principal in order to affect budgeting and strategic long-range planning. These persons must understand the value of the school library media program to the education of students from the first day of each school year throughout the year. The school library media specialist who works closely with the principal and other administrative staff to provide the best resources and information literacy experiences for students will remain essential to the school when budgets are reduced or when a different resource allocation process is put into place. This public relations effort is not a once-a-year effort; it is ongoing.

Efforts are expanded when the library media program is brought to the attention of the school board, and individual members are given demonstrations of effective activities in media centers, thanked for funding special projects, or made aware of needs for the district's media programs. Suggestions for conducting an advocacy plan are covered in chapter 12.

When school library media specialist positions and programs are threatened—whether the threat moves into action, an attempt to replace the professional with a clerk or to close the program—it is too late to begin public relations efforts. The evidence of the value of the school library in the lives of students and teachers must be constant and well documented. The program must be supported by others in the school community and not just the school library media staff. The members of the school community must be made aware of what will be lost long before the threat appears so that they will be prepared to help lobby for the survival and maintenance of the program and staff.

To secure the consideration of state-level funding agencies and legislators requires a more sophisticated organization of efforts. At this level, more groups are demanding attention from these agencies and individuals, and one's message can easily be ignored. For this reason, novice lobbyists need to remember that legislators at any level are still elected officials. They serve at the pleasure of their constituents, and, as voters, school library media specialists are constituents.

The second thing to remember is that these officials work for us. They are interested in helping make things better for their constituents. They are elected officials in a democratic society that they and all other citizens wish to remain democratic. To do this, citizens must be informed voters, and, as the leaders who developed the U.S. education system believed, this depends on teaching reading and offering reading opportunities. In an information society, it also means citizens who are information literate, and that requires access to information resources as part of the education process and access in and through the library media center. Elected officials need to be kept aware of the central role of the library media center in the education of youth. This is the responsibility of library media specialists—to organize efforts and to be effective lobbyists.

Articles, books, and pamphlets are available from a variety of sources to help understand the lobbying process. The ALA Washington office maintains a legislative e-mail list, and messages are sent regularly to members requesting their action. Office staff will tell you that congressional offices are interested in hearing from constituents; they often do not understand the issues involved in particular pieces of legislation. Staff members in the ALA Washington office explain to school library media specialists that sometimes legislators receive no comments from any constituents concerning certain legislation. In some cases, opponents of legislation affecting education may send a few persons to state a case against a bill, and the legislator acts in their favor because no one from the education community has offered another viewpoint.

Most legislators now have e-mail addresses and fax numbers for receiving messages. Writing such a message takes only a little time and is of great help in communicating with a legislator. Some suggestions for writing a letter are given in Appendix I. It is no longer a speedy process to send a letter to a legislator in Washington. Since the threat of anthrax, all mail addressed there goes to a site for checking before being forwarded to the legislator's office. It is better to look up the legislator's name in the local telephone directory's government pages and send the letter there if you aren't sending it by e-mail or fax. However you are sending it, follow the ALA's "Five Basic Rules for Effective Communication."

1. Be brief. A legislator's time is limited. So is yours.
2. Be appreciative. Acknowledge past support, and convey thanks for current action.
3. Be specific. Refer to local library and district needs.
4. Be informative. Give reasons why a measure should be supported.
5. Be courteous. Ask; do not demand or threaten. Be positive but polite.

State and national associations often support Legislation Days, when members of the association go to the Capitol to call on legislators; this can be effective. Although school library media specialists often cannot be away from school on these days, that does not mean they cannot be effective lobbyists. Indeed, it may be even more effective to meet legislators at their local offices. The local offices of state legislators and members of Congress are listed in the government pages of telephone directories (usually blue pages).

Legislators most often hear from constituents when they want something. It is desirable to establish communication with legislators and their office staff before a need or crisis arises. This can smooth the way for a visit in time of need. Again, remember that legislators need information from their constituents to better understand issues. As a reliable information provider, you can convince your legislator that library media specialists are friends of lawmakers, there to help them understand the educational needs of students.

Sometimes the library media specialist must move to block proposed legislation. Professional associations usually have a legislative network in place to notify members when it is necessary to visit legislators, write letters, or make telephone calls against, as well as for, a bill. When a call comes, it is important to act quickly.

For the library media specialist who becomes immersed in local, state, and national politics, there are some simple rules:

1. Give legislators carefully researched and correct information. To tell a state legislator that the average per-pupil expenditure for media materials in a state is a very low figure only to have incorrect information contradicted will be embarrassing to everyone, perhaps critically so to the legislator.

2. Follow legislation of interest to school library media specialists from introduction through signature. Carefully choose legislators to support the issue. Learn to gather support from news media—local newspapers and television—as well as lawmakers.

3. Learn to write letters to lawmakers, and then write them. The image of library media programs must be a positive one, and lobbying will help create a positive image of library media specialists and their programs.

For library media specialists who have never considered it necessary to lobby, one is reminded of the Little Red Hen. People are out there planting the wheat, gathering it, and making bread. When it is time to eat that bread, they will not be eager to give away slices to those who have not been active participants in the process. For the continued improvement of information services for students and teachers in schools, school library media specialists must lobby every day with their meaningful programs, demonstrating to students, teachers, administrators, and parents that they and the services in the media programs make a difference in the lives of children. School library media specialists also must keep reminding their community members how important information resources are in schools for the education of future taxpayers. Finally, state and national government officials must be told that cutting funds for information resources for school library media centers reduces the ability of youth to become effective citizens in a global community and persons interested in and capable of lifelong learning.

This is a formidable assignment, but one that must be undertaken. If school library media specialists wish to make a difference in students' academic achievement, they must ensure that attention is paid to the program. As Lance and others have pointed out in many states,

- The size of a library media center's staff and collection is the best school predictor of academic achievement.
- The instructional role of the library media specialist shapes the collection and, in turn, academic achievement.
- Library media expenditures affect library media center staff and collection size and, in turn, academic achievement.[2]

SCHOOL LIBRARY MEDIA SPECIALISTS IN THE GLOBAL COMMUNITY

Many school library media specialists in the United States are aware of the need to participate in the global community. The world is shrinking with the expansion of access to communication and movement of resources from one country to another. Language may not remain a problem as computer programs translate texts. Students in schools today need to know how to interact with their peers in other nations. School library media specialists need to be models of interaction with others throughout the world.

Attending annual conferences of IASL and IFLA provides an opportunity to meet school librarians from other nations. Those attending from developing nations point out the need for active school library media centers in their schools in the face of no funding, no collections, and no perceived value. With the increased capability of electronic transfer, many persons providing service from their small school libraries will become part of the global community as transmission of information becomes available through the Internet. School library media specialists in the United States should become aware of the problems of schools without libraries and should begin to help plan solutions to these problems.

Perhaps one of the greatest pleasures of being a school library media specialist is being able to expand horizons of students and teachers through the activities that go on in the library media center and the opportunities to move out of the media center into their local and world communities. Making students aware of opportunities that will be available to them both as citizens of the United States and of the world is opening a door to a successful future.

LOOKING LIKE A PROFESSIONAL, MAKING YOU A PROFESSIONAL

Like the old adage, if it looks like a duck and quacks like a duck, it must be a duck, if library media specialists are to assume our rightful place in the professional community, we need to make sure that we look like a professional and sound like a professional. At some recent school library media conferences, this author has presented a program called "Fifty Ways to Succeed @ Your Library." Because most of them have no real cost attached, implementing these will help you become the professional you should be. They are divided into four categories: managing, teaching, public relations, and "that extra effort."

Managing

1. Make your library media center appealing to all who enter. Close your eyes and do a virtual walk into your media center. What does the visitor see? How can you make it more attractive?

2. Don't put up with broken, scarred, wrong size mismatched furniture and shelving. This one could cost you some money, so you need to take your principal, a teacher, and a member of your advisory committee to a national or state association meeting where many furniture vendors display their wares and show what the library could look like. Be prepared with the amount that would need to be raised and have some thoughts about how you would raise that money.

3. Improve your signage. If you don't know how to do this, look around at local bookstores and see what they do. You could ask the art teacher to help with this.

4. Take some hints from public librarians. Some children's librarians put their bookshelves on wheels to make rearranging spaces quite easy. They also sometimes hang book racks on the end of shelves and do other things to make spaces more useful.

5. Merchandise your collection. Visit the local bookstore or a local department store and look at how they attract customers to want to buy their products.

6. Weed your collection. Nothing is as negative as shelves and shelves of old, unattractive, out-of-date things that nobody wants. Shelves crowded with "dogs" will keep your teachers and students away because they won't think you have anything that is modern.

7. Change displays, bulletin boards, and exhibitions frequently. What's on that bulletin board or in that display case will draw students into the media center.

8. Help students learn about continuing their educations. Guidance counselors cannot reach students as easily as you can because their offices are small and usually require an appointment to enter. You can help every student find something to do when they finish high school. If students knew how to enroll in programs after high school, quitting school might be less an option. Most of us came from homes where parents let us know what we were supposed to do after high school, so we stayed in high school. You need to do this for students who don't have parents who see any advantage (or possibility) for study after high school.

Teaching

9. Work with teachers and students to make the teaching job easier for teachers and the learning job easier for students. Collaborate with teachers.

10. Meet with teachers informally and formally and plan. Collaborate with teachers.

11. Teach, with their teachers, things students need to learn. Collaborate with teachers.

12. Teach your teachers all the new bells and whistles technology has to offer. This makes you the hero in the battle to stay current.

13. Welcome all teachers with a smile. Yes, the football coach does like to get rid of classes before the Friday game. You should be thankful that you aren't responsible for the arms, legs, neck, back, and head of 100 young men who may come away from that game with something wrong with any or all of those body parts. Make sure you have a collaborative assignment for the class, and be a good sport.

14. Share with teachers new articles from your professional collection. They will look to you for leadership in educational innovation.

15. Dream up new ways to approach same old same old. A teacher may be bored to death with some, if not all, assignments, which means students are going to be equally bored. Help spruce up assignments, and learning will increase.

16. Be especially helpful with new teachers or things new to a teacher. In both cases, the teacher may be quite anxious. It is an easy way to become a hero and leader.

17. Encouraging reading has always been the assignment of library media specialists. Students today are bombarded by so many opportunities to do anything except read, while many of these opportunities require the ability to read. Use all the ideas you can think of and find on the Internet, in professional books, and in other publications to increase students' reading skills.

Public Relations

18. Copy Wal-Mart's greeter policy. Assign students to stand at the door and welcome students into the library. This might be a good assignment for an escapee from study hall if your school still has them.

19. Watch rules. My principal always told me that a rule meant a punishment for breaking the rule, and keeping up with those who break ineffective rules and their punishment is more difficult than not having the rule in the first place. Two all-encompassing rules are: Do unto others what you would have others do unto you, and do not do unto others what you would not want others to do unto you.

20. Watch and remove rules that limit students, such as "two weeks checkout only," "you can't come to the library if you have an overdue book," or "one book only."

21. Make sure the students understand it is *their* library. This means you ask them what they want and then you try to provide it. After all, it is *their* library, isn't it?

22. Overcome overdues. If you lengthen the checkout time (as you do for teachers) and only require that a student return the book when another student requests it or at the end of the semester, you won't have overdues.

23. Forget fines. Fines cost more in bad public relations and bookkeeping than you could possibly earn.

24. Resist broadcasting negative messages over the public address system. Make these messages about good new books, new things available, and new opportunities.

25. Resist negative reminders in the library. If your library media center has rules, they should begin with something other than "No" or "Do not."

26. Have great programs. Schedule exciting events in the media center. Shopping centers and airports bring automobiles in for people to see. Ever think about a motorcycle in the library?

27. Encourage students to volunteer in the library media center. This helps them understand what goes on in there. If they understand a database well, they can teach others how to search, effectively easing your teaching load. It also makes the media center *their* media center.

28. Keep the principal informed of exciting things going on in the library media center. Give him or her things to brag about to other principals.

29. Maintain a great Web site with links to great information. If you can't do this alone, draft a reliable student or two.

30. Keep your principal informed about what is new in the professional literature. When principals are cutting-edge aware of all the newest educational trends, they won't be embarrassed at a district meeting when something new is proposed that they haven't heard of.

31. Have an advisory committee for the library media center. What they can help you do will surprise you. They become your advocates.

32. Provide at least one event in the library each semester for parents. Make sure the students are involved.

That Extra Effort

33. Watch for opportunities for proposal writing. This can be time consuming at the start, but once you get a list of places and their offerings, you can pick and choose. Also, you need not do this alone. Get your advisory committee members or other teachers to help you, or, if you want to get a bigger grant, recruit other media specialists in the district to join you.

34. Find out about contests in which your students can participate. You may have to help the teachers collect and submit entries, but a winning student makes the newspaper.

35. Find out about field trips. Sometimes you can tell teachers about special opportunities for students and how to go about getting to the place. Sometimes you can take the training offered by the museum or gallery and become the teacher for all the students, thus relieving all other teachers in your building from participating in the training.

36. Don't miss school events. Students know who attends their special functions, whether it is a football game, the class play or musical, or a field trip. Attending school events is an easy way to become a mentor.

37. Show your worth. You may have to gather some statistics, but when you make a difference, you need a record of that.

38. Keep records of your successful experiences. If something worked well, do it again.

39. Conduct real research. For this you may need to find a local college or university and an assistant professor in need of research for tenure, but what you discover may have more value than action research you did on your own.

40. Make frequent reports. These should be short and sweet and interesting.

41. Visit your legislators. Take students, teachers, and parents to show off your program. The legislators will know who and what you are when you need to ask for legislation.

42. Invite the school board and legislators to your school. This needs to have your principal's approval, but it may not have occurred to your administrators that having the school board or your legislators visit the school and library just to show off the great programs there would bring applause to your school. It is another way to help them understand education and school library media programs.

43. Be a problem solver for little, middle, and big problems. Gain a reputation for getting things corrected, made better, made possible. You may not always be able to do this alone, but you should learn who are the best people to work with to make things happen.

44. Volunteer to present a session at your state conference. You should be able to get funding to attend. If you really want to ensure this, ask your principal and a teacher to present with you.

45. Volunteer to write for a professional periodical. Your teachers, principal, and community will love seeing their school featured.

46. Bring in the media as often as you can. When you do something in the library, perhaps invite legislators to your building, the media will come mostly because the legislator will want this featured in the media.

47. Make sure students understand Frances Henne's description of the ultimate in information literacy: "For some students, and in certain schools, this may be many students, the only library skill that they should have to acquire is an awareness, imprinted indelibly and happily upon them, that the library is a friendly place where the librarians are eager to help." This is what we are all about.

48. Think before you whine; then don't.

49. Most of all, enjoy your job, all day, every day. The contribution you are making to the teachers and students in your school cannot be measured.

50. Smile.

Library media specialists open the world of information to students, teachers, administrators, and the community. We can and do make a difference in the lives of students every day of every school year. What an exciting role to play.

Exercises

1. Review the charges to AASL committees found in the ALA Handbook of Organization. Compose a letter to the president-elect of AASL, who will make new appointments, volunteering to serve on the committee of your choice. Be sure to state your qualifications for this committee as well as your desire to serve.

2. Compose a one-page document for your school board requesting support for an increase in the per-pupil allocation for materials. Statistics from matching costs of materials from purchase orders for the past three years will demonstrate the rising costs of materials and can be used to support your position.

3. Find out the latest legislation in Congress that would affect school library media services, and write a letter supporting the position that would most help improve these services.

4. Gather together evidence of the recent activities in your library media center, and plan how to present them to your state or national legislator. Call your legislator and request an appointment or plan an activity to invite your state or national legislator to your school library media center.

5. Plan an activity that will open a library media center to the larger world community.

6. Choose one or more of the "Fifty Ways" and implement them or add other ways to the list.

NOTES

1. Helen R. Adams, "Money Talks," *School Library Media Quarterly* (Winter 1994): 127.

2. Keith Curry Lance, Lynda Welborn, and Christine Hamilton-Pennell, *The mpact of School Library Media Centers on Academic Achievement* (Castle Rock, CO: Hi Willow Research and Publishing, 1993), 92.

Appendix A
Writing a Technology Plan

Here are some questions to consider before coordinating the writing of a technology plan:

- How often should the planning committee meet? Consider all the logistics. When will meetings be held? Where can they be held? How long will they last? Who will attend? Who will chair the meeting? Who will design the agenda? Will you use a professional consultant?

- Can you collect sample technology plans from similar schools or districts? Is it possible to visit a benchmark school or district? Will committee members be able to attend expositions, conferences, or professional development opportunities to observe best practices?

- What technology resources are currently available in your school and district? How are these resources being used? Are there varying levels of expertise in using these technologies present in your committee—the expert, the average user, the reticent?

- Will the plan be evaluated and assessed by the same committee after completion?

The Instructional Technology Plan, as a physical document, can run from as few as twenty to several hundred pages long, depending on the size and complexity of the school or district. There is no template to follow when writing the plan, but it will be helpful to look at other school or district documents and use a similar writing style. Match the layout, type, and overall design to what the stakeholders are used to seeing. Share the document in draft status to allow everyone in the group to contribute to and proofread the plan. If possible, send drafts in hard copy as well as posting the draft to a Web site. Get feedback in any way possible, and use technology to do this (e-mail, discussion boards, wikis, etc.).

The Instructional Technology Plan can be long and overwhelming to nontechnical people, and ultimately the school board will need to approve it. Be sure to include an executive summary, which contains concise descriptions of the major initiatives, budget, and timeline.

Typically, the Instructional Technology Plan consists of:

- Cover sheet
- Title page
- Table of contents
- Acknowledgements
- Executive summary
- Committee membership
- Vision and mission statements (might include philosophy)
- Demographics (community, schools, academic ranking)
- Data collection, analysis, and reporting
- Critical issues
  o Infrastructure and facilities
  o Equipment
  o New and emerging technologies
  o Networking and security
  o Funding
  o Acceptable use policies
- Implementation
  o Public relations
  o Professional development
  o Incentives/reward system
  o Purchasing
  o Community resources
  o Legal aspects
  o Curriculum, instruction, and evaluation
  o Maintenance
- Evaluation
- Budget
- Bibliography or reference list
- Glossary
- Appendices
- Index

Appendix B
Sample Letter of Application

Your Street Address
City, State ZIP
Date

Dr. _____, Superintendent
yyy Schools
Street Address
City, State, ZIP

Dear Dr. _____:

Our University Placement Office has indicated that you are seeking applications for a position as school librarian in one of your elementary schools, and I am very interested in being a candidate for this position. My resume is enclosed.

I have a bachelor's degree in elementary education from the University of Z. When I finish my master's degree in library science in the School of Library and Information Science at the University of A, I will be applying for (K–12) school library certification as an endorsement on my Instructor I certificate in elementary education.

During the past year, I have prepared a portfolio of work completed in my program, including a proposal for funding (group project), an in-service education workshop to show teachers and students how to use a digital camera, a Web site for a fictional school, and a 45-minute speech written to present at a professional association meeting. During my practicum, I prepared two teaching units, collaborating for one with a high school science teacher and the other with all first-grade teachers who were revising their unit on community helpers. I also have three examples of students' senior research projects.

241

My experience with technology includes extensive experience with ____, ____, ____, and ____. In addition, both schools in which I completed my practicum experience offered extended reference services as members of the statewide online library of resources from two database vendors, ____ and ____, as well as an OPAC database with interlibrary loan.

I'm looking forward to hearing from you.

Sincerely,

Appendix C
Questionnaire

Circle the correct response to each question.	-1	0	1	2	3	4	5
How does the center compare to others in district?	not very well	don't know	almost as good as	as good as	better than	much better than	best in district
How many books per student are in media center?	don't know	1	3	5	10 student	15	more than 15
In general, the collection of books is:	out of date	Peripheral value	few recent titles, fair condition	some recent titles, some relevant	mostly relevant, most in good condition	mostly recent titles	recent, relevant, good condition
How many databases do you have?	none	1	2	3	4	share with public library	Connected to statewide resources
Do users produce learning materials?	teachers only	groups of students	only when assigned to do so	teachers produce many materials	students sometimes produce visuals	teachers produce multimedia lessons	teachers produce lessons; students produce portfolios

We have a new technology plan.	don't know	why?	I think so	library media center gave a survey	Answered survey	made suggestions	voted on plan
We have new technologies.	don't know	computers	fax machine	online resources	wireless cart	24/7 references	all plus media center Web site
Media collection is weeded.	don't know	we never discard anything	we rarely discard anything	occasionally	yearly	semi-yearly	constantly evaluate and discard
Media center is used for:	discipline	study hall	entertainment	supplementary use	support for curriculum	extension of learning	integral to learning
Media center is used by __% of potential users.	don't know	0–9	10–20	21–40	41–60	61–80	over 80
Media collection is used by at least 50% of students.	don't know	never	once a year	each semester	once a month	every two weeks	once a week
Students enjoy going to the media center.	don't know	never	occasionally	some of the time	often	most of the time	always
Media center is used by 50% of teachers.	don't know	never	once a year	each semester	once a month	every two weeks	once a week
Teachers choose time for use of the media center based on instructional needs.	Never; they follow a rigid schedule	occasionally	when reminded	some of the time	often	most of the time	always
Media center is open before and after school.	never	only for faculty	by special plans	either before school or after school, but not both	often	most of the time	always
Media specialist may leave the center.	no, has study hall	don't know	only for lunch	sends classroom collections	seldom visits classrooms	often visits classrooms	regularly visits classrooms
Media specialist serves on curriculum committees.	don't know	no committees exist	sends suggestions	attempts to assist when asked	serves on one committee	is an integral part of planning	leads curriculum planning
Media specialist and principal Have a five-year plan for the media center	don't know	no plan	principal speaks to media specialist when passing	principal meets with media specialist yearly to discuss program	media specialist submits annual report	media specialist keeps principal informed of needs	Plan is provided by media specialist; principal approves

The principal supports the media program.	never	occa-sionally	when-ever re-minded	some of the time	often	most of the time	always
Teachers support the media program	never	occa-sionally	when-ever re-minded	some of the time	often	most of the time	always
Students support the media program.	never	occa-sionally	when-ever re-minded	some of the time	often	most of the time	always
Media center has an effect on the school.	Never con-sid-ered	don't know	perhaps	occasion-ally	often	most of the time	always

Appendix D

Presentation of a Five-Year Long-Range Plan

FOR LIBRARY MEDIA CENTER DEVELOPMENT

Goal: To bring the Thomas Alva Edison Middle School Library Media Center staff, program, and holdings to meet the needs of students and teachers.

Thomas Alva Edison Middle School is one of 25 schools in the Washington Area School District. This district has a varied population, from inner-city to upper-middle-class residential areas. Three of the 20 elementary schools, 1 of the 10 middle schools, and 2 of the 5 high schools are designated magnet schools serving children with exceptional skills in one or more areas. One high school is designated for the performing arts and the other for students interested in science and math. Students interested in vocational training attend a vocational program supported by the county.

All schools, elementary through high school, have classroom art, music, and physical education instruction as well as band and chorus for interested students. Students may also participate in intramural sports.

Four high schools, excluding the performing arts magnet, participate in Class A football and baseball programs for boys. Girls' and boys' teams provide opportunities for basketball, indoor and outdoor track, soccer, swimming, and volleyball at all five high schools.

Edison Middle School, the designated magnet middle school, has 1,245 students. Because of its geographical location, 50 percent of the population comes from upper-middle-class homes in the immediate area, and the remaining 50 percent matriculates through an application and testing process. The school features strong science and math programs and offers four foreign languages. Spanish, French, and German are taught by on-site instructors, and Japanese instruction is delivered via an interactive video

246

classroom. Because of the strong foreign language component, other areas of the curriculum stress a more global view than in the other, more traditional middle schools.

The international emphasis of this school means that students may be given priority for attendance if they are international residents or recent emigrants to the Washington Area Schools. A strong Teaching English to Speakers of Other Languages (TESOL) program resides here.

PERSONNEL

The Edison Middle School's media specialist is a licensed professional who chairs the School's Curriculum Committee. This person is assigned the management of the media program and those assigned to work in the program. In addition, the media specialist attends departmental meetings as often as possible, and always when changes in curriculum are to be discussed.

Because of the strong technology component, the transmittal of instruction for some classes and the online resources in the media center, a full-time technology manager is assigned to the media center to handle technology problems and to oversee the computer lab. Two clerks handle routine assignments: one is assigned responsibility for distributing and collecting textbooks for and from use in the classrooms.

The professional, technical, and clerical tasks can be accomplished with the existing personnel for the first two years. However, by the third year, the use of the information resources at school and from teachers' and students' homes will require additional materials and hardware. Training teachers and students on how to make the best use of these resources as well as the circulation and maintenance will require an additional .5 professional media specialist and a .5 technology manager. It is hoped that a single individual can be hired for half-time assignments. The additional clerical staff member will be able to assume responsibility for communication contacts as the distance program expands to add more variety to the school's curriculum.

2009	2010	2011	2012	2013	2014
1 FTE Prof	No change	No change	1.5 FTE Prof	No change	No change
1 FTE Tech			1.5 FTE Tech		
2 FTE Clerk			3 FTE Clerks		

FACILITY

The media center at Edison Middle School was recently remodeled so that the facility, with 10,000 square feet, easily accommodates 120 seats in the media center reading room, 30+ seats in the library classroom, and 30 work stations in the computer lab. With the installation of a wireless network in the school, students may use their own computers throughout the library. The shelving provides easy access for students to all the print materials in the library.

Because most of the newspaper and periodical collection is available online through the statewide database and the additional databases to which we subscribe, the library media center provides multiple copies of only 20 of the most often requested periodicals. The center's periodical storage has been greatly reduced.

When the area was remodeled, ergonomic desks were installed for students and teachers in the computer lab and at the online public access catalog (OPAC) stations in the library. The reading room has some new tables and chairs, but most of the old tables remain. Although they have been sanded and are in good condition, new groupings separating old from new might help make the library more attractive.

We have made no budget allocation for the facility in our five-year plan. We believe that other items are of higher priority at this time.

EQUIPMENT

At present, the Edison Middle School Library has a classroom with 30 desktop computers with Internet connectivity. We also maintain a collection of 30 laptop computers on a wireless cart for checkout to classrooms or for student use in the library if a class is using the lab. These laptop computers may be checked out at the end of the day for home use, but they are to be returned before the beginning of the school the next day.

In the reading room, five stations support the OPAC and one station is for circulation. Another station is available in the office of each professional and each clerk (four stations until 2011).

Because all forms of media can be transmitted from the media center to classrooms, there is little need to provide televisions, VCRs, or DVD players. We do have a television with VCRs and DVD players in case the system should malfunction.

We recognize that equipment purchases must be carefully planned so that equipment remains compatible. New items on the market are carefully tested to see that they provide a needed service and fit the current software collection or have the type of information needed to support the curriculum.

We also recognize that the estimated costs for equipment will seem high. However, the continuous upgrading of both software and hardware dictates a critical need for regular, sustained replacement of equipment.

BUDGET

Salaries for personnel must be estimated from the district's salary schedule for years of service and professional education. We've used $40,000 as a base salary for both professionals and $20,000 for the clerks just to help you understand how the increases would look. Calculations were to add

3 percent to each year's salary until 2011. Then salary increases include the additional half-time professional positions and for the one additional clerical position.

2009	2010	2011	2012	2013	2014
	+3%	+3%	+.5 position	+3%	+3%
$40,000	$41,200	$42,436	$65,368	$68,829	$70,893
40,000	41,200	42,436	65,368	68,829	70,893
40,000	41,200	42,436	87,155	89,769	92,462
$120,000	$123,600	$127,308	$207,891	$227,427	$234,258

TRAVEL

A budget item also provides support for the media specialist and the technology assistant to attend workshops, conferences, and training sessions to learn about changes in media center management, new technologies and their applications, new resources, and methods of teaching. The media specialist also holds office in the Association of State Library Media Specialists. This funding supports travel to board meetings, conference planning sessions, and conference attendance. A higher increase is made in the year 2010 to accommodate the new persons in the media center.

2009	2010	2011	2012	2013	2014
$7,000	$8,000	$9,000	$10,000	$11,000	$12,000

EQUIPMENT

We anticipate that the cost per computer for our lab will be reduced in the immediate future. However, for our other computers, we would like to continue to continue to purchase a higher level of computer. We plan to purchase new equipment yearly as follows: six computers for the lab (1/5 of the collection), six laptops, one replacement OPAC and one replacement for administration. Note in year 2011 a new server will be added. The only purchase in 2013 is another wireless cart with 20 laptops.

	Lab Stations	Laptops	OPACS	Admin.	Server	Total
2009	6 = $12,000	6 = $12,000	1 = $1,200	1 = $1,200		$26,400
2010	6 = 9,000	6 = 12,000	1 = 1,200	1 = 1,200		23,400
2011	6 = 9,000	6 = 12,000	1 = 1,200	1 = 3,600	$10,000	35,800
2012	6 = 9,000	6 = 12,000	1 = 1,200	1 = 1,200		23,400
2013	Additional wireless cart with 20 laptops					30,000
2014	6 = 9,000	6 = 12,000	1 = 1,200	1 = 1,200		23,400
				Computer hardware total		$162,400

COMPUTER SOFTWARE

Computer software purchase for upgrading systems and for renewal of the existing online newspaper/magazine service will cost at least $25,000 per year for the next five years. If we change circulation systems or the online public access catalog, a larger amount could be needed in this category.

Total: $125,000

COLLECTION

Analyzing the library collection is carried out to determine the quality of the collection to meet the needs of students and teachers. A schoolwide selection committee assists in the review of new materials that may be considered appropriate for purchase. Teachers and students are queried concerning their expectations for subject areas and interest levels to be met. Weeding procedures ensure that the collection is relevant, up-to-date, accurate, relevant, as interesting as possible, and provides the research materials needed to support and enhance the curriculum.

Our collection includes 32,000 books, or 25 books per student. We have not recently calculated the number of titles held per pupil, but books, when duplicated, are purchased in paperback, and these numbers are not counted in the 32,000 total. For this reason, we will allocate $30 per pupil per year for the five-year period, or $37,350 per year.

Total: $186,750

As stated earlier, most of the periodicals and newspapers are available online through the statewide database. The cost of this item includes the duplicate copies of 20 periodicals for a yearly cost of $2,400 per year.

Total: $12,000

Budget Analysis

	2010	2011	2012	2013	2014
Salaries	$123,600	$127,308	$207,891	$227,427	$234,256
Travel	6,000	7,000	9,000	11,000	13,000
Hardware	26,000	23,400	35,800	30,000	23,400
Software	25,000	25,000	25,000	25,000	25,000
Print/books	19,000	19,000	19,000	19,000	19,000
Magazines	2,400	2,400	2,400	2,400	2,400
	$202,400	$204,108	$299,091	$314,627	$317,056

Total without salaries $619,200

Grand total (includes salaries) $1,337,282

Appendix E
Volunteers

Volunteers may be asked to assist in the library media center program in many school districts. Care must be taken to make sure that the use of volunteers does not violate the teachers' contract and that the school administration is aware that volunteers are being recruited. A districtwide policy about the use of volunteers in schools may exist. If the district provides orientation and coordination, the library media specialist can be relieved of responsibility for this part of the process.

If no districtwide program is in place, the library media specialist must do the following:

1. Inform the principal and other appropriate administrators of the scope of the volunteer program and the person or persons designated to take responsibility for it.

2. Develop job descriptions of the tasks expected of volunteers so that interested people may anticipate their activities once they volunteer. These job descriptions will help the library media specialist plan the training for volunteers.

3. Recruit volunteers through the parent-teacher organization in the school, notes sent home with students, pleas to service organizations in the area, and any other means available.

4. Recruit a manager of volunteers. That is, enlist another person to assume responsibility for the attendance of volunteers. The volunteer coordinator frees the media specialist of such time-consuming tasks as volunteer scheduling and rescheduling, accepting telephone calls for volunteers who cannot appear on their scheduled day, and so on. Otherwise, the volunteer program could become more trouble than it is worth.

5. Ask volunteers to complete an information form (sample follows).

6. During orientation, explain your expectations to volunteers. If there is no district orientation, volunteers *must* be informed of their expected behavior toward students and information they may learn about students. All information about the school, teachers, or the program must remain confidential and should remain at school. Volunteers must not discuss the activities in the media center with their friends and neighbors, because this may be a violation of students' rights. Any volunteer who is unable to come at the designated time should call the volunteer coordinator well in advance to allow opportunity to call a substitute. Volunteers should also recognize that they will serve as "media specialists" while in the media center and should dress and behave appropriately.

7. Careful records should be kept of volunteers' attendance, activities, and comments concerning possible revisions and volunteer program improvement. Careful evaluation can help reinforce good work by volunteers, encourage better performance, and help remove those who are not adding value to the program.

8. Plan a reward system for volunteers. Parties to honor them or other acknowledgements of their efforts will be appreciated and will encourage them to continue. The true test of volunteer devotion is continuing after one's children leave the school.

9. Remember at all times that volunteers are directly linked to the school and to those people who can support the library media program. Volunteers can be enthusiastic advocates of media activities.

Parent Volunteer Form

Please complete this form and return it to the library media specialist.

Name _____

Address _____

Telephone Number _____

Cell Phone _____

Days you are available to volunteer: _____

(Please indicate 1, 2, 3 for your preference)

Monday   Tuesday   Wednesday   Thursday   Friday

Times you are available to come to the library media center:

_____

A.M. only   P.M. only   A.M. and P.M.

Grades you prefer to work with:

Primary   Elementary   Middle School   High School

I would like to (check as many as apply):

___ read stories to children   ___ type orders and book lists

___ prepare a bulletin board   ___ assist with computers

___ duplicate learning materials   ___ help circulate materials

___ other, please specify

Appendix F

ALA Intellectual Freedom Policy Statements[1]

53.1 LIBRARY BILL OF RIGHTS

The American Library Association affirms that all libraries are forums for information and ideas, and that the following basic policies should guide their services.

1. Books and other library resources should be provided for the interest, information, and enlightenment of all people of the community the library serves. Materials should not be excluded because of the origin, background, or views of those contributing to their creation.

2. Libraries should provide materials and information presenting all points of view on current and historical issues. Materials should not be proscribed or removed because of partisan or doctrinal disapproval.

3. Libraries should challenge censorship in the fulfillment of their responsibility to provide information and enlightenment.

4. Libraries should cooperate with all persons and groups concerned with resisting abridgment of free expression and free access to ideas.

5. A person's right to use a library should not be denied or abridged because of origin, age, background, or views.

6. Libraries which make exhibit spaces and meeting rooms available to the public they serve should make such facilities available on an equitable basis, regardless of the beliefs or affiliations of individuals or groups requesting their use.

7. Adopted June 18, 1948. Amended February 2, 1961, June 27, 1967, and January 23, 1980, by the ALA Council.

53.1.1 Challenged materials that meet the criteria for selection in the materials selection policy of the library should not be removed under legal or extra-legal pressure. Adopted 1971, revised 1990.

53.1.2 Expurgation of any parts of books or other library resources by the library, its agent, or its parent institution is a violation of the Library Bill of Rights because it denies access to the complete work, and, therefore, to the entire spectrum of ideas that work was intended to express.

53.1.3 Members of the school community involved in the collection development process employ educational criteria to select resources unfettered by their personal, political, social, or religious views. Students and educators served by the school library media program have access to resources and services free of constraints resulting from personal, partisan, or doctrinal disapproval. School library media specialists resist efforts by individuals or groups to define what is appropriate for all students or teachers to read, view, hear, or access via electronic means. Adopted 1986, amended 1990, 2000, 2005.

53.1.4 Denying minors equal and equitable access to all library resources available to other users violates the Library Bill of Rights. Librarians and governing bodies should maintain that parents—and only parents—have the right and responsibility to restrict the access of their children—and only their children—to library resources. Lack of access to information can be harmful to minors. Librarians and library governing bodies have a public and professional obligation to ensure that all members of the community they serve have free, equal, and equitable access to the entire range of library resources regardless of content, approach, format, or amount of detail. This principle of library service applies equally to all users, minors as well as adults. Librarians and library governing bodies must uphold this principal in order to provide adequate and effective services to minors. Adopted 1972, amended 1981, 1992, and 2004.

53.1.5 Evaluation of library materials is not to be used as a convenient means to remove materials presumed to be controversial or disapproved by segments of the community. Adopted 1973, amended 1981.

53.1.6 Attempts to restrict access to library materials violate the basic tenets of the Library Bill of Rights. Policies to protect library materials for reasons of physical preservation, protection from theft, or mutilation must be carefully formulated and administered with extreme attention to the principles of intellectual freedom. All proposals for restricted access collections should be carefully scrutinized to ensure that the purpose is not to suppress a viewpoint or to place a barrier between certain patrons and particular content. A primary goal of the library profession is to facilitate access to all points of view on current and historical issues. Adopted 1973, amended 1981, 1991, 2000, and 2004.

NOTE

1. American Library Association, the Voice of America's Libraries, *ALA Handbook of Organization 2007–2008: An Annual Guide to Member Participation* (Chicago: American Library Association, 2008).

Appendix G
Publications List

This list has been prepared to assist building-level library media specialists to facilitate information sharing about exciting programs and activities. By reviewing the information concerning topics of interest to the editor and requirements for submission of papers, media specialists may choose an audience for any article they might produce. The list contains the name of the periodical and, when available, the address, telephone number, URL, editor, information concerning the editorial policy, and requirements for publication. Journals published by professional associations have editors who tend to rotate frequently, because the task is often a volunteer position. Commercial publishers, in contrast, hire editors to fill regular positions. Because topics for issues change frequently and submission guidelines may also change, it is wise to use the URL to get the most up-to-date information about publishing in each periodical.

Children and Libraries: The Journal of the Association for Library Service to Children

Association for Library Service to Children
A Division of the American Library Association
50 East Huron Street
Chicago, IL 60611-2795
Telephone: (312) 944-6780
URL: www.ala.org
Editor: Sharon Korbeck Verbeten
820 Spooner Court
DePere, WI 54115
Telephone: (920) 339-2740
CALeditor@yahoo.com

The official journal of the Association for Library Service to Children is published three times per year. *Children and Libraries* (CAL) primarily serves as a vehicle for continuing education of librarians working with children, which showcases current scholarly research and practice in library service to children and spotlights significant activities and programs of the association.

- Submit manuscripts that are neither under consideration nor accepted elsewhere.
- Send four copies of the manuscript to the editor at the address above (one copy if sending by e-mail).
- Editor will acknowledge receipt of all manuscripts and send them to at least two referees for evaluation.
- Accepted manuscripts with timely content will have scheduling priority.
- During the production phase, page proofs will be sent to authors to confirm copy accuracy and answer copy editor queries.
- Authors receive two complimentary copies of the journal at publication.

Knowledge Quest

American Association of School Librarians
A division of the American Library Association
50 East Huron Street
Chicago, IL 60611
Telephone: (312) 944-6780 ext. 4386
Fax: (312) 664-7459
URL: www.ala.org
Editor: Debbie Abilock

Devoted to offering substantive information to assist school library media specialists, supervisors, library educators, and other decision makers concerned with the development of school library media programs and services, articles address the integration of theory and practice in school librarianship and new developments in education, learning theory, and relevant disciplines.

KQWeb, the online component of *Knowledge Quest,* is dedicated to enhancing the print publication with expanded articles and original content.

Submit all manuscripts via e-mail attachments in Microsoft Word or rich text format to the appropriate editor. The subject line should include the column or issue name, if appropriate. Although the peer-review process and decision on submissions can take up to six months, authors should receive acknowledgment of their submissions within a week. Authors who do not hear from an editor at *KQ* should assume that their e-mail has not been received and should write again.

Check the Web site for the personal information that must be submitted with articles, requirements for formatting, and writing the abstract. Consult the *Chicago Manual of Style, 15th ed.* (Chicago: University of Chicago Press, 2003) for bibliographic style, capitalization, abbreviations, and design of tables.

An example of a state (Pennsylvania) association (Pennsylvania School Librarians Association) publication is shown below:

Learning and Media

Pennsylvania School Librarians Association
URL: www.psla.org
Editor: Michael Nailor
nflncfl@ptd.net

Writing for *Learning and Media* is simpler than many media specialists might think. If you have information that others in the profession need—ideas, expertise, experiences—consider writing a piece for *Learning and Media.* Forward a Microsoft Word document attached to an e-mail. Pictures may be sent as .jpg files attached to a separate e-mail.

Library Journal

Library Journal
Division of Reed Business Information
360 Park Avenue South
New York, NY 10010
Telephone: (646) 746-6819
Fax: (646) 746-6734
URL: www.libraryjournal.com
Editor-in-Chief: Francine Fialkoff
ljarticles@reedbusiness.com

Library Journal welcomes the best feature articles that reach out to the profession in a broad way or offer useful information and ideas to others in an accessible and readable style. Send either queries or finished articles, via e-mail if possible. A query can consist of just a paragraph or several. Describe what you plan to cover and your approach. Describe your connection to the topic and your expertise. The editors will reply and let authors know whether they are interested within four to six weeks. If you have completed a draft of the article, send it in attached to your e-mail. Most of the features run two or three pages in the magazine, which translates into 1,800 to 2,700 words.

Library Media Connection

Linworth Publishing, Inc.
3650 Olentangy River Road, Suite 280
Columbus, OH 43214
Telephone: (614) 884-9995
Fax: (614) 884-9993
URL: www.linworth.com

In all articles, emphasis should be on the author's actual experience or personal observation. Manuscripts (usually 1,200 to 3,000 words) must be submitted electronically in Microsoft Word or ASCII text. Indicate on the manuscript your name, date, and title of the article. Articles may be submitted as attachments to the e-mail address shown above.

Phi Delta Kappan

Phi Delta Kappa
408 North Union Street
Box 789
Bloomington, IN 47402-0789
Telephone: (812) 339-1156
Fax: (812) 339-0018
URL: www.pdkind.org/kappan/kappan.htm
Editor: Bruce M. Smith

The professional journal for education, the *Phi Delta Kappan* provides a forum for debate on controversial subjects. The editors are looking for two qualities for the publication: educational significance and readability. The article should deal with real problems and be factual, logical, and well focused, avoiding the use of jargon and using concrete examples. Manuscripts may be submitted either by U.S. mail or by e-mail. Please use double-spaced format. Send one hard copy to the editor. If you want your manuscript to be returned if it cannot be published, enclose a stamped, self-addressed envelope. In your cover letter, provide sufficient information about yourself for a standard author-identification paragraph. For e-mail, send an e-mail cover letter to manuscripts@pdkintl.org, including sufficient information about yourself for a standard author-identification paragraph, and attach a file of the manuscript (Microsoft Word preferred). Featured articles run between 1,500 and 5,000 words. Please use the *Chicago Manual of Style*.

The Reading Teacher

International Reading Association
Headquarters Office
800 Barksdale Road
Newark, DE 19714-8139
Telephone: (800) 337-READ
Fax: (301) 731-1057
URL: www. reading.org/publication/n/
Editors: Robert B. Cooter and J. Helen Perkins

This peer-reviewed journal welcomes well-written original instruction that improves the literacy of children through age 12. Manuscripts must provide an appropriate blend of practical classroom application and solid theoretical framework. The journal editors will not consider book reviews, literary analyses, class projects, term papers, dissertations, endorsements of commercial products or services, previously published work, or manuscripts under consideration elsewhere.

Manuscripts will be judged on their contribution to the field, timeliness, freshness of approach, and clarity and cohesiveness of presentation. The acceptance rate is approximately 10 percent. Manuscripts for full-length articles should run between 5,000 and 6,000 words, including all references and other materials. These should provide *RT*'s practitioner audience with classroom ideas for literacy development, based on sound theory and research. The primary style manual is the fifth edition of the *Publication Manual of the American Psychological Association*. All manuscripts must be submitted electronically.

School Libraries in Canada: The Journal of the Canadian School Library Association

Canadian Library Association
328 Frank Street
Ottawa, ON K2P 0X8
Telephone: (613) 232-9625
Fax: (613) 563-9895
Interim Editor: Richard Beaudry
960 East 39th Avenue
Vancouver, BC V5W 1K8
Telephone: (604) 713-4799
Fax: (604) 713-4801

Send a manuscript (using the *Publication Manual of the American Psychological Association*, 5th ed. as a guide for formatting and references) to the editor shown above.

School Libraries Worldwide

School Libraries Worldwide
Department of Elementary Education
University of Alberta
551 Education South
Edmonton, Alberta T6G 2G5 Canada
URL: www.iasl-online.org/slw.hml
Editor: Dianne Oberg
doberg@ualberta.ca

School Libraries Worldwide, the International Association of School Librarianship's international journal for school librarianship, is issued twice yearly in January and July. Contributors are invited to submit manuscripts for publication on current research on any aspect of school librarianship. Each issue of the journal usually includes a theme section, introduced by a theme editor and including three or four articles on the theme. *School Libraries Worldwide* primarily publishes new scholarly works, such as research reports and literature reviews. On occasion, due to the nature of the theme chosen, the theme editor may invite the submission of other types of papers, including personal narratives, commentary, and opinion.

- Manuscripts should be word processed or typed, double-spaced throughout, and should not exceed 6,000 words, excluding graphics and references.

- The first page of the manuscript should include the manuscript title and an abstract of approximately 100 words. To ensure anonymity in the review process, the author's name should not be placed on the manuscript.

- Where appropriate, the author may provide the title and abstract in a language other than English, in addition to the English title and abstract, for inclusion in the published article.

- A separate cover page should be provided with the title of the paper, the author's name, affiliation, mailing address, and other contact information (including e-mail address, fax number, and telephone number, where possible); and a brief biographical note (50 to 100 words) about the author, suitable for publication with the manuscript.

School Library Media Activities Monthly

Libraries Unlimited/Greenwood Publishing Group
88 Post Road West
Westport, CT 06881
Telephone: (800) 225-5800 ext. 4488
Fax: (203) 454-8662
Managing Editor: Deborah Levitov
3401 Stockwell Street
Lincoln, NE 68506
Office: (402) 327-2324
deborah.levitov@lu.com

The following format guidelines for each of the sections of *School Library Media Activities Monthly* should help you write your contribution.

Feature Articles: Feature articles should be about some aspect of teaching library media skills or library media practice related to skills instruction. In-text citations and reference lists, where appropriate, should conform to the bibliographic style of the *Chicago Manual of Style*. A very short vita of the author should be included. Black-and-white photographs and/or line drawings to illustrate the content are welcomed.

Activities Almanac: Very brief descriptions of library media activities related to a particular day of the month (birthdays, holidays, historical events, etc.). Maximum of 150 words.

Into the Curriculum: The activities included in this section will be fully developed and in lesson-plan format, including the following components: library media skills; curriculum (subject area) objectives; grade levels; resources (with complete bibliography information);

instructional roles; full description of activity listing all procedures; all necessary reproducible teaching aids; all necessary line illustrations and/or illustrative photographs; and descriptions of ways of evaluating student performance of objectives.

Information Skill of the Month: Ideas and activities that will help reinforce a skill or promote learning or teaching new skills related to information literacy (should be sent as an attachment with an explanation of their application and use).

Notes from the Field: Brief descriptions of activities, ideas, and suggestions related to teaching information literacy skills, professional development, or library media program development.

The Advocate: Articles related to advocacy for the library media center. Share how you have recruited others to be advocates for your program. Provide ideas for using public relations or marketing to gain attention and support for the library media center.

School Library Media Research

American Association of School Librarians
A Division of the American Library Association
50 East Huron Street.
Chicago, IL 60611
Telephone: (312) 944-6780 ext. 4386
Fax: (312) 66–7459
URL: www.ala.org
Editors: Jean Donham and Carol L. Tilley

This official journal of the American Association of School Librarians is the successor to *School Library Media Quarterly Online.* The purpose of *School Library Media Research* is to promote and publish high-quality original research concerning the management, implementation, and evaluation of school library media programs. The journal will also emphasize research on instructional theory, teaching methods, and critical issues relevant to school library media. Please submit manuscripts to:

Carol L. Tilley
SLMR Coeditor
The Graduate School of Library and Information Science
University of Illinois at Urbana-Champaign
501 East Daniel Street, MC-493
Room 220
Champaign, IL 61820–6211
ctilley@uiuc.edu
Telephone: (217) 265-8105
Fax: (217) 244-3302

Teacher Librarian

4501 Forbes Boulevard, Suite 200
Lanham, MD 20706
Telephone: (301) 459-3366
URL: www.scarecrowpress.com
Editors: David V. Loertscher and Esther Rosenfeld

A manuscript, including references, bibliographies, charts, figures and tables, should not exceed 15 double-spaced pages, in 12-point type with one-inch margins. Please include a 100- to 200-word abstract for the manuscript and a word count. References follow the American Psychological Association format. For book titles on lists of recommended materials, include ISBNs. Drawings, cartoons, and photos are welcome. Please include suggested captions and photographer credits, where appropriate. If copyrighted material is used in the article, written evidence of permission to use the material must be included. E-mail the manuscript as an attachment (preferably Microsoft Word for Windows, but any format is acceptable) to admin@teacherlibrarian.com.

Tech Trends

Association for Educational Communications and Technology
1800 North Stonelake Drive, Suite 2
Bloomington, IN 47408
Telephone: (812) 335-7675
URL: www.aect.org
Editor: Sharon Smaldino

This is a publication for professionals and seeks authoritative articles that focus on the practical applications of technology in education and training. Manuscripts of the following types are considered for publication:

1. Reports of innovative and/or exemplary practice.
2. General articles discussing matters of concern to practitioners.
3. Critical reviews of important literature, materials, and devices related to the field.
4. Summaries of research translated into practical application.
5. Reports of developmental programs and trends of national and international significance.
6. News of the latest products—both materials and devices—for use in the field.
7. Articles of use to managers and various specializations within the general educational communications and technology field.

Manuscripts should be approximately 1,000 to 4,000 words in length (or 10 to 15 manuscript pages) for regular articles. Manuscripts must conform to the *Publication Manual of the American Psychological Association*, 5th edition.

VOYA

Scarecrow Press, Inc.
4501 Forbes Boulevard, Suite 200
Lanham, MD 20706-4310
Telephone: (301) 459-3366 ext. 5706
URL: www.voya.com
Editor: Stacey L. Creel
screel@voya.com

Book lists are usually arranged by the **VOYA** editor with committees or contributors as annotated bibliographies/Webliographies that appear annually. Occasionally, book list submissions on current topics of teen appeal are considered via query. Submissions must conform to the house bibliographic style sheet, which is available upon request. Columns are planned by the editor. New column ideas are welcome as queries.

Young Adult Library Services: The Official Journal of the Young Adult Library Services Association

Young Adult Library Association
A Division of the American Library Association
50 East Huron Street
Chicago, IL 60611-2795
Telephone: (312) 944-6780 ext. 2128
Editor: Valerie Ott
Send manuscripts to Stephanie Kuenn
skuenn@ala.org

Submit manuscripts that are neither under consideration nor accepted elsewhere. Send copies of the manuscript to the addresses above; send one copy electronically via e-mail or one copy on a disk. Use the note-style references as described in the 15th edition of the *Chicago Manual of Style*. Submit manuscripts up to 20 pages, double-spaced (including references, tables, notes, and bibliographies) on a 3-1/2-inch disk, CD, or as an e-mail attachment in either Microsoft Word or WordPerfect.

Appendix H

Budget Information Needed for Grant Applications

Project Director:

Organization:

Salary and Wages:

Name/Title of Position	Number	How Cost Was Calculated	Funds Requested	Funds Matched	Total
Project Director[a]	1	50% of yearly salary	$15,000	$15,000	$30,000
Project Manager[b]	1	20% of yearly salary	0	7,000	7,000
		Subtotal	$15,000	$22,000	$37,000

[a] The project director is a district employee and will be working on the project half-time or 50 percent of yearly salary. You are asking the funding agency to provide one-fourth of the project director's $60,000 salary, and the district is going to cover one-fourth of the salary as cost sharing or matching funds.

[b] The project manager is also a member of the clerical staff and will be working on the project one-fifth time. You are going to provide 20 percent of the $35,000 salary as cost sharing or matching funds.

Fringe Benefits					
Rate	Name	Salary Base	Funds Requested	Funds Matched	Total
30%	Director	$60,000	$9,000	$9,000	$18,000
30%	Manager	35,000		10,000	10,000
		Subtotal	$9,000	$19,000	$28,000

Because you have split the director's salary, it is reasonable to split the fringe benefits between the funding agency and the district.

The manager's salary is a cost benefit, and the 30 percent fringe is matching funds.

Consultant's Fees					
Name/Type of Consultant	Number of Days	Daily Rate	Funds Requested	Funds Matched	Total
Project Evaluator	5	$1,000	$5,000	$0	$5,000
		Subtotal	$5,000		$5,000

Travel							
From/To	Number of Persons	Number of Days	Food/ Lodging[a]	Travel	Funds Requested	Funds Matched	Total
x to x	2	2	$800	$1,000	$1,800		$1,800
Various[b]	20	20	20,000	10,000	30,000		30,000
	Subtotal		$20,800	$11,000	$31,800		$31,800

[a] For food and lodging, use the district's per diem established travel amount. Districts sometimes use the government rate for the state. In this example, the flat rate of $200 per diem for lodging and meals is calculated.

[b] One purpose of the project is to bring school librarians to the district for a five-day institute. Therefore, the 20 librarians must have travel and per diem, and you won't know at the application stage from where or how these persons will be traveling. Establishing a flat amount of $500 for travel expenses would mean that most travel was within the state. To make sure you have budgeted enough for all participants, take the highest cost for a ticket within the area your participants live and $1,000 for per diem.

Supplies and Materials[a]				
Item	How Cost Was Calculated	Funds Requested	Funds Matched	Total
Office Supplies			$4,000	$4,000
Flash Drives		500		500
Software		20,500		20,500
	Subtotal	$21,000	$4.000	$25,000

[a] This would be an estimate of what you thought you would be spending based on use of materials in your district's offices for a year. The flash drives are for your participants to take their work home with them. You might need to purchase new software for the institute and to send home with the participants if they need it to continue what they learned at the institute.

Services[a]				
Item	How Cost Was Calculated	Funds Requested	Funds Matched	Total
Telephone			$1,000	$1,000
Duplication and Printing			4,000	4,000
Books		15,000		15,000
	Subtotal	$15,000	$5,000	$20,000

[a] Here you estimate what you will spend to make calls to get participants to the institute, travel arrangements, and what it might cost to duplicate materials for the institute, perhaps to buy books for the office to plan the institute, or even to buy books to give to participants.

Other Costs				
Item	How Cost Was Calculated	Funds Requested	Funds Matched	Total
20 laptops	Bid price	$20,000	$20,000	$40,000
Stipends[a]	Per diem	5,000		5,000
	Subtotal	$25,000	$20.000	$45,000

[a]Allocated for the participants' districts to hire substitutes @ $50 per day for 5 days times 20 participants = $5,000.

Total Direct Costs			
Item	Funds Requested	Funds Matched	Total
Salary and Wages	$15,000	$22,000	$37,000
Fringe Benefits	9,000	19,000	28,000
Consultant's Fees	5,000	0	5,000
Travel	38,000	0	38,000
Supplies and Materials	21,000	4,000	25,000
Services	15,000	5,000	20,000
Other Costs	25,000	20,000	45,000
Total Direct Costs	$128,000	$70,000	$198,000

Indirect Costs			
Item	Funds Requested	Funds Matched	Total
Direct Costs	$128,000	$70,000	$198,000
Indirect Costs			19,800
Total Project Costs			$217,800

The indirect cost rate for this project is the state government rate of 10 percent.

If this was a multiyear project, you would need to make those calculations and then submit a figure for the entire grant period.

Appendix I
Sample Letter to Legislator[1]

Although legislators' Washington addresses are given here, letters will arrive much faster if they are sent to the legislators' local addresses in your state.

To Your Senator:

The Honorable (full name)
United States Senate
Washington, DC 20510

To Your Representative:

The Honorable (full name)
U.S. House of Representatives
Washington, DC 20515

"Sincerely yours" is in good taste as a complimentary close. Remember to sign your given name and surname. If you use a title in your signature, be sure to enclose it in parentheses.

Forms similar to the above, addressed to your state capitol, are appropriate for your state representatives and senators.

If possible, use your official letterhead. If this is not appropriate and you write as an individual, use plain white bond paper, and give your official title following your signature as a means of identification and to indicate your competency to speak on the subject.

---

[1] This information is available from the American Library Association, Washington, DC, office.

Dos

1. Your legislators like to hear opinions from home and want to be kept informed of conditions in the district. Base your letter on your own pertinent experiences and observations.

2. If you are writing about a specific bill, describe it by number or its popular name. Your legislators have thousands of bills before them in the course of a year and cannot always take time to figure out to which one you are referring.

3. Legislators appreciate intelligent, well-thought-out letters that present a definite position, even if they do not agree.

4. Even more important and valuable to legislators is a concrete statement of the reasons for your position—particularly if you are writing about a field in which you have specialized knowledge. Representatives have to vote on many matters with which they have little or no first-hand experience. Some of the most valuable information they receive comes from facts presented in letters from people who have knowledge in the field.

5. Short letters are almost always best. Members of Congress receive many, many letters each day, and a long one may not get as prompt a reading as a brief statement.

6. Letters should be timed to arrive while the issue is alive. Members of the committee considering the bill will appreciate having your views while the bill is ripe for study and action.

7. Follow through with a thank-you letter.

Don'ts

1. Avoid letters that merely demand or insist on votes for or against a certain bill or letters that say what vote you want but not why. A letter with no reasoning, good or bad, is not very influential.

2. Threats of defeat at the next election are not effective.

3. Boasting about how influential the writer is is not helpful.

4. Do not ask for vote commitment on a particular bill before the committee in charge of the subject has had a chance to hear the evidence and make its report.

5. Form letters or letters that include excerpts from other letters on the same subject are not as influential as a simple letter drawing on your own experience.

6. Congressional courtesy requires legislators to refer letters from non-constituents to the proper office, so you should generally confine your letter writing to members of your state's delegations or members of the committee specifically considering the bill.

7. Do not write too many letters. Quality, not quantity, is what counts.

Index

About the Author

BLANCHE WOOLLS is Director and Professor Emerita, School of Library and Information Science, San Jose State University, past president of the AASL and IASL.

CPSIA information can be obtained at www.ICGtesting.com
Printed in the USA
LVOW032300040912

297387LV00005B/44/P